Hardeman's Tabernacle Sermons

Volume IV

N. B. Hardeman

Gospel Advocate Company
P.O. Box 150
Nashville, Tennessee 37202

HARDEMAN'S TABERNACLE SERMONS

VOLUME IV

Eighteen Sermons Delivered at Ryman Auditorium at Nashville, Tennessee, from October 16 to 31, 1938

By

N. B. HARDEMAN, President
FREED-HARDEMAN COLLEGE
HENDERSON, TENNESSEE

Manuscripts Taken and Prepared Under the Direction of
L. O. SANDERSON
NASHVILLE, TENNESSEE

Original Dedication:

To Brother R. W. Comer, Nashville, Tennessee, who, probably, was more responsible for the meetings in which these sermons were preached than any other man, and whose devotion to the "old paths" is ever a source of inspiration – to him, my friend and benefactor, this volume is sincerely dedicated.

N. B. Hardeman

Hardeman's Tabernacle Sermons, Volume IV
Gospel Advocate Reprints, 2001

Published by Gospel Advocate Co.
P.O. Box 150, Nashville, TN 37202
www.gospeladvocate.com

ISBN: 0-89225-489-0

N. B. HARDEMAN

BEN H. MURPHY

FOREWORD

In the words of a great Bible character, I am sure we feel, and are ready to say: "It is good for us to be here." This occasion is vividly reminiscent of similar efforts in other years, when the churches of Nashville came together with a commendable unity of purpose, to stand solidly behind like meetings, to make them a triumphant success. As I look over this vast concourse of people here assembled, I am persuaded that the same unity of purpose is again to characterize you in this meeting.

We are moved immeasurably as we contemplate ourselves standing, as it were, amidst the sepulchres of our fathers in the gospel. Near by, "upon the lap of earth," rest the heads of Lipscomb, Sewell, Elam, Smith, and McQuiddy. These esteemed men of God sacrificed their lives on the altar of loyalty to the word of God to prevent the removal of the ancient landmarks of Holy Writ. It is altogether fitting and proper, therefore, that this great meeting—the object of which is to add emphasis to the restoration plea—should be conducted in the shadow of the monuments of their endeavors.

Modernism today is removing the ancient landmarks of Biblical facts. The spirit of compromise, and of halting between two sides, is removing the ancient landmarks of Biblical commands. The church, therefore, needs constant admonition to "contend earnestly for the faith." Christendom, my friends, needs more Nehemiahs to rebuild the walls around Jerusalem. She needs more Ezras to restore the law of God. Christendom needs more Zerubbabels to rebuild the temple of God. In your selection of a preacher to lead you in your gesture here toward these ends, you have chosen a man who has combined in himself the qualities of the afore-mentioned three. Like Nehemiah, he would rebuild Jerusalem's fallen walls; as Ezra, he would uncover and restore the "law of grace"; like Zerubbabel, he would rebuild the temple of God. In this all important work, Nashville for the fourth time becomes the field of assertion. And now it is my very great pleasure, ladies and gentlemen, to present to you the speaker of this occasion, N. B. Hardeman.

J. LEONARD JACKSON.

Franklin, Tennessee.

INTRODUCTION

The same motive prompts the publication of this volume of eighteen gospel sermons preached by N. B. Hardeman in Ryman Auditorium, Nashville, Tennessee, that prompted their delivery. To know why the meeting was conducted is to know why the book is published.

To refer to it as the Fourth Tabernacle Meeting might be a trifle misleading. More than ten years had elapsed since the last of the three previous meetings. Those meetings were unique in some respects, including their physical proportions. All had been conducted by the same man in the same building and the audiences attending were largely the same.

In addition to the three meetings, Brother Hardeman had engaged in a public discussion there with Ira M. Boswell of the Christian Church, with Instrumental Music in the Worship as the issue. He had also delivered a series of lectures based upon a trip to the Holy Land. Five volumes had been published and offered to the public. All had met a hearty response.

The affinity between the man and the building is interesting, if not unique. Possibly no other man has used this remarkable building more; certainly none has put it to a better use. On the other hand, the building has surely received the cream of the best thoughts of his life. He has received more from the building, and the building has received more from him, than from any other man or building. His every utterance there has been published.

A knowledge of these facts may have weighed in some hearts. Some may have felt that it was fitting to add another meeting and another volume of sermons to that record. Neither is there any way to determine the spirit and motive of those who attended the fourth meeting. But with the general indifference that pervades the church, to say nothing of any other consideration, it is doubtful if the latter meeting would have been suggested upon these grounds.

The members of Eleventh Street Church in Nashville, and the individuals and congregations who cooperated with them in arranging for and supporting this meeting, prefer to believe that this was a special meeting with a special purpose. It was in no sense a "spite meeting." Believing that the church is drifting away from its doctrinal moorings, and contracting the spirit of sectarianism, the supporters of the meeting hoped to awake some to the situation, and crystallize sentiment for a return to original ground.

They were unanimous in believing N. B. Hardeman to be the logical man to achieve such a purpose. In fact, their confidence in him was such that there was no official conference with him as to the ends sought. They felt that the experiences of the past decade had suggested to him the same needs as to themselves. In this they were correct, for the preaching done fitted the purpose of the meeting better than if the supporters had undertaken to outline and suggest what Brother Hardeman should say.

The meeting was successful from every standpoint, in so far as it is possible to judge from appearances. The number baptized was not disappointing, as the meeting was primarily directed toward the amelioration of internal conditions of the church. The fundamentals of the gospel were restated. By example and exhortation distinctive preaching and active opposition to all error was encouraged. Crowds exceeded the expectations of both speaker and supporters. It was not the best attended of the four meetings, of course; but considering the general indifference of church members to all preaching, and the diminishing number of regular churchgoers, as well as the divided sentiment prior to the meeting, the attendance was remarkable. At the six Sunday meetings no more could have conveniently been accommodated, and at some of the other sessions the great auditorium was practically filled. The singing, led by Ben H. Murphy of Nashville, was very effective and inspiring. Incidentally, it was the second of these meetings in which Brother Murphy was the song leader.

The reactions following the meeting have been favorable. There is a better feeling among brethren in Nashville. A firmer stand is being taken by many. All have been awakened to trends and issues. A number of private and semi-public studies in premillennialism have been started recently. There has been more preaching on this subject. Many seem to have decided that the only way to settle this issue is to investigate it and settle by the Divine Standard.

Prepublication sales of the book of sermons bid fair to approach the three thousand mark by the date of delivery. There were perhaps more out-of-Nashville and out-of-Tennessee visitors at this meeting than any of the previous meetings. Interest in the meeting seemed to be more intense throughout the brotherhood, proportionately, than in Nashville. It is expected that many of the books will be sold, and it is the prayer of those who labored to promote the meeting that the spiritual harvest from the distribution of the sermons in printed form may even exceed the good which resulted from their delivery.

W. E. BRIGHTWELL.

CONTENTS

The Purpose of This Meeting — 7

Is the Bible the Word of God? — 18

The Reception of Any Truth Depends upon Our Attitude Toward It — 32

Teaching the Word of God — 46

Is the Gospel, as God Gave It, Adapted to Man, as God Made Him? — 60

Unity Among Brethren — 71

Cost of Discipleship — 85

Essentials and Non-Essentials — 99

"The Spirit of Christ" — 109

The Blood-Bought Institution of the New Testament — 122

The Establishment of the Kingdom — 134

Premillennialism — 149

How God Speaks to Man — 167

The First Sermon Under the Commission — 179

The Church — 192

The Vine and the Branches — 205

Is Christ with Us? — 219

The Final Exhortation — 235

HARDEMAN'S TABERNACLE SERMONS

THE PURPOSE OF THIS MEETING

Friends and brethren, I want to acknowledge my profoundest gratitude for such a magnificent audience this afternoon. I count myself exceedingly fortunate, in the providence of God, to have been preserved for this hour, and I appreciate, far more than I can express, the confidence in me on the part of brethren in and around Nashville responsible for this occasion. I have never heard a more fitting introduction than that delivered by Brother Jackson. I now read to you from the tenth chapter of Acts as an introductory scripture. Cornelius was the first Gentile convert. An angel appeared to him, bidding him to send to Joppa to call for one Simon, who lodged in a house by the seaside. "When he comes," the angel said, "he shall tell thee what thou oughtest to do." Upon receiving that instruction from the angel, Cornelius dispatched messengers to Joppa. They met with the preacher, were lodged overnight, and after they had started back to Cesarea I begin with the story. "And the morrow after they entered into Cesarea. And Cornelius waited for them, and had called together his kinsmen and near friends. And as Peter was coming in, Cornelius met him, and fell down at his feet, and worshipped him. But Peter took him up, saying, Stand up; I myself also am a man. And as he talked with him, he went in, and found many that were come together. And he said unto them, Ye know how that it is an unlawful thing for a man that is a Jew to keep company, or come unto one of another nation; but God hath shewed me that I should not call any man common or unclean. Therefore came I unto you without gainsaying, as soon as I was sent for: I ask therefore for what intent ye have sent for me? And Cornelius said, Four days ago I was fasting until this hour; and at the ninth hour I prayed in my house, and, behold, a man stood before me in bright clothing, and said, Cornelius, thy prayer is heard, and thine alms are had in remembrance in the sight of God. Send therefore to Joppa, and call hither Simon, whose surname is Peter; he is lodged in the house of one Simon, a tanner, by the sea side: who, when he cometh, shall speak unto thee. Immediately therefore I sent to thee; and thou hast well done that thou art come." Now note: "Now therefore are we all here present before God, to hear all things that are commanded thee of God. Then Peter opened his mouth and said, Of a truth I perceive that God is no respecter of persons: but in every nation he that feareth God and worketh righteousness, is acceptable with him."

This is from the record of the first Gentile convert. That occasion was fraught with momentous circumstances. The apostle, in response to the call, and by order of the Holy Spirit, was treading upon dangerous ground. There was bitter opposition to any Jews going among the Gentiles. But Peter went, believing in God and dreading not any sort of trial that might follow. And when he arrived at the place, found out what it was all about, and that a great company had assembled, he asked the purpose of their sending for him. Cornelius told him, and said: "Now, Peter, here we are—all of us present before God." Brethren, there was a fine company assembled. It was made up of kindred and friends of Cornelius. They were conscious of the fact that they were in the presence of God Almighty. So they said, "We are all here before God." It was a solemn occasion. They were conscious of their responsibility. We have sent for the preacher, and we are prepared to hear all things commanded of God.

Note: Cornelius did not say we are all here to listen to any kind of theory that you may have; or to listen to varied philosophies that might be yours; but we are here for one purpose, and that is to hear all things commanded thee of God. I believe, friends, that the adoption of that sentiment on our part would be an explanation to our friends everywhere as to why we are assembled.

I am made this afternoon to recall some of the meetings of years gone by. It has been sixteen and a half years since I first came to the Ryman Auditorium, wherein a wonderful meeting was held. That was followed by another in 1923; and that meeting immediately followed by a discussion of some points of difference among those who claim to love the Lord. Then ten years ago, another meeting was held. Most of the sermons of each meeting were put in book form. The influence of those meetings is, I think, yet going on. As I recall, first of all, it made the brethren of Nashville conscious of their strength and who they really were. I believe it told to the people of Nashville, as nothing else could have done, who we were. I believe these efforts impressed the people of Nashville and the great brotherhood far and near who earnestly accept the faith once for all delivered to the saints. And throughout the length and breadth of the land these have served as a great encouragement to the cause of Christ. And here we are for a repetition of those efforts.

"When I came unto you then, brethren, I came not with excellency of speech or of wisdom, declaring unto you the testimony of God. For I was determined to know nothing among you, save Christ and him crucified." Such is the sentiment prompting my presence this afternoon. I have not come to discuss the social problems which challenge our attention day by day. I am not here to talk about political affairs, nor of world-wide relationships, only as incidentally and illustratively such might come. Neither am I here to discuss personal matters or individual differences. "For though I preach the gospel, I have nothing to glory of: for necessity is laid upon me; yea woe is unto me, if I preach not the gospel!" I am fully aware of the fact that if an angel from heaven were to come to the city of Nashville and preach any other gospel than that which you have received from inspiration, the very curses of God would rest upon him. I want you brethren and friends to be fully aware that Hardeman is not unmindful nor unconscious of the responsibility assumed in this meeting.

But you ask: Why have a meeting of this sort? Well, first, it is customary to have protracted meetings, and to engage in a series of such efforts to accentuate further the principles that we believe to be correct. But so far as I am concerned, I am not here conforming to custom. I care but little about that. This meeting ought to be held, first, because there is great enthusiasm aroused by a congregation of this kind. One stick of wood may burn pretty well, but if you want a rip-roaring fire that will make you sit up and take notice and talk about it, pile them on and then sit back and watch it blaze. The influence of it radiates as it could not possibly from a single stick, however well it might burn. So for this reason the meeting is advisable. Then again, in the great distressing times that have been on for the last ten years, conditions have served to take the minds of people from things sacred and center them on matters purely material. And because of this common distress, not only among us here, but also among the nations of the earth, those who have proclaimed the gospel for years and have stood for it when bitterness was against them on every hand, think that congregations of this land are drifting away from the old landmarks, and from pioneer principles characteristic of apostolic times and, likewise, of the great Restoration Movement that, more than a hundred years ago, shook this old earth from center to circumference, and made the world to tremble in all phases of error. I think, friends, that it is very timely, therefore, for us to reexamine the platform upon which our campaign was launched.

Paul said to the Corinthians, "Examine yourselves whether you be in the faith; prove your own selves!" I used to ride the trains much more than now. When they pulled into the city of Nashville, I could see a man come along by the car, with hammer in hand, tapping every wheel. I did not get alarmed over it. I knew the purpose of it—not that he thought the wheels were faulty, but there was so much at stake that he just wanted to tap it to see if it rang clear again. Now I appreciated the thoughtfulness therein manifested. That is the preventive idea—that

precaution taken for security. I know there are men who have deeds and mortgages and various kinds of papers, upon which they rely, who frequently open up their deposit boxes and go through again, checking over—what for? Not that they doubted, but they just want to see again how these things stand. I believe, therefore, it is certainly worth while for us to examine the fundamental planks of our platform and to see whether or not we are steering clear of counterfeits or deviations from the old paths.

I think another reason for this meeting is to restate those old fundamental principles, and I have here, with rather an apology for reading, a declaration and address, delivered by Thomas Campbell, in September, 1809, upon which, as a foundation, ringing true to God's word, the movement, known as the Restoration, was launched. The purpose of this movement was to uproot denominationalism and to turn back to the principles delivered in the long centuries gone by. May I read to you several statements, to which I subscribe one hundred per cent—not because Campbell said it, but because he spoke the truth in denouncing error? Hear it: "From a series of events which have taken place in churches for many years past, as well as from what we know in general of the present state of things in the Christian world, we are persuaded that it is high time not only for us to think, but also to act for ourselves, to see with our own eyes, and to take all measures directly and immediately from the divine standard. To this alone we feel divinely bound to be conformed. As by this authority we must be judged. Moreover, being weary and fully aware of the sad experience of the heinous nature and pernicious tendency of religious controversy among Christians, tired and sick of bitter jarring and janglings of the party spirit, we would desire to be at rest, and were it possible, we would desire also to adopt and recommend such measures as would give rest to the brethren throughout all the churches as would restore unity, peace,. and purity to the whole church of God."

Now note again: "It is a pleasing consideration that all the churches of Christ which mutually acknowledge each other are not only agreed in the great doctrine of faith and holiness, but also materially agreed, as to the positive utterances of God's institution, so that our differences at most are about the things in which the kingdom of God does not consist. That is, about matters of private opinion or of human invention. What a pity that the kingdom of God should be divided over such things! Who would not be the first among us to give up human invention in the worship of God and to cease from imposing his private opinion that our breaches might be healed? Who would not willingly conform to the original pattern laid down in the New Testament for this happy purpose? Furthermore, let us declare that we will receive as a matter of faith or practice nothing which is not expressly taught and enjoined in the word of God either in express terms or approved precedent, that we would not relinquish that so we might return to the original constitution of unity of the church and in this happy unity enjoy the full communion with all brethren everywhere."

And then again: I beg your indulgence, because I think it is timely, to state some fundamentals. First, "that the church of Christ upon this earth is essentially, intentionally, and constitutionally one." Again, "that nothing be inculcated upon Christians as articles of faith; nor required of them as terms of communion which is not expressly taught and enjoined upon them in the word of God." Also, "that the New Testament is as perfect a constitution for the guidance of Christians under Christ as was the Old Testament for the guidance in the days of Moses; that division among Christians is an evil. It is antichristian, as it destroys the visible unity of the body of Christ as if he were divided against himself, excluding and excommunicating a part of himself. It is antiscriptural as being strictly prohibited by his sovereign authority, a direct violation of his expressed command. It is antiscriptural as it excites Christians to condemn, to hate, and to oppose, one another." And further, "that ministers duly and scripturally qualified inculcate none other things than those very articles of faith and holiness which are expressly revealed."

Friends, brethren, I have read to you from that original document some of the fundamental principles upon which the Restoration of a century or more ago was launched. To those principles preached down the ages, we owe our existence today. Some good brethren think that a spirit of yielding is abroad in the land; that there is a tendency to compromise with evil; and because of that fact, I think it very well and exceedingly timely that these matters be restated and enlarged upon for the next two weeks.

But there is another purpose prompting this meeting. All of us are conscious of the fact that Christian people need to be revived. We have been up against it—beset on every side by problems confronting us, as we have been, until many have grown cold and careless, indifferent and unconcerned, regarding their eternal welfare. Such is characteristic of man's nature. Therefore, the warnings of the Bible were given. Peter said, "Brethren, this second letter write I unto you to stir up your pure minds by way of putting you in remembrance of the things spoken both by the holy prophets of old and by the commandments of us the apostles of Jesus Christ." Paul went to the district of Galatia, preached the gospel unto them, and turned them from the Jewish religion to that of the gospel of Christ. But with the passing of time and the cooling of their ardor, they became unmindful of duty. So in writing to them, he said: "Brethren, you did run well; what has hindered you" —what has come to pass that has caused you to be indifferent? So Jude said that it was manifest that he should write and exhort that "ye earnestly contend for the faith once and for all delivered unto the saints."

Let me say to you, friends, that if judgment begin at the house of God, Peter raised the question: "What shall be the end of them that obey not the gospel of Christ?" And "if the righteous scarcely be saved where shall the ungodly and the sinner appear?" "It is a fearful thing to fall into the hands of the living God." Instead, therefore, of our efforts being centered entirely on the matter of new recruits for the banner of the Lord, I think the call is from every part of the country: Let us try to save ourselves, and revive

Christian people with a presentation of a lively hope once again. If, then, this meeting shall serve to make one follower of the Lord more devout, more determined to continue in his footsteps, I think it will not be a failure.

But I pass from that. Another purpose that all of us have in mind is that of trying to convert sinners to and by the gospel of our Lord Jesus Christ and thus extend the borders of the church until the sons and daughters of men, lost, ruined, and recreant, may come within the bounds of gospel promises. In order to do this, what we call primary principles should be repeated. And I want to suggest some things that I think are exceeding worth while. Why preach again first principles of the gospel of Christ? I look out over the audience and see silver-haired sires along with other brethren that have been knowing the truth for numbers of years, and I wonder if you do not think: "Is he to preach again on faith, repentance, confession, and baptism for the remission of sins? Why, Brother Hardeman, we understand that." Doubtless a large part of you do; but mark it: There are people attending this meeting now and shall hereafter, who know no more about the gospel today than some of you preachers did twenty-five or thirty years ago. It is just as necessary to show this present generation the distinctive plea of the gospel of Christ as it was for our ears to have been greeted by it in the years gone by. Second, there are people accountable to God today that were not accountable last year, and for that reason let us tell it over and over again. In the third place, there are people interested now who were not, at the last meeting in Nashville. Well, how do I know that? By general observation. I know there are experiences and things that come to pass in our lives that make us feel more keenly that we are rushing on down to an open tomb, that make us more conscious of the fact that we are beating funeral marches to the confines of the dead. Some spell of sickness, the burial of some loved one, some tragedy has come so close as to make people recognize the danger, thus prompting them to resolve within themselves: "I expect to become obedient unto the gospel of Christ." Therefore, preach the first principles. Why? People attending that never have before; some accountable now that were not when the last meeting was held; some by virtue of varied and sundry circumstances interested now who have not hitherto so been.

With these several reasons stated, I have another matter, all of which is purely preliminary. I want to raise the point: How shall I proceed? And what endorsement shall you lend? There are two schools of thought right along that line. Denominationalism, as it has expressed itself in the various creeds and writings of men, has this to say: Jesus Christ was begotten of the virgin, incarnated in the flesh, lived upon this earth, suffered, sorrowed, bled, and died, was buried, and rose again. Now watch it—that he might reconcile his Father unto man. Now that's one side of the matter. Hence, some of you can recall how we used to meet at early candlelight and start the meeting by various ones telling their experiences, then carrying on until the wee hours of the morning sometimes, begging God, pleading with Christ, imploring the Holy Spirit, with one petition after another, "Lord, come down, convict sinners and convert mourners, and, therefore, be reconciled." And after working at it until midnight, some good brother arose to say: "Thank God it is not of works" and generally added, "lest any man should boast." Now that is one conception—that the whole business is an effort on our part to get God reconciled to man. Friends, hear it! There is not a syllable of truth in that theory! The Bible is absolutely and positively to the contrary. There is not a line in God's book on the matter of reconciliation, but is exactly and precisely the opposite of that sentiment. The scheme of redemption drafted by Jehovah as the great architect included every son of Adam upon the face of the earth. So, then, God already is willing for man to be saved, so much so that his love for mankind prompted the sending of his only begotten Son. Jesus Christ came to this earth—and note the purpose of it—that he might do, not his will, but the will of the Father that sent him. Hence, when he died the tragic death on the tree of the cross, poured out his blood which he freely shed, and cried, "It is finished!" I wonder

—actually wonder—is there any soul so thoughtless as to want to bow down this afternoon and pray God Almighty to get up another scheme of redemption? Are you satisfied with what he has done? Do you think his plan is big enough and broad enough and inclusive enough for you to share its benefits? All right. Would you kneel this afternoon and pray Jesus Christ to come to this earth and travel over Judean hills and Samaritan plains again, suffer the shame and the ignominious things of this life; would you plead that he might die another death, and his body be suspended between the heaven and earth; that his side be pierced again and the life-giving current freely flow that you might live?

That, my friends, is already done. Why plead for such again? Would you bow down and pray God's Spirit to come to this earth and make another revelation of God's will? Jude said, "This is that which *once for all* was delivered unto the saints!" When the pen of inspiration was dropped from the hand of John, on the lonely Island of Patmos, never again to be grasped by mortal man, it was the doxology and the valedictory of God's revelation unto man. The scheme of redemption was complete! I am not, therefore, a subscriber to the thought of that school which teaches that we should plea with God, or Christ, or the Holy Spirit, to make us another plan of salvation. I am not here to plead with Christ to try to get his Father reconciled to man. That has already been done. Now listen to the scripture: "All things are of God who hath reconciled us unto himself, and hath given unto us the ministry of reconciliation: to wit, that God was in Christ, reconciling" —now observe the direction—"the world unto himself!" Friends, is this a movement on the part of God toward man? Or is it intended to be a movement on the part of man toward God? "We are, therefore, ambassadors for Christ as though God did beseech you by us, we pray you in Christ's stead, be ye reconciled unto God." "Knowing the terror of the Lord, we persuade men." Hence, the purpose of this meeting is not to plead with God for another scheme of redemption, nor with Christ to execute the Father's will again, nor with the Holy Spirit to make another

revelation, but we urge upon those who may chance to hear, a full acceptance of that which the Spirit of God has already revealed.

Therefore, I lay down this afternoon five planks in our platform. I beg you to hear them. First, let us resolve to take God at his word. Second, to believe what he says. Third, to become and be what he requires. Fourth, try to live as he directs, and, number five, trust him implicitly for the fulfillment of the promise. Upon that kind of a platform our campaign for the next two weeks in now launched. And to the further deliberation and consideration of such matters as shall grow out of these fundamentals, I solicit your attention, your presence, your prayers, and your interest everywhere.

Should there be one or more present this afternoon who, from former teaching or study, understands the will of the Lord and has it in his heart that he wants to become and live a Christian, to accept Jesus Christ as his leader, the Bible as his guide, resolves to worship God as it is written, and to practice the principles of pure and undefiled religion, the invitation is to be extended while we stand and sing.

IS THE BIBLE THE WORD OF GOD?*

Several years ago our greatest audiences that assembled at their respective places of meeting were at night. With the passing of the years, however, and the interest of humanity in other affairs, such is not true in modern times. In view of all of that, I am delighted most wonderfully tonight with such a fine audience, even in the absence of the additional delegations that were here this afternoon. I rejoice and congratulate myself always in being permitted to share in a service of this kind.

I have for our study tonight that which I believe to be the supreme issue before Christians at this hour—"Is the Bible God's Word?" Is it true? All of us have been interested in many matters, and issues of different kinds, and we wish not to lessen their importance; but there has never been anything to challenge the consideration of men equal to the question as to whether or not the Bible is the word of God. Have you ever stopped to think just what depends upon that? If this book that I have here before me is not God's word, then it must, of course, be the work of man. If the work is of man, it is the greatest imposition and the grossest deception upon which I have ever gazed; because, from beginning to end, it claims to be by inspiration given. If that claim is untrue, then this volume must be relegated, not only to the level of man-made books, but far beneath them. The result will be that the odium attached thereto can never be removed because of its false claim to be given by inspiration, and that holy men of old spake as they were moved by God's Spirit. It is rather strange that any of us should think it is definitely in order to discuss a matter of this kind, for time was when we were called upon to discuss matters that are taught *in* the Bible altogether. It was then assumed that the Bible was the word of God. But in

*The general outline of this address is based on notes made while hearing William Jennings Bryan speak along this line.

these modern times, of independent thought and infidel considerations, the Bible itself has been brought up and subjected to various criticisms and doubtful questionings.

I feel like suggesting, as did Elijah when he called upon the people, asking why they halted between two opinions—if God be God, recognize and serve him; if Baal is God, then serve him. He challenged the worshipers of Baal, the opponents of God, to a showdown. Let it be said that they were good sportsmen—they accepted his proposition. "Let us build two altars," he said. "You build one to your god, and call upon him; if he answer, him will we serve. Then I will build an altar and call upon my God. Whichever answers our prayers, by fire, will be the true God." They replied that the thing was well spoken—"we will agree to a matter of that kind." "Now there are 450 of you prophets of Baal, and just one of me, so you go first." They prepared the altar, got all things in readiness, and then began to call upon their god to touch it off with fire. They started early and prayed earnestly, until after a while Elijah began to emphasize the matter and to make it uncomfortable for them. "Why," he said, "you fellows are not praying loud enough. Cry a little bit louder—maybe your god does not hear well, or, if not that, perhaps he is asleep—rouse him up. Or maybe he has gone on a long journey." Thus they continued to pray, agitated and aggravated, until finally they inflicted punishment upon themselves, hoping their god might finally answer; but ultimately they gave up.

Well, it came Elijah's time. He built the altar and put the wood at the proper place, and then said to them: Bring a barrel of water and let us saturate the whole thing. They did it, and then he said: "Get another—put two barrels of water on it; and then do it three times, until it is soaking wet." The water filled all the ditch round about. Then he bowed and prayed unto God Almighty. The result was that high heaven heard his call and answered that wonderful prayer. And all the people said, "There is no God but Elijah's," and he ordered those 450 prophets to be slain.

Now then, to all enemies of the Bible, I make this kind of a challenge: If this book is an imposition, and not the word of God, man ought to be able to write a book that would bring more comfort to the sorrowing and more consolation to the distressed and point us to brighter prospects of the by and by than hitherto we have had. Now if some man cannot do that, instead of proving that man has evoluted, if he does not mind he will prove the opposite of that, and I suppose that word would be "devoluted." With all the advantages of the twenty centuries, the opportunities and experiences of life, if we tonight cannot produce a better book than did those of the days gone by, it shows that we are making progress—in the opposite direction. My friends, all is at stake. If the Bible be not true, our conception of God is all wrong. There is no such character as Christ. We worship in vain, and we have nothing toward which we can point the youth of the land, if, indeed, the Bible be a book fraught with error from beginning to end.

But let me say to you: In this Bible, there are those things that are worth more to humankind than all things written in other books the world over. The Bible is worth more to our civilization, to the progress and to the happiness of the human family than all other books that have ever been written upon this earth. We could better afford, as someone has said, to cast aside every volume in the libraries of the land, and be robbed of the whole human collection, than to have the Bible blotted from the face of the earth.

There are three verses, the first, twenty-fourth, and twenty-sixth, in the first chapter of Genesis that mean more and answer more satisfactorily the inquiries of mankind than all other books and chapters the world has ever produced or seen. And in addition to those, we have the rest of the Bible from which we glean great thoughts as well. Now I mention them for your careful study and analysis. The world tonight is wonderfully interested in the origin of things with which we come in contact and observe. There are different theories on every hand—the Christian has one idea, one faith, and one basis for it. All others have different ideas as varied almost as there are individuals. You turn to a Christian tonight and ask him what he thinks regarding the origin of things, and without hesitation he turns to the first chapter in the Bible and the first verse "In the beginning, God . . ." That is as far back as anyone can go. Back of that no one has dared to make a suggestion. So we launch out into the fathomless depths of the eternal and urge "In the beginning, God!" There we have a character, all-wise, all-powerful, all-loving, and all-divine. Accepting him, the Christian can explain anything, however miraculously it may follow in the stream of affairs.

But someone says, "That is an assumption." I grant that I assume one thing—that is, the existence of a God, the like of whom I have just mentioned. With that as an idea for beginning let me say that it is the only sensible one, so far as we know, that has ever been penned, the only statement that any boy or girl can believe, or upon which he can rely. I assume the fact that God is, and was, and will ever be; and in the beginning he was responsible for things created as they are. Now you take the opposite of that, the atheist, the one who denies the existence of God Almighty, and begin to make inquiries of him. Generally, he accepts what is called "the nebular theory," and assumes at the very beginning two things: first, the existence of matter, and second, the existence of force. Then he will assume a third thing without asking your permission, and that is this: that force acted upon matter, and the result was "all things as we behold them tonight." Now, I want to ask: Why can I not assume the existence of one thing, namely, the God of the universe, with as much intelligence, with as much degree of scholarship, as any pretended scientist or what not can assume the existence of two things neither of which he can possibly explain? With my idea of the matter, nothing is mysterious. As Paul says in Hebrews 11: 3, "Through faith we understand that the worlds were framed by the word of God."

Boys ask me, "Brother Hardeman, do you understand how the world was wrought into existence?" Why, certainly, son. "Well, how was it?" Through faith I understand that the worlds were framed by the word of God!

That is the kind of character with whom I take my stand. Hence, I repeat that this is the most sensible statement ever penned to mortal man regarding the existence of the worlds. That is the only one that moves on down the line unvaried, unmodified, and for which no man has to make apology.

Well, you take the second verse referred to in that first chapter of Genesis, which is verse 24. There is the truth regarding the continuity of things created; the perpetuity of all things wrought in the handiwork of God. What is it? It is a simple statement. God said that everything shall bring forth after its kind, hence the existence of life upon the earth and the perpetuity of the same. Now, let us pass down through the ages of the distant past and let them be twenty-four millions of years or three hundred and fifty millions—and my reason for mentioning those figures is this: Scientists in their calculations are nearly together on how long in the distant past these things were. One of them says twenty-four millions of years, and the other says three hundred and fifty. But what does three hundred and twenty-six million years amount to with a scientist! Now a man can walk squarely up and accept that with three hundred and twenty-six million years of variance, and yet if in the Bible it is one time spelled B-o-a-z, Boaz, and the next time B-o-o-z, Booz, he rises up in holy horror: "The Bible contradicts itself and I have found things incongruous in the pages of the same." Nothing under heaven but a willful effort to be dishonest and to fail to give justice to the evidence would prompt an attitude of that kind. But you go back into the eternal past, trace down the stream of human generations, as well as all things else, and—mark it!—the world has never yet found a single violation of the God-given principle that everything shall bring forth after its kind! Man with all his ingenuity has never been able to persuade that intangible something-or-other to violate that law of continuity upon this earth. Scientists in their best efforts have told us about the multiplied millions of species. I have read several of them, and I am certain that they do not know much more about it than I—and

that is saying quite a little bit regarding it; but suppose there are millions of species, many of them living, others traceable in their fossilized state back in the rocks, and various places of the earth. Mark it! There has never yet been found a single solitary thing in process of transition from one state to another. If, for instance, you dig in the rocks and find a skeleton that you might designate as a fish and analyze him. He is just like one caught down here in the Cumberland River. If you go back and find some bones, fossilized in the long distant past, then what? It is exactly after the kind that has been borne on down the line. Hence, there is absolutely no possibility of man's finding where anything has ever violated the law of perpetuity of life.

Well the third verse that means so much to the thoughtful student is that one accounting for the existence of man. The Bible simply says that "God made man out of the dust of the earth"; that he breathed into him the breath of life, and there he was a living soul. With all the theories and guesses and the speculations, there has never been an idea one-thousandth part as sensible as the acceptance of the divine record. I am sure you have read extracts along the line, and have heard others speak possibly more intelligently than I can regarding the matter; but I have read their many theories, and it is amusing—if it were not so serious—to think how some men's minds run along with ideas of this type.

A prominent theory is that one single cell came into existence someway, somehow.

But you ask the sponsor of that idea: "How came it to exist?" Well, he is up in the air, and either will tell you that it was a spontaneous matter bursting forth, or it came to this earth from some other planet. Well, we wonder then why that thing does not continue. They go so far as to tell us that that one cell had two children—that one was a vegetable, and the other was an animal. And I have just thought about what a family that must have been. A bunch of dog fennel and a little puppy dog are brothers and sisters, all in the same home, starting down life's way together—which, of course, is absurd, ridiculous, preposterous, nonsensical, and an insult to an intelligent being. But that is the theory as given by some. One time, it is said, a little animal made its way out of the water upon the coast. There it lay, in the bright, brilliant, golden sunlight, and upon its head there was a little pigment, or freckle. The sun played upon that more directly than it did anywhere else. As a result, that little freckle became irritated, more than any other part of the body, and as a result of that irritation, there burst forth an eye, and the little animal had one eye and began to see. Now that is the explanation. When, in the course of time, another freckle occurred—just happened to be in the right place, on the top side instead of the bottom—and the sun likewise played on that, and in response to the call of the sun and just as a mere accident, that eye came out; so it had two eyes! I suppose, now, that the sun went into eclipse and has been that way ever since, or we would still have eyes coming out! It is certainly strange that the process stopped with just two operations!

They tell us further that in the course of time that little animal wanted to move and it found that it had a wart on its belly (and it is very fortunate that it was not on its back—the whole thing would have been upside down). By the use of that wart, it found that it could have locomotion and move position more easily. By exercising the wart, a leg came out. That was beneficial, but it was all lopsided. Then there chanced to develop another wart, and after a while, by wiggling and using it, that also developed into a leg. So, as time went on, there happened to be four of them. Now that provokes a smile on the part of anybody. But, they say, that little animal developed into a higher one with other features, more and more cultured and developed, finally getting up into the monkey stage and on to the higher classes of the monkey family. Ultimately, the monkeys lost their tails—and here we are! That is the theory. Just look at it and trace our ancestors.

Now, ladies and gentlemen, you ask in all candor: "Who teaches that kind of stuff?" Hear it! Dr. Harry Emerson Fosdick, a Baptist preacher, in a Presbyterian meeting-house, in a little book called "Faith," page 128, endorses that idea. And yet he is the speaker, sponsored by the Federation of the Churches of Christ of America, over whom the world goes wild and listens to every Sunday afternoon. A theory, a guess, that is unworthy of consideration, is galvanized into prominence, into respectability, by men of that type occupying the pulpit and claiming recognition of the Bible. It is an insult to divinity and a mockery to God's word. Friends, let me tell you: the thing that is in opposition to the Bible tonight is not crime, though this world is cursed with it, because the more crime we have, the greater need we have of condemnation from the Bible respecting the same. Sin is not the great opponent of the Bible, for the more sin there is, the more we need the divine standard of condemnation. The greatest enemy of the book of God is a class of men claiming to be superior in their intellect, trying to apologize and find a scientific excuse for rejecting the Bible as the word of God. There is our trouble tonight.

May I now suggest to you, my friends, another line of thought? It would be almost impossible for me to undertake to trace the progress that has been made in all things material, beginning with the very first, and coming down from generation to generation. Time forbids and my ability likewise hinders a recitation of those things with a degree of accuracy that others might be able to picture. But even in our day and in the days of our fathers, we note the progress made in all the physical and material world. Take the simplest things of life, for instance, our method of travel. Long ago, it took months and months to cross the mighty Atlantic—and now in twenty hours we hop from America to Europe. Years ago, months were consumed in passing from the Atlantic seaboard to the Pacific—now within thirteen hours we eat one meal in New York and the next in San Francisco. Our method of travel round about Nashville would cause those who passed away even in our early days to rise up in amazement and wonder as to what can be done.

Take our manner of living, no longer is it characterized by the drudgery of the days to which our grandmothers belonged. Why some of you can perhaps remember when the wool from the backs of sheep was cut by hand clippers; that it was then combed and burred and trimmed, then carded into rolls, taken thence to the old spinning wheel. And then by physical foot power on the old loom woven into fabrics for the household. Then with a brass lamp and a yellow light, not bigger than your finger, with the eye of the needle in the wrong end, our grandmothers there sat and sewed and eked out a miserable existence for their families. All of that has not been so long past. But what about it now? Those days are gone forever, due to the progress of our modern civilization. That is but a sample of every phase and feature of things material with which you might have to do.

But, friends, I want to ask of you: What progress has there been made in those more sacred and solemn and important relationships of man? What more do we know tonight about heaven, God, Christ, the Holy Spirit, or the angelic host around the throne of God, than we did twenty centuries ago? Absolutely nothing! What do you know about God that you did not read from the Bible? What do you know about Christ other than the story penned by inspiration? What conception of heaven have you other than that gained from the Bible? What has all our education, our theories, our philosophies brought to us regarding the things that transcend the realms of time? Nothing! What do you know about man that was not known and written in that book called the Bible? What attribute or characteristic, passion, lust, appetite, desire, does he have—and what do you know about it—that is new to the Bible? Hear it! You know nothing! What do you know about sin that you did not learn from the book of God? What do you know about salvation outside of God's book? Not a thing! What progress has the human family made in analyzing our ownselves and figuring out a destiny that will bring to us the sweetest joys that earth can possibly have? Absolutely nothing. What commandment has ever been given since Christ and the apostles quit the walks of men? None. What promise is there after life's fitful fever is over that is not found in this blessed book? Not a single one.

When you begin to study, therefore, the progress in the material world, from any point of consideration, it is marvelous to make comparison and the ratio is not a hundred nor a thousand, but thousandsfold of progress along every possible line of human thought and endeavor; but when you turn to those matters that outlive our existence here, and talk about the by and by, we have moved forward not one solitary hair's breadth. This suggests to us that the Bible comprehended and surveyed the whole field of human endeavor and our relationships one with another, and to our God, and pictured to us the golden glories of the eternal home beyond. There has been nothing added to what is found in the Bible.

But another thing: There are statements made in this Bible as matters of prophecy that have come to pass and are verified by profane history that could not have been made with that degree of accuracy other than by the fact of inspiration. There are things revealed upon the pages of holy writ concerning which there was the densest ignorance and the greatest skepticism imaginable. I shall just mention two or three simple ones. Job lived about fifteen hundred years before Christ. In his writing he said some things that are marvelous, one of which we find in chapter 26, verse 7. When Job was enlarging upon his conception of Jehovah and picturing his grandeur and glory, and transcending superiority, in a voice and sentiment of ecstasy, he said: "He stretcheth out the North over empty space, and hangeth the earth upon nothing." Well, that is a very simple statement. Job just said that God stretched out the North over that vacant place and that he hung the earth on nothing. World scientists, so called, have made fun of Job for three thousand years and talked about that ignoramus discussing matters of that kind. But do you know what has come to pass? With modern science and invention, especially with the invention of the great telescope, astronomers have turned that mighty telescope upon the various parts of the heavens, and always there are stars and worlds and systems that have been brought to view—but when they have turned it directly, as Job said, to the North, to their utter surprise and chagrin, there is absolutely nothing but an otherwise inexplicable vacancy. They have been "up in the air" trying to explain all of that. How does it happen that if you turn it East or West or South, millions of stars are beheld which are not visible to the naked eye, but when you turn that mighty lens on the North, the precise point, the biggest telescope fails to reveal one solitary thing.

Now as a verification of this fact, just last spring, I wrote to the Scientific Research Bureau of Los Angeles, California, stated the case, from Job 26: 7, and raised the question: Is that statement scientifically correct? I had an answer in reasonable time that it *is* correct and has been one of the problems baffling the skill of the scientist with his great telescopic invention. Now then, Job was not an astronomer. He did not even have a high school diploma, and was not president of any college; but Job said that God Almighty, the creator of heaven and earth, stretched out the North over the empty space—there it is, acknowledged by modern science. They have come down from their lofty pinnacle, and now say: "Job must have known something about this matter." No, he did not know it—God told him! God caused him to write it.

Well, the other part of the verse is so simple that you marvel at it. "He hangeth the earth on nothing." Think a minute. Until the days of Columbus, Sir John Mandeville and the Italian geographer, Toscanelli, everybody thought this earth was flat—that it had four literal corners, that it sat upon four posts, and those posts rested on the back of a big turtle. Hence, even old Mrs. Columbus—I take it a good woman—lived and died believing the earth was flat, possibly ridiculing and rebuking her boy for having such wild dreams as to think this earth was globular and spherical in nature. Well, what happened? By sailing on the deep Columbus demonstrated that the earth absolutely is round and that it is suspended on nothing! Why that is as simple to us as anything—but when did we catch on? About four hundred years ago! Who found it out before we did? Why Job could say, "You ignoramuses, I said that fifteen hundred years before the birth of Christ. I was not a geographer; I did not claim to be a scientist; but I know that God said he hangeth the earth on nothing."

Here it is, out in space tonight, rotating on its axis, at the rate of a thousand miles an hour, turning in its annual revolution around the sun at the rate of about eighteen miles a second, and ever since I can remember, it has never been behind time, never had a wreck, a puncture, or a blowout, in all these years. What is the philosophy of it? God put it that way! It did not happen by chance, and the very universe declares the glory of its creator.

Friends, I want you to think about it: Here is a watch, upon which I look and tell the hours, the minutes, and the seconds of the day. I know good and well that this watch did not just happen to be. Suppose I would tell you this: One time a man gathered up a whole lot of scrap iron, a little gold, and other metals and piled them up together. Then some fellow got drunk, lost control of his automobile, and came down the street and hit that junk pile in just such a way that when it was all picked up, there was found a watch as the result. Now you know that is not so. That thing could not possibly happen. There is the watch that counts the hours, minutes, and seconds. Somebody designed it. It declares the glory of a creator. That thing did not occur just as an accident or by chance—some power, some intelligence, was behind it! Who was it? Well, you cannot tell to save your life who made that watch. You know someone did it, but who? There was an intelligence back of it. Is it revealed? The watch itself does not tell. But after all the works are put in, with everything in shape, the designer and maker placed the name thereon—Hamilton! Now what do you have? There is the thing that declares there was a designer. The writing identifies it! It was not Mr. Smith or Mr. Johnson, but Hamilton! Now watch the application: When you look out on this old world in which we live and on the sister planets you become convinced of what David said: "The heavens declare the glory of God!" The existence of some wonderful power is certain. Who was it? Oh, you can look out on the sun, moon, and stars, and you cannot identify him.

But when you take the physical exhibitions of his handiwork and the physical universe declaring the glory—these supplemented by the Bible, which reveals his identity—what do you have? That in the beginning God was responsible for all of this. He stretched out the North over the empty place, suspends this old earth on nothing, except on the invisible and the immutable laws of gravity.

Friends, that is but a sample. Time tonight forbids illustrations further along that line. I want to commend to you who shall have an interest in this meeting an absolute, undaunted, unquestioned faith in God's book. I want you to be so thoroughly set upon the correctness of it that you are willing to put your hand, one on Genesis and the other on Revelation, and say, "Lord, I believe it all." Further, "I have no apology to make for any statement found upon the pages of sacred truth." I love to talk about the Bible, I love to study about it. I love to teach young men and women things *about* the Bible. But far beyond that, I love to teach them the Bible itself! I am not so much interested in your learning all about the Bible—I want you to learn what it says, to know what is *in* it. I would love to have those who favor me with their presence to recognize that this is God's book, by inspiration given; that it is a lamp to our feet, a light unto our path, beside which there is none other book or person to whom we can go. I would love for you to accept it wholeheartedly, without apology, without reservation. Let us take our stand upon the statements found therein, be circumscribed by its authority, and resolve, deep down in our hearts, that we will accept nothing, we will believe nothing, we will do nothing other than that which is clearly revealed on the pages of God's truth. Further, let each one determine: "I will demand a 'thus saith the Lord' direct, or an approved example, or a necessary inference from the gospel. I will not be among that number who conjecture what it might imply. I will not be with that company which philosophizes as to what it might mean. I will take its plain statements, believing confidently that revealed things belong to man and unrevealed things belong to God. For their fulfillment, I will wait until God sees fit to make known clearly that in which I have an interest tonight."

Friends, this Bible teaches all men everywhere the plan of salvation. The very tenor of this book is to get you to believe that Jesus is the Christ, the son of the living God. May I just add this: I am not especially interested in Jesus Christ as a great teacher; nor Jesus as the man of Galilee; nor Jesus as the philosopher. I think all statements of that kind are intended by infidels to draw away men from the issue. Hear it! I am wonderfully interested in the fact that Jesus is God's Son. Though the greatest teacher that ever lived, if he be not God's Son, my interest is wonderfully lessened. Though the matchless Philosopher of all ages, if he be not the Son of God, I have no hope whatsoever centered in him. Therefore, that blood-bought, heaven-born, and world-wide institution, the church of the Bible, is founded upon the fact that Jesus Christ is God's Son. I bid you believe it with all your heart; accept its teachings by turning from every sin away; render that obedience enjoined in this Bible; and then stand upon the promises of our Lord.

Friends, that is our hope tonight. That is the purpose of our assembly and I rejoice over the interest you manifest thus far. Now together we are standing for the invitation hymn.

THE RECEPTION OF ANY TRUTH DEPENDS UPON OUR ATTITUDE TOWARD IT

There was handed to me tonight, just before I approached the stage, a query, with a special request that it be answered tonight. Nothing pleases me more than to enter into a meeting where all things are favorable for the answering of almost any type of sensible query. The program of this meeting, however, is such as to preclude that procedure. It is possible that I might discuss, during the remaining nights, the very thing about which someone would like to ask. I will read this with a word of comment.

"Does a man see the Holy Spirit when he is born again?" The word "see" is used in two different senses. Not knowing just which the person had in mind when he asked, it would be impossible for me to anticipate the thought about it. If you mean it in the sense of enjoy, I would say yes. Then the latter part: "Have you seen it yet?" I enjoy *his* comforting influence and exceeding great and precious promises.

In the thirteenth chapter of Matthew, we have an account of the Savior's speaking a series of parables by the Sea of Galilee. He got into a boat, and went out, and there sat while the multitudes stood on the shore. And he spake to them first the parable of the sower, which is so simple that all of us can easily grasp it. And when he had finished the disciples came to him and said this: Master, "why speakest thou unto them in parables?" Now that was unusual—he had not been doing it that way, and they were a little bit surprised and troubled over the method of his procedure. Why speak to them in parables? "He answered and said unto them, Because it is given unto you to know the mysteries of the kingdom of heaven, but to them it is not given. For whosoever hath, to him shall be given, and he shall have more abundance: but whosoever hath not, from him shall be taken away even that he hath. Therefore, speak I to them in parables: because they seeing, see not; and hearing they hear not, neither do they understand. And in them is fulfilled the prophecy of Esaias, which saith: By hearing you shall hear and shall not understand; and seeing you shall see and shall not perceive: For this people's heart is waxed gross, and their ears are dull of hearing, and their eyes they have closed; lest at anytime they should see with their eyes, and hear with their ears, and should understand with their heart, and should be converted, and I should heal them." That is the reading from verse 10 down through verse 15 of the chapter.

Now based upon that reading—and I think easily drawn from it—is a proposition that I want to state, and have you study for the time allotted. Our reception of any proposition or truth depends upon the attitude that we assume toward that thing presented. Now if you will get that statement, you have the foundation of the talk tonight. Our reception of any matter, from whatsoever source, depends wholly upon the attitude that we have toward the character who presents it. I hope to make clear to you the development of that principle.

I know that in our social relationships, and the ever-changing characteristics of the same, many of us are unprepared to meet the rapid changes and to endorse the radical things that members have seen come to pass regarding these very things. Our methods of entertainment in social relationships are not always appreciated, not always endorsed—well, why not? Our attitude and conception of such matters forbid a hearty reception of that which is presented for our consideration. I know good and well that in our political relationships, my prejudices and my partisan spirit, formulated in years gone by, prevent me from giving full faith and credence to a statement made by any representative of a party with which I am not affiliated. For instance, I am somewhat against dictators. I have not any too much use for Hitler, Mussolini, or any other of that would-be autocratic type. Hence, I am not in very good position to accept anything with full credence that might emanate from such a source. I think anything that Hitler might say, regarding governmental problems, should be taken with the proverbial pinch of salt. Why? Because my attitude toward his method is not good. And there is a prejudice, I grant, which must be removed if I am to walk out wholeheartedly and accept any declaration that he might announce.

I think you could take an old-time, standpat Republican, and it would be very difficult for any representative of the New Deal to put across to that man anything, however true it might be, with full confidence of genuine acceptance. Always there is suspicion that you are trying to put something over; that you have sinister motives back of it; I am afraid of you—I fear that you are not sincere. Now that principle is true regarding individuals. You may have prejudices against some man, or against some place, or some relationship, and however truthful a sentence might be spoken with reference to it, you take it with some degree of caution. For instance, when Philip actually found the Savior, a real fact, and was so elated over that discovery, and ran to tell Nathanael, "I have found him who is called the Christ"—that did not register. Nathanael was not prepared to receive that. And his reply was: Surely not. "Can any good thing come out of Nazareth?" You must be mistaken about it. Now what is the matter with him? "I am just not ready for the reception of a truth of that sort." He had opinions to the contrary. "Why I have been educated—things have been put into my mind—that forbid a hearty acceptance of your statement."

May I suggest to you, friends, that a principle like this prevails in matters religious as it does in all things else? Many cannot accept the truth. Why? It is against their former teaching. "I have never heard it after that fashion." They have not been thinking thus of it. Hence, however true and plausible and reasonable it might on the surface appear, "I just know there is something the matter with it somewhere. I cannot receive it." The Savior talked about this same principle when he said (John 7: 17), "If any man *will* to do his will, he shall know the doctrine." It depends a great deal on how you read that. Not if any

man will do his will, he shall know the doctrine; that would make the doing of his will in advance of knowledge. But the other is the preparation of heart. Do I have a desire tonight to do God's will? Am I really hungering and thirsting after heaven's truth? Am I free from prejudices and a partisan spirit to that extent that I can say: Lord, speak, and I will hear; command, and I will obey? Let the matter be round or flat, wet or dry, hot or cold—I care nothing about how it may be—I simply want God's word, and to that I attach my hope for eternity. I have got to reach that point of honesty with myself—perfect candor toward the truth and an attitude favorable to the reception of God's word, no matter whether it is in harmony with what I have previously understood, or in harmony with my party, or any other interest. If I ever get to heaven, I must first of all reach the point where I have no theory, no ax to grind, no interest in anything except the very truth of God Almighty. Hence, if any man *will* to do *God's* will!

Now I think there are many who would not mind becoming Christians if God would let them dictate the terms on which that should be brought about. I think numbers of people would be perfectly willing to live what they call the Christian life if God would allow them to set up the standard. Plenty of people are willing to worship God if God will let them do as they please and have whatsoever may strike their fancy. There is deception and delusion in all that. It is my firm belief that no man can possibly reach heaven until he gets to the point where he can say, "Lord, here I am, what is my duty? What does the Bible teach? Show me the way—I want God's truth!" Jesus said if a man gets in that attitude, that position, with reference to truth, that man "shall know the doctrine." I verily believe there are angelic spirits to minister unto all such as shall be heirs of salvation.

The Ethiopian officer, the secretary of the treasury of Queen Candace's government, was exactly of that type. He was studying the Bible, wanting to know what the will of the Lord was. And when it was unfolded, then and there, he was ready to obey it. I think Cornelius, at the head

of the Italian band, was another. He wanted the truth, and was seeking for it, hungering and thirsting for it, and doing what he could to learn it. God saw to it that he learned the truth and understood the will of the Lord. Christ therefore said, "If any man will to do his will"—what about it?—that man "shall know it"—not may, nor might, nor perhaps, but in the providence of God, the light of truth shall shine round about him and the path of duty will open up clearly before him.

Now let us get back and see if that has any connection with the reading. Jesus had spoken the parable of the sower, and the disciples came and said, "Master, why do you speak to them in parables?" Why not come out and tell it with all directness? Here is the answer: Because "unto you it is given to know the mysteries of the kingdom of heaven," but unto them it "is not given." Now shall I conclude that there is partiality on the part of God and that some represent the very elect who from before the foundation of the world were designated unto eternal life? And of those to whom it is not given to know, we must say they were "nonelect," and regardless of all things, it is impossible for them to receive the truth? That would be foreign to the teaching of the Bible, and a conclusion hastily drawn, and wholly unwarranted. Why was it given unto some to know and not given unto the others? Well, the same thing is true tonight, and that scripture is just as applicable this very hour as it was when spoken on the shore of Galilee.

Study the matter just a minute. To whom was it given to know? To the disciples. Well, why? Some months before that, they had bidden good-by to things of this earth and to the material concerns of the world. They had left their respective occupations and had followed after the Savior, sitting at his feet, learning the wonderful lessons, watching the performance of miracles, with mouths, ears, and eyes open, anxious, ready, willing, wanting every word that came from his precious lips. They were studiously seeking the truth. What about them, Lord? Unto them it is given to know! To that very kind it is given tonight.

Well, why is it not given unto the others? You heard me read exactly why. "This people's heart is waxed"—or become—"gross." "Their ears are dull of hearing, their eyes *they* have closed, lest at any time they should see with their eyes and hear with their ears, understand with their heart, and should be converted, and I should heal them." Well, what about them? It is not given to that class to know the will of the Lord. They shut their eyes and stopped their ears and barred the door of their hearts—hear it!—a man of that kind cannot learn—it is impossible for that man ever to learn the truth. Why? He does not want the truth. He will not have teaching. He will not sit and hear and weigh honestly what might be said. He is opposed to the proposition. He closes his eyes and ears and heart for fear he might learn something which he does not want to know. Therefore, unto that man, Christ says, it is not given to know.

Now, then, that puts the responsibility, friends, upon every individual present. Do I tonight, solemnly and seriously, personally and individually, want to go to heaven when I die? No one on earth can answer that but me. Do I want to know what the will of the Lord is? Or am I such a partisan that I want my party to prevail, to triumph regardless? Do I gloat? "I expect to win out! I will down the other fellow!" Now a man of that sentiment is certain to go to hell. Do I want God's will to prevail, even though it might go contrary to my opinion? I must reach that point where God's will is supreme if heaven is ever mine in prospect to share, and I pray God tonight that each one may be able to say, "Lord, I am ready to give up all preconceptions; I am ready to forget any prejudices or former ideas; I want to come with open, honest frankness and say, 'Lord, speak; let me hear thy truth; command, I will obey,' and I will not stop to figure out why nor wherefore nor raise the point, 'Will not something else do, and cannot I get by with this?' "

Now then, with that as a setting, I just want to ask you some things tonight, for personal investigation. Friends, what is your attitude toward this book? First, with reference to its inspiration. Do you believe that this book is inspired of God? Do you believe this Bible was by inspiration given? Are you sold on the idea that holy men of old spake as they were moved by the Holy Spirit? I trust that I am speaking to a company who have not a doubt respecting this. Do we not believe that the Bible was breathed into men of old—that this book is not the product of man, but God's word, directed, inspired, and prompted by the Holy Spirit?

Assuming now that the audience is a unit on that, there is another point right in connection with this. There are two schools of thought at this place: The position of one is that it is ideally inspired. What is meant by that? That God gave the writers the idea and allowed them to frame it in their own language and to present it according to their conception and relationship toward the same. Then there is another school. Here is its view: That the Bible is inspired, word by word, verbal inspiration of God's book. Much depends upon your attitude toward these matters as to what you will be, what you will do, and what you will practice out in life. Well, the strongest argument against verbal inspiration is this: That verbal inspiration would destroy the individuality and the style of the different writers. Clearness of thought and accurate selection of words are essential to the expression of truth; but peculiarities of style have nothing to do with such. If that objection be valid, it would follow that God would be unable to tell Peter the very words that he desired told and that it must be left to Peter to arrange them after the general manner and make-up of Peter's decision along those lines. What is style? Well, it has to do with the arrangement of sentences and phrases; the use of connectives and the selection of synonyms. You might as well say that God could not make two styles for different blades of grass or leaves of the trees or two people, absolutely different, as to say that God was unable thus to fit his words, one by one, suited to the method by which Paul, Peter, James, or John might express themselves.

We have many illustrations of that kind that reduce the professed argument to nothingness. I heard someone tell this story that seemed to me to illustrate the very point. A gentleman from the country once walked up to the postmaster and inquired about a letter. He was handed one. He went off and stayed for ten or fifteen minutes trying to read it, but could not. Finally he brought it back to the postmaster and said, "I am unable to read this letter. I think it is written in some foreign language. And I would love to get you to help me decipher it." The postmaster said, "The only language I know is American. I do not know anything about foreign languages such as French, or German, or English, but I will do the best I can with it." So he took the letter and, with the aid of a dictionary, carefully studying it for a while, called the patron and said, "I think I have this thing worked out. I do not want you to take it too seriously, because it might not be this way; but I think your letter says this, 'Your Uncle James, being advanced in years and being debilitated, physically and intellectually, by reason of the frailties that attach to the encroachment of senility, and having suffered severe financial reverses, in a moment of temporary dementia, precipitated his own demise.' I think that is it, but in American language here is what it means, 'Your Uncle Jim got old, lost his wad, went nerts, and bumped himself off.' " Here are two ways of telling the same thing, as you can see. Now you get the two styles. The very same thing is told, but the idea is clothed in quite different styles. The point is made just the same, and while one fellow went way around by the Joneses and finally got to the point, the other one cut right through—his style was to rob it of all superfluity and go straight to the point.

Without further discussion tonight, I believe without a shadow of doubt, God spoke every word, one by one, unto those to whom he had assigned the task of penning his will toward man. I am told that the expression "Thus saith the Lord" is in the Bible some two thousand times. Let me just quote to you one or two passages. 1 Cor. 2: 12, 13, "Now we have received not the spirit of the world, but the spirit which is of God; that we might know the things that are freely given to us of God; which things also we speak"—now watch it—"we speak not in the words which man's wisdom teacheth, but which the Holy Spirit teacheth; comparing spiritual things with spiritual." Now, Paul, what have you said? We have received the Spirit of God, and we teach those things, not in the words of man's wisdom, but in words which the Holy Spirit hath spoken. But again, 1 Thess. 2: 13, "For this cause also thank we God without ceasing, because, when you received the word of God which you heard of us, you received it not as the word of men, but as it is in truth, the word of God, which effectually worketh also in you that believe." Not the idea—but the word! Brethren, that is not merely it—that is it! Why argue or have misgivings or doubts about a thing concerning which the Bible is so clear?

Well, again, my friends, what is the attitude that you have tonight toward the Bible with reference to this point: its completeness, all-sufficiency, fullness? Is the book of God complete? Is there something to be added? Do you accept this as a complete revelation of God's will to man and man's duty to God? Do you subscribe to the statement of Jude when he urged that men ought to contend earnestly for the faith which was *once for all* delivered unto the saints? Is that your attitude and disposition? Doubtless you say "yes." Don't you then see that you could not accept the Mormon idea that a revelation was made to Joe Smith? Jude said it "was *once for all* delivered to the saints." That settles it—there hasn't been anything since. Do you not see that you cannot subscribe to the idea of the Christian Scientist that God told Mrs. Eddy something and told her to repeat it. Contrast that with Paul's statement—"I was caught up unto the third heaven, I heard things that were unlawful for men to utter." But this woman says "God told me to tell it—he would not let Paul utter it, but he gave it to me." And that is a long time after Jude said, "Once for all delivered to the saints." Friends, the acceptance of the Bible teaching precludes the addition of revelation since the pen of inspiration was dropped from fingers weary on the lonely Isle of Patmos, almost twenty centuries gone by. That settles it.

Well, again: If you subscribe to the idea and have that attitude toward the Bible, that here is a full revelation of God's will to man, and in it there is programmed our duty to ourselves, to our fellow men, and to the God of our being, subscribing to that and believing that God has given unto us all things pertaining to life and Godliness, and that "the scriptures are profitable for doctrine, reproof, correction, and instruction in righteousness that the man of God may be perfect, completely furnished unto every good work," you cannot endorse any other attitude. If you cherish those statements, which I have read with little comment, then what? Do you not see that you cannot subscribe to any sort of human booklet in the form of a creed, discipline, confession of faith, or church manual? Do you not understand that you already preclude the possibility of such? When a man comes along with any kind of human document, supplementary to the Bible, and declares allegiance, and subscribes to that, what does it spell? The Bible is not as complete as it should be. It is lacking in some matters; therefore we have adopted this human booklet by which to be governed. Now I bid you think on that just a moment, and see whether or not you really believe the Bible to be complete.

But all manner of excuses are offered. Why I have heard them say, "Brother Hardeman, now I know that I have done that, but don't you think that we ought to have our articles of faith written down?" I surely do. "Well, then, here is our booklet." Do you mean to say by that that you have articles of faith which are not in the Bible? If so, you had better look out for your articles of faith—something wrong somewhere. I would be ashamed of myself tonight if there was a single article of faith to which I subscribe that I could not turn to in God's book and read. And if I can have it in the Bible, why do I have to have some "big men" get off in the corner and write it down again? "But, Brother Hardeman, we must have some rules and regulations governing our church." Now just wait a minute—what does that spell? First, we have got a church that God knew nothing about, and in his Bible there are no rules or regulations governing our church—I know that is the truth, there is none "governing our church." Do you mean to say, though, that in the Bible there are no rules or regulations governing the church bought with his blood? If there are, then what is the excuse for having a human book, be it called this, that, or the other? Friends, that is the wrong attitude toward God's book. What you need is faith implicit, undoubted, absolute in the all-sufficiency of the word of God.

Well, let us see again. What is your attitude toward the Bible with reference to prophetic matters? I know there are prophecies galore in God's book and what conception do you have of them? Just what approach do you have respecting the same? Well, what is a prophecy? First, it is the unveiling of events in the distant future that would preclude the possibility of accident, or merely coming to pass as a guess. Second, a prophecy must be sufficiently far in the future to preclude the prophet's living long enough to have any part in the fulfillment of the same. Third, there must be such a sufficiency of events and characteristics of it as to preclude the idea of chance. And fourth, prophecies are not to be accepted until they are fulfilled.

Friends, there are four statements regarding prophecies that are absolutely true. First, what it is. Second, how far distant must it be, beyond the realm of the life of the man making it, to prevent his serving as an agency in bringing it to pass. Third, not simply one point, but a sufficient number of points to prevent its being an accident. And, fourth, prophecies are not to be given full credence until after they are transformed into historic certainty. Now then, what is your attitude toward the Bible? Do you believe the statement made by Moses (Deut. 29 and verse 29) when he said: "Revealed things belong to man, unrevealed belong to God." Now where is my fear and what is my disposition toward matters of that kind? Well, I believe the Bible. God said in effect, "Hardeman, if you believe the Bible, you speak those things that are revealed."

That is what belongs to man. And don't you seek to be wise above that which is written, and whenever a prophecy comes to pass, then what? Believe it and recognize the fact that it is no longer prophecy, but is now a matter of history. Friends, that is the right attitude to assume toward all that, and my reception of any statement whatsoever, by any man made, depends upon that attitude! Now if I am disposed to search my own wisdom, draw my own conclusions, play upon my imagination, and paint pictures by my own ingenuity, then what? I transcend my authority and likewise the realm of Holy Writ and get out into the farthest depths of those things concerning which man absolutely knows nothing. But, when that thing has come to pass and sufficient evidence of its fulfillment is produced, then what? I preach that as an historic fact. Well, that is my attitude toward it.

Now again, what is the attitude that anybody ought to have toward error, be it whatsoever kind it may? I just regret that on all of these points there are divisions in our land—first, division regarding the inspiration of God's book; that is lamentable. Second, regarding the completeness of it, therefore the excuse of supplementary books in the form of church manuals and directories, etc. And again, with reference to prophetic declaration and on to the last regarding error. I think, brethren, that there is growing up among us a sentiment that my duty as a preacher is this: preach what you believe, what you conceive to be true, but let all things else alone. Now if preachers and those who advocate such were consistent about it, I would have more respect for them. But that very same fellow who may offer such counsel to me, and urge such procedure to be my duty, does not hesitate to criticize and condemn evil in general. He considers it error to have marble machines in Nashville. He opens his mouth about the liquor issue, and fights all kinds of evil. To be consistent with his principle, he should just go ahead and be sober himself and say nothing about the other fellows drinking liquor. And if some man wants to put up a saloon next door to him, he should not open his mouth. His theory is: preach your own doctrine and let the other fellow alone. And if someone wants to put a race track in Tennessee and license gambling, say nothing about it. Did you ever notice that very kind that are so wonderfully particular and object to any preaching against religious error are out on the public platform condemning all the errors in the social, in the political, and in the general realm of human affairs? Why not be consistent? There is a growing disposition to apologize for truth when preached and error when condemned. Friends, that is the most dangerous idea and the most pernicious attitude threatens the peace and the unity of the church of God tonight.

In the very same charge that Paul gives Timothy to preach the word he also said: "Reprove, rebuke, and exhort." Now Paul did not say, "Son, preach the word, preach the truth, let everything else alone." That disposition, friends, would never have planted the cause of truth upon the face of God's earth. When Paul, when Christ, when all of them were in the midst of the Jewish controversies of their day, they kept not silent respecting error. "Them that sin, rebuke before all, that others may fear." That is the teaching of God's word. It is the duty of the church to expose error and to declare the truth. Any preacher who will not do both is unworthy of the name. Every member of the church must do likewise.

That is what Paul said to Timothy. It is as much my duty to point out the error of young men, of young women, as it is to teach them the truth of God's word. I want to sound it out now. Boys and girls who come to Freed-Hardeman College, with which I have a connection, are not only taught the truth—they are taught the pitfalls, and the doctrines, and the errors that are along the pathways, so that they can stand out like a stonewall, immovable, absolutely firm and solid against every wave of doctrine contrary to the teaching which we have received. Now that is my attitude. I, of course, believe it the right one.

But again, friends, what is your attitude tonight toward the Bible with reference to its being a book of *Absolute Authority?* Is the Bible just a book of general directions, outlining the general policy, with all details to be worked out by sanctified common sense, or is the Bible specific in those things that would lead a man out of darkness into the kingdom of God? Is it specific and does it go into detail with reference to how the child of God ought to worship the Father? What do you think about it? Is it just a general broad-gauged book of principles with the details and specifications left to every man's own idea, or does God Almighty outline the path of duty from the time we leave the world of sin until by and by we sweep through the gates into his everlasting and eternal presence on the other shore? Think on these things.

I want those in this audience who are not to become Christians by obedience to the will of God. If you desire to do his will, if there is a disposition of heart and mind to accept it tonight, the invitation is gladly tendered.

TEACHING THE WORD OF GOD

Far beyond my power to express it, do I appreciate the fine audience assembled tonight, and I most earnestly hope that every service may be, within itself, the strongest possible invitation for your return. As Brother Acuff so well said there is nothing characteristic of this meeting intended to appeal to the gallery other than simple gospel singing of spiritual songs, the reading of the scriptures, and an earnest presentation of matters that ought to challenge the concern of every person who wants to go to heaven when he dies.

I am reading to you from the last part of Matt. 28—one of the most familiar paragraphs that I could select—"Then the eleven disciples went away into Galilee, into a mountain where Jesus had appointed them. And when they saw him, they worshipped him; but some doubted. And Jesus came and spake unto them, saying, All power is given unto me in heaven and in earth. Go ye, therefore, and teach all nations, baptizing them in the name of the Father, and of the Son, and of the Holy Ghost: Teaching them to observe all things whatsoever I have commanded you; and, lo, I am with you alway, even unto the end of the world."

My friends, there was never a more sacred, solemn charge clothed in human language delivered to mortal man than that which I have read in your midst. It is the language of their king, who was soon to be crowned at God's right hand. It is a charge to the disciples which meant either salvation or damnation to all accountable, responsible beings. Jesus Christ was ready to introduce and to inaugurate a new religion unlike that of the Patriarchal period or that of the Jewish age. It was new in all phases and the foundation of it was the obligation to teach the word of the Lord. May I just say to you that the very basic principle of Christianity is that of teaching, learning, grasping. Therein it differs from all other kinds of religion, and, be it said, that the church of God makes progress proportionate to the intelligence of the people and to the light revealed to them from God's word. It is a principle true everywhere that if you are conscious of the fact that you have the truth regarding any matter you seek the light and want all the evidence turned on because as a result it shines out with greater brilliancy. If there is error anywhere about our system, we seek to clothe that in darkness and to conceal it. Christ knew that he had a message to mankind, and he solemnly said to these disciples: "Go, therefore, and teach all the nations"—every creature in all the world.

I am talking, therefore, tonight, about that commission, not as ordinary preachers do. Teaching is the theme for discussion. The Bible abounds with statements embodying that principle. The prophet said prior to the times of Christ "they shall be all taught of God." Jesus quoting that said, "Therefore every man that heareth of the Father, learneth of him, cometh unto me." Becoming a Christian is not an accident. It is not a step of blindness, nor of ignorance, nor of mere passion, but it is a matter of true, calm deliberation upon the facts of the gospel. Hence, the very foundation of all work committed to the apostles and disciples was: they were to teach all men everywhere. Jesus himself went about teaching and preaching and confirming what he taught by the performance of miracles. A severe rebuke is administered in Heb. 5: 12 when the writer said: "The time is that you ought to be teachers of others, but instead of that, ye have need that one teach you again, which be the first principles of the oracles of God." If, my friends and brethren, the church of the Lord is not making the progress that we would desire, if you think there is a trend toward drifting and variation, I think the little end of the taproot of it is a lack of study and of teaching just what the will of the Lord is on the part of those who assume the responsibility for the same. Paul said to Timothy, "Now, therefore, my son, be strong in the grace that is in Christ Jesus, and the things that thou hast heard of me among many witnesses." The same thing, not something different, not something nearly like it, not something that sounds *almost* the same, but the *same* thing, "Commit those same things unto faithful men able to teach others also." Therefore you have the two qualifications of a gospel preacher. Here they are: First, faithful, loyal, true to God's word. Second, with an acquired or a native ability to put it across. Therefore Timothy handed it on down the line, sire to son, generation to generation, to faithful men, able to teach others also. Then he said again, Son, "continue thou in the things that thou hast learned, and been assured of, knowing of whom thou hast learned them." Men learn their religion. They are what they are because that is the way they have learned it. I have gone into Catholic cathedrals and have observed their peculiar manner and method of worship. I sat in old St. Peter's Cathedral for more than two hours and watched the secretary to the pope direct the service, going through all of their performances. I sat there and meditated—"that is not the way we do it back at Nashville, Tennessee, in the churches of our Lord, and hence, why do they perform after this fashion?" Now here is the answer: That is the way they learned it. Well, I have gone into Mohammedan places of worship and have watched their exceedingly peculiar form of worship. I have heard them read from the book called the Koran and go through their respective items and their peculiar postures of prayer. I then raise the point: What makes you do it that way? And the answer is: That is the way they learned it.

Now just apply that all over the land. Why do people in Nashville vary in worship and carry on differently? That is the way they learned it. Now if you were to ask me tonight: "Hardeman, why do you occupy the place you do and worship God according to the form characteristic of you?" Here is the answer: Friends, I learned it this way. So Paul said: "Timothy, continue thou in the things that thou hast learned and been assured of." Now watch it: "Knowing of whom thou hast learned them." Now mark this: It is not sufficient for me to simply say that I learned a certain system of worship, but right after that, I should raise the all-important point, where did I learn it, and what is the source of that information? From whom was I taught it? Did I receive it from the word of God? If so, I can check up on every item that I claim to follow and find it in God's book; but if perchance I start out and fail to find even that very organization of which I am a member, and in which I delight, and to which I lend my encouragement and my time, and influence, and money, then what do I know? I surely know that I learned this from the wrong source—I did not get it out of God's book because there is not a hint, nor a word, nor a syllable that even mentions my church. I know then that my teaching has been wrong, and I am not to continue in a thing other than that which I learned from the right source. So the whole thing is a matter of teaching.

Now, then, brethren, I want to raise this question: Upon whom, tonight, does the responsibility rest for executing the commission of our Lord? On whom does it depend? Who must carry out what the Savior said when he declared, "Go, teach all the nations?" Do you suppose that President Roosevelt and the cabinet assembled about him are conscious of this responsibility? Does the President say: "Gentlemen, we have got to carry out the commission of our Lord and teach all nations the gospel of Christ"? You know that commission was not given to the Democratic party, old dealers or new dealers. And, by the way, none of you Republicans ought to think that it was given you because God had no such things in mind. Hence, this is not the obligation of some political party. Well, I just wonder if the Odd Fellows ever felt keenly that it is their duty to carry out the command of our Lord and Savior Jesus Christ? To mention such a thing carries the negative answer.

Who, then, is responsible for the execution of the commission of our Lord? Is some modern, human, organization designated as a church? Did God give it unto them? Was he talking to some modern denomination when he said go teach all nations? Why, they were never heard of then and for hundreds of years afterward no such things existed on the face of the earth. Hence, they are eliminated on the ground that they did not exist when the Savior gave that solemn charge. Then it comes back to us: Upon whom does it rest? I think you will agree that these disciples were to be charter members of that institution called the church of our Lord. And on all such as are members of it that obligation is in force tonight.

But let us get this clearly fixed in mind, brethren: The church of the Bible is not some artificial, corporate body, from which we are distinct. I sometimes think we look upon it as such and stand back and criticize what the church is doing and what it is not doing. Wait a minute and raise the point: What is the church? It is that spiritual realm over which Christ is head and in which the Holy Spirit dwells. And every man or woman, boy or girl, who has been born again, born of water and of the Spirit, is a member of it. The very fact that I claim membership makes me and forces me to assume the obligation upon my part to execute the commission of our Lord.

The problem is: What am I doing along that line? Not what is the church doing—what am *I* doing? Because I claim to be a member of it, and the combined effort of individual Christians is the result or cause of all that the church may do. If, therefore, every individual becomes aware and keenly conscious of the fact that "I am a part of the church of the Lord, and the obligation rests upon me," I think that carelessness and indifference, that lack of familiarity of God's word, would cause us to shudder and get down to studying that we might show ourselves approved unto God, workmen that need not to be ashamed, rightly dividing, or handling aright, the word of truth. Hence, the obligation is upon the church. I am not expecting the Masonic fraternity to carry out the commission —I think they were never charged with teaching God's word. I think no human society was ever bidden to preach the gospel, but the church of the Lord, the only institution known in the Bible, was. It is that through which the wisdom of God was to be manifest unto all the nations of the earth—God's wisdom is to be made known by the church!

Hence, God's promise of salvation, God's scheme of redemption, God's teaching to the human family, is revealed to us and it is to be executed and maintained and continued through God's heaven-born and blood-bought institution, namely, the church. And that was not simply an accident, be it remembered. Let me call attention to this. There is a theory prevalent among our premillennial friends that the church was never intended by the Lord Almighty to exist upon this earth and was purely an accident; that Jesus Christ came to establish a kingdom, and the Jews having rejected him, he turned aside and established the church in its stead. Therefore, we are in the "church age" as a "spiritual contingent"—a thing not intended on the part of Jehovah.

Now will you just listen how plainly the Bible contradicts that? It says openly that such is untrue. I am reading to you from the third chapter of Ephesians, verse 10, but I begin at verse 8 for the connection: "Unto me, who am less than the least of all saints, is this grace given, that I should preach among the Gentiles the unsearchable riches of Christ; and to make all men see what is the fellowship of the mystery, which from the beginning of the world hath been hid in God, who created all things by Jesus Christ." To the intent—now watch it—"to the intent that now unto the principalities and powers in heavenly places might be made known *by the church* the manifold wisdom of God, according to the *eternal purpose* which he purposed in Christ Jesus our Lord."

Why, friends, from the foundation of the world God purposed the church as a missionary agency through which the wisdom of God, the teaching of heaven's will, was to be made known to the sons and daughters of men. Paul, therefore, said that the church is God's medium and it was so intended from the very foundation of the earth. It was in the beginning! Away, then, with the idea that the church is a "contingent." The church is God's institution and according to his eternal purpose it existed that it might teach the world the unsearchable riches of Christ.

Well, let us think of some other phases and decide from these considerations. When I study the Bible and become conscious of the fact that the religion revealed in it is a taught religion, I begin to wonder: How does God teach us? What are the methods by which heaven's instruction are to be made known unto man? And may I suggest to you now that there are three ways by which God teaches us his will, his word, his way. Now hear them: First, he teaches by direct statement, by positive command, saying the thing in so many words. Now that is one way. Well, there is another. You might not have a direct "Thus saith the Lord," but if you can find an example approved and inspired of God, that concrete example comes to us with all the power and force of divine authority. That is God's way of teaching. Then again, if there is a passage in the Bible from which a necessary conclusion and inference must be drawn, I am willing to accept the statement that the Bible teaches that thing. So watch then. How does God teach us? First, by direct statement. Second, by approved example. Third, by a *necessary* inference. And now it is mine to demonstrate those three methods tonight. I trust that it will make you appreciate the Bible all the more and give you standards by which you can determine whether or not anything presented merits your approval in the light of God's truth.

Suppose I were to raise the question tonight: Does God teach all men to repent of their sins? What do you think about it? Why, of course, you would say yes. Well, how does he teach us repentance? Why, here is how: He comes out openly and says so. Paul stood on Mars Hill (Acts 17: 30) and said, "The time of this ignorance God winked at [or passed it by], but now God commands all men everywhere to repent." Now that settles it. Well, does God teach us anything about assembling? In Heb. 10: 25, "Brethren, forsake not the assembling of yourselves together, as the manner of some is, but exhort one another, and so much the more, as ye see the day approaching." Does God teach that? Certainly he does. How? He plainly says it.

Well, ought brethren and Christians to contribute of their means to the support of the gospel? Surely! Does the Bible teach it? Yes! How? 1 Cor. 16: 1, "My brethren, concerning the collection for the saints, as I have given order to the churches of Galatia, even so do ye." "Upon the first day of the week," that is the *time*, "let every one of you," that is the *who*, "lay by in store," that is *getting ready*, now mark it, "according to ability," or to prosperity. Does the Bible teach that? Certainly it does.

What about lying? "Lie not one to another, speak the truth in your heart, do not bear false witness." God says it. Now that is what I mean by the Bible teaching a thing by *direct statement*.

Well, now let us get some other things. Brethren, does the Bible teach Christians to observe the Lord's Supper on the first day of the week? You answer, "Yes." Now, have you stopped to think just how that is done, and how the Bible teaches it? Christ told the disciples, and so did Paul, "Take and eat" and thus we are commanded by direct statement to eat of the bread and to drink of the fruit of the vine. But I just want to ask some of you "old-timers" where did Christ ever say, "Eat of the Lord's Supper on the first day of the week?" Had you ever stopped, brethren, to meditate upon a thing like that? Where is the command to partake of it on the first day of the week? I can find you a command to eat of it, and to drink of the fruit of the vine, but where is the *direct statement* to do that on the first day of the week? And do you know that the fellow that knows where that is is not present tonight and has not been here and is not going to come? Now why? Because there is no such statement in the Bible, and I trust none of you, brethren, will get shaky over Brother Hardeman's announcement of that fact. Yet, the Bible teaches—mark it—the Bible teaches the observance of the Lord's Supper on the first day of the week. But how does it teach it? Now here is the way: By giving us an *approved example* of the brethren at Troas meeting on the first day of the week to break bread. Therefore, that example of their doing it under the direction of the Holy Spirit comes with all authority. Now, if I would meet with God's approval, as did they, I will do likewise, and on the first day of the week partake of the supper of the Lord. What is my authority? A heaven-inspired example! Now let me carry along with that this idea. I do not know whether you have had to meet it or not, but I have. After teaching that way, and preaching after this fashion, I have had men to ask me, "Well, Hardeman, why don't you folks then wash one another's feet if you are going to follow an example? Don't you know that Christ instituted the supper and the washing of feet about the same time?" Yes! "With the same persons?" Yes! "And did he not tell them that he left them an example that they should follow in his steps?" Yes! "Then why is it that you hold on to one example, namely, the observance of the supper, and reject the other example of washing feet?" I think that is a legitimate question, and I can appreciate any man's asking a thing of that kind. Now, watch it—why is it that the church of Christ accepts the example of eating the Lord's Supper on the first day of the week, but does not wash feet as a church ordinance? Well, I will tell you why! Here it is: Both of those examples were given before the church of the Lord was organized. During the personal ministry of Christ, the supper was instituted and the washing of feet was inaugurated. Now then, after the church was organized I find where brethren met together on the first day of the week to break bread. Whenever somebody in Nashville can find where the brethren, after the church was established, met to wash their feet, I will agree to do it or admit that I am wonderfully inconsistent. But that man does not live in Nashville; he has never heard of Nashville. Therefore, I am on positively safe, legitimate grounds, consistent grounds, when I accept the example of eating of the supper and reject the perpetuity of the washing of feet. So much for that.

Now, there are some things that I think the Bible teaches and yet, if you were to ask me to read it in so many words, I could not do it. If you were to ask me to give a direct example for it, I could not do it, and yet I would say it teaches it. Well, how? By a necessary deduction or inference. Now, I grant you that you have to be careful in studying matters of this kind. Inferences are of two kinds, may I say, *logical* or *reasonable*, and second, *necessary*. Let me illustrate: My home is at Henderson, Tennessee, 140 miles west of here. Well, here I am at Nashville. That is a fact. Now with that fact you may begin to infer how I got here. Someone said, "He came on the train." Well, I did not tell you I did, but how did you decide that? "Oh, I just inferred that you came on the train." That is a reasonable inference. That is not silly. And someone else said, "I just have drawn the conclusion that you rode the bus." Well, people do ride the buses and that is a reasonable inference, and I might have come that way. And another infers and decides, "He came in a private car." Now all of those are sensible, but I want to ask you, "Which one of them is necessary?" Not a single one! Why? Because I could have walked and not have come either way, or I could have ridden a mule as I have done. Now can you see the difference between a *reasonable* inference and a *necessary* one? And right there, I believe is the ground of much of the confusion in the religious world tonight. Inferences, if hastily drawn, and not carefully thought out, will lead you into error of the most dangerous type whatsoever. Now, I can illustrate what I mean by a *necessary* inference. In the twelfth chapter of Genesis we have an account of a famine in the land of Palestine, so much so that Abraham and Sarah, his wife, went down into the land of Egypt, and because of her beauty, there was trouble with the Pharaohs. After all that is over the first verse of the thirteenth chapter of Genesis says this, "And Abraham went up out of Egypt, he, and his wife, and all that he had, and *Lot* went with him, into the south." Now what is the statement, "Lot went with him up out of Egypt?" Now question, did Lot go down into Egypt? The Bible is as silent as the twinkling stars. There is not a word ever said about it. Someone said, what do you think about it, Hardeman? I think he did. Well, what makes you think it? Because of the statement the Bible says, "Lot came up out of Egypt," and I am forced to the conclusion, therefore, that he must have gone down into the land else the statement of the Bible that he came up out of it could not be true. I infer, therefore, with all the right of Bible authority, Lot went down into Egypt. But I can give you brethren one that you know more about than you do that. In the third chapter of Matthew it is said, "And Jesus, when he was baptized, went up straightway out of the water." Did you know, brethren, that the Bible never did say that Christ went down into the water? And yet, you will argue that he did, and, I think, argue correctly. But if you were called upon to read "where did Christ ever go down into the water" you could not do it. That is not in the Bible. Well, someone said, "Another fellow did, and that is the example." No, the example of someone else would not prove that he did. "Well, I know he did." How do you know it? Because the Bible said he came up *out* of it, and physically, it is impossible for a man to have come up out of Egypt or out of the water unless previous to that he had gone down into it. Therefore, the Bible teaches that Jesus Christ went down *into* the water and was baptized and came up *out* of it. Let us see another source of error on the part of many people that do not think logically and correctly. In Acts 16 the Bible says that "Lydia and her house were baptized." That is the statement made after Paul had preached to her and God opened her heart so that she attended unto the things that were spoken. All right, "Lydia and her house were baptized." Now note one system of reasoning. Lydia was a married woman. How do I know? I assume it. What made me assume it? Why, it said "she and her house," and I infer that if she had a house, she must have been married. And Lydia had children. Why? The Bible says "she and her house were baptized," and I infer that if she had a house, she must have had children, and some of those children were babies. Well, how do I know? Well, I just infer that she had a house, and had children, and some of them were babies. Now the Bible says "she and her house were baptized," therefore I reach the conclusion that there is a case of *baby baptism.* How did I get that? By inferring it! Well, was the inference silly? No, not at all. Every one of those things sometimes happens. But raise the point: Is it necessary for the statement of God's word to be true that Lydia must have been married? Can a woman have a household and not be married? Well, I know they can and I can name you some. Again, can a woman have a household and not have children? Surely, and there are plenty of them in Nashville. Furthermore, in a household where there are children, is it necessary that some of them are infants? How about it at your house? Any infants at your house? Friends, did you know this? You can canvass the City of Nashville, up one street and down two and then across over to three, and you will not find an infant in every fifth home. Therefore, the conclusion that because the Bible says "Lydia and her house were baptized" there must have been babies is a dangerous conclusion and not necessarily so. Why? The facts of the Bible can exist without that, and yet, as a good Pedobaptist preacher friend of mine once said to me, Hardeman, that is the strongest argument I know of in the Bible for baby baptism. Then he added, I will admit that it is an inference wholly unnecessary. That is what all ought to think.

Now then, let us make application of some of these things in the time that is left tonight, and get some matters further before us. Brethren everywhere teach that the church, or the kingdom of God, was set up, inaugurated, established on the first Pentecost after the resurrection of Christ. I will affirm that any day with a respectable opponent and feel certain of my ground. Well, some one said, Does the Bible say it was set up on Pentecost? No, it does not say it. Well, is there an example of something else having been set up on Pentecost? That would not prove that the church was. How do you reach that conclusion then? By a necessary inference. Some one said, "Let us see you go about it." Well, that is not the theme tonight, but just a word. "There be some of you standing here which shall not taste of death until the kingdom of God shall come with power." (Mark 9: 1.) Christ said in effect, "Some of you folks are not going to die until God's kingdom will come, and it is going to come with power," and then he said, "Tarry in the city of Jerusalem until ye be endued with power from on high." Now note: The kingdom is to come with power, the power came with the Spirit, and the Bible says, "the Spirit came on Pentecost." Therefore, I am forced to the conclusion that if God's Spirit came on Pentecost, the power came with it and God said the kingdom would come with the power. Therefore, the kingdom of God was established upon this earth on the first Pentecost after the resurrection of Christ, and away with the man who declares no such thing is yet in existence.

Well, does the Bible teach that baptism to a penitent believer is for the remission of sins? It does and I will affirm that with any respectable opponent. Well, how does it teach it? There is not any inference about that at all. God just comes right out and says it. Unto those who had heard the gospel, who had been cut to their hearts and cried out, "Men and brethren, what shall we do?" Peter said, prompted by the Holy Spirit, "Repent and be baptized, everyone of you, in the name of Jesus Christ for the remission of sins, and you shall receive the gift of the Holy Spirit." No inference about that; no example about it; there is the straight statement itself. I believe that. Why? That is what the Bible says.

Well, let us try again. At the time to which I referred as being in old St. Peter's, I saw our Catholic friends count their beads, one by one, and say a little sentence prayer with each bead pulled down the string. Now, without any prejudice against it or anything unkind to say about the practice, I ask: Does the Bible teach that? It will have to teach it in one of three ways: First, is there any command in God's word bidding folks to count their beads as a religious rite? And I turn to the Bible, unbiased and unprejudiced, and try to find that. No, no such statement. All right. Does the Bible teach it by direct statement? No. Is there any example approved under heaven where they were counting beads and God smiled graciously upon it? Absolutely none. Well, again, is there any statement in all the Bible from which I must conclude, therefore, they surely did count beads? Now there is not a sign of a statement like that in the Bible. Therefore, what? I say the Bible does not teach it. Why? I have checked up on the three methods of teaching and each one is like old Belshazzar "weighed in the balances and found wanting."

Brethren, try any kind of a theory. With those who use mechanical devices to worship God, I raise the point: Is there a direct statement in the New Testament where God orders men to play upon human devices? Well, search the Bible. What is the answer? None.

Again, is there any example where an apostolic church or inspired church had mechanical devices wherewithal to worship God? Search again. What is the answer? None. Well, you are not done yet. Is there any statement in the New Testament from which I am forced to the conclusion they must have had mechanical devices? Not one. Therefore, with an intelligence that carries conviction, openness and frankness, *hear* it—the Bible does not teach it. That man does not live that can find it. Now that is the way to get at things all along the line. Try any kind of a newfangled theory, any kind of a speculation, any kind of a guess—check up on it and you will find it is the easiest matter in this world to determine whether or not the Bible teaches it. But that is enough for tonight.

Now the Bible does teach, my friends, that all people everywhere should believe on the Lord Jesus Christ; that they should repent of their sins, confess his name, acknowledge him as leader or Master, and be buried with him, from which burial they arise to walk in newness of life. That is in the Bible clearly taught and if there is one or more tonight present, desirous of doing that very thing, the invitation is gladly tendered while together we sing the song.

IS THE GOSPEL, AS GOD GAVE IT, ADAPTED TO MAN, AS GOD MADE HIM?

I am quite certain, my friends, that possibly those of us most directly interested in this meeting, have not yet realized the wonderful importance of it and the results that are to follow. Brethren all over the United States are looking to this meeting. They are anxious regarding it. In view of their interest, I want to appeal to all friends to make whatever effort is necessary to lend your presence at every service you possibly can. We all understand the setting and the crisis through which, apparently at least, the church of the Lord is passing. Hence, with the keen responsibility and a consciousness of it, we ought to move step by step in the light of that eternal judgment toward which we are so rapidly passing. I am delighted with the company here tonight, and I think, though the rain should come, we ought not let that interfere.

I am trying to speak along lines that will not only be interesting and, perhaps, profitable to you, but which will be read by thousands whose influence will extend far beyond that period in which I live. In the light of all that, with God as my witness, I want to speak forth the words of truth and soberness and declare only God's will and word to mortal man.

I have two statements to read tonight from the Bible. Here is the first one: Gen. 1: 27, "God created man in his own image, in the likeness of God created he him; male and female created he them." I think nobody here doubts that. I believe that there is not a soul who subscribes to the idea that man's existence is accounted for on any other grounds than that God created him out of the dust of the earth, breathed into his nostrils the breath of life, and he stood forth a living soul. Now the next passage that I have for you is Rom. 1: 16-18. "I am not ashamed of the gospel of Christ, for it is the power of God unto salvation to everyone that believeth; to the Jew first, and also to the Greek. For therein is the righteousness of God revealed from faith to faith, as it is written, The just shall live by faith." I have read those two passages to get a matter before you for study, in the form of a question. Here it is—Is the gospel, as God gave it, adapted to man as God made him? Will you think on that for just a moment and get it well fixed in mind? Away back yonder, in the far distant past, God made man. After forty centuries there was presented a plan of salvation. Now question: Is the plan adapted to the man? Is it suited and commensurate with his needs? I think implied in this is the very foundation of difference between the church of Christ and most religious denominations of our land. Brethren everywhere, who have subscribed 100 per cent to the Bible, answer that theory in the affirmative. The world about us would answer, No, that the gospel is not adequate, and therein is the first difference between, what I believe to be truth, and error. Now, you ask, Upon what grounds I make that statement? Well, here it is: The denominational world teaches that in conviction and conversion there must be a power in addition to and distinct from the word of God to bring about the conversion of the alien sinner, that you may know I am not mistaken about it, I give you this concrete evidence. I held a four-days' debate last April in the city of Little Rock with Dr. Ben M. Bogard of the Missionary Baptist Church. That debate is published, and I notice today, it will be ready for mailing next Monday. The first proposition in that was affirmed by Bogard, and here it is: "The Bible teaches that in conviction and conversion there must be a power brought to bear upon the heart of the sinner in addition to and distinct from the word of God." What does that imply? That the plan of salvation, as revealed in God's word, is not sufficient—that it is lacking somewhere, and before a sinner can be converted, God must move and bring about supernatural and additional power to the gospel as revealed in the Bible, to accomplish the salvation of the man. Hence, the question implies a fundamental matter, and I repeat it. When God made man, and after forty centuries developed the plan, I ask: Was that plan, and is that plan fitted, suited, and adequate to the needs of the man whose soul he was seeking to save? Now if it be not commensurate and adapted, I want to raise this point with you: Why is it not? God made man; God made the plan, Why didn't he fix the plan suited to the man for whom it was intended? If you say that God *could* not thus arrange a plan, you reflect upon His ability, and limit His power. If you say that He *would* not draw up the plan suited to the man, you reflect upon his goodness and you take the responsibility from man and transfer it wholly to God. If, therefore, anybody is damned, God will be responsible for it. If, for instance, here is a man unable to render obedience to the gospel of the Lord until high heaven moves in some supernatural way, then if God ever moves upon him and brings about his conversion, He is under obligation to convert also this other man by a supernatural power; and if He converts two men beyond and above what is written for their consideration, then the obligation extends to two hundred, to two thousand, to two million, and to the entire human family, on the ground that God is no respecter of persons. If, therefore, at the judgment bar of Jehovah, I should be denounced, and hear Him say: "Depart into everlasting fire," I could truly answer, "Lord, I am not to blame. There I was waiting, longing, and begging for you to send that miraculous power by which I might be enabled to render obedience to the gospel of Christ." So, all of that, I think, is implied in this question, and it's striking at the very foundation of whether or not human organizations are in error or whether or not the church of the Lord has been mistaken in such proclamations.

Now, you ask, "How can we study a thing of this kind?" And, so far as I know, there is only one way. Here it is: I have to learn something about that man which makes him a subject of gospel address. I must analyze him and find that which must be converted. Then, I need to analyze and to understand what the gospel is. After an analysis of each of them, it looks to me as if I then ought to be the more able to determine whether or not the plan fits the man, as also he has been analyzed. So with that setting before us, I am calling your attention now, to the man. What have you to say regarding that? I think we all agree that it is not his physical make-up or being that needs changing. This body of mine is not a subject of gospel address. It is not subject to the law of God, neither, indeed, can it be. Hence, that eliminates the physical part of it. What, therefore, must be converted? And without being tedious about it, I think we all agree, it's that thing in man called the *Heart*. Note its condition. "The heart is deceitful above all things, and desperately wicked." Therefore, before man can be saved, that heart that goes to make up the part addressed and that is taken into consideration by high heaven, must be converted. But that brings up the point now as to what the heart is? And I am not going to reflect upon your intelligence by talking about this muscular organ, this engine in my physique that pumps the blood to the extremities of my body. Let's eliminate that on the ground that nobody wants that thing tampered with or changed in the least bit. I don't even want any organs of mine changed. They have been functioning pretty well for forty-two years and then some, and I have no desire to have any change, whatsoever, wrought in my physical organism. So what is the heart, the thing to be converted? Well, the Bible is not like a dictionary. You can't just take up the alphabet and run down to the H's in the book of God and find a direct, straight-forward definition of the heart. But we learn what a thing is by learning what it does. If, tomorrow on the streets of Nashville, I were to meet a man with a hammer, saw, plane, and other tools, I would say that fellow is a carpenter. I would think he's a carpenter. Another person comes along with a little grip in his hand and there's an array of medicine cases and surgical equipment in it, I would draw the conclusion that that man is a surgeon, or a physician. And if I were to see some man up before the judge of the court, pleading the cause before the gentlemen, or even the women, of the jury, I would sit there and say, "I know what that fellow is." Well, who told you? Nobody. Then, what is he? I answer, a lawyer. How do you know? Because I have seen what he does. Now that's very simple and yet there is a great principle involved in it. What is the heart? I propose, to-night, a survey of the Bible, that we may learn about it. Now commencing in Genesis 6: 5, very early in the record, we have this statement; mark it—"God saw that the wickedness of man was great upon this earth, and that every imagination of the thoughts of his heart was evil and that continually." Now what have you learned from it? God said that the *thoughts* of the heart, not the thought of some other part of the man, but the thought originates in the heart. Now there isn't any use for comment. A man who believes the Bible won't deny that. The heart is that part, therefore, about me that does the thinking. Who said so? God did, and that's the end of it. "The thought of the heart"—What are you exercising right now? Why, the heart, in that you are thinking with me along this outline which I am trying to present.

Well, in addition to that, get this statement. In the second chapter of Mark, just after the Saviour had said to the man sick of palsy, "Son, thy sins be forgiven thee, arise and walk," the scribes sat there, "reasoning in their hearts." Christ said to them; "Why reason ye these things in your hearts." What do you learn now? Just from the Bible direct, without any comment upon it, you have learned that the heart is that part about man that *thinks*, and is that thing about him that *reasons*.

Well, again, Matt. 13: 15. "This people's heart is waxed gross, their ears are dull of hearing, their eyes they have closed; lest at any time they should see with their eyes, hear with their ears," now watch it—"and should understand with their heart, and thus be converted, and I should heal them." What does the heart do? It *thinks*, it *reasons*, it *understands*. Well, "what doth hinder me to be baptized?" That's a Bible question. Here's the answer. "If thou believest with all thine heart, thou mayest." Therefore, with the heart, man believeth, as with the mouth he makes the confession. Now look at it! What is the heart?

It's that part about us that *thinks,* that *reasons,* that *understands,* that *believes.*

Now in man's analysis of his fellows, he says that is his Intellect, the part about him that thinks, reasons, believes, understands. That's the intellect of man, thus functioning, and thus exercising itself. Well, all right. Now hold that in mind, will you? Is that all that the Bible says about the heart? Absolutely not. Heb. 4: 12, "The word of God is quick and powerful, sharper than any two-edged sword, piercing even to the dividing asunder of soul and spirit, and of the joints and marrow," now watch it—"and is a discerner of the thoughts and intents of the heart." Where was the origin and whence the seat of all that? With what were you thinking and intending? God says, with the heart. Did you ever have any plans and purposes? If so, hear II Cor. 9: 7, "Every man according as he purposeth," where? "in his heart, so let him give." Now what have you learned? The heart is that thing that intends. It is that which purposeth. Watch again, "you have obeyed from the heart." Rom. 6: 17. What is that? Obedience has back of it the heart of man, doing the act. So what have you learned? The heart is that part about us that intends, that purposes, that executes. Now what does man call that? He says, that's the willpower. The part that thinks, and reasons, and understands, and believes, he calls the Intellect. That part which intends, purposes, executes, he calls the Will. Now is that all? No!

Rom. 10: 1, Paul said, "Brethren, my heart's desire," your what's desire? "My heart's desire," the desire of my heart. Now where are desires in the origin? In the heart. Who said so? Paul did. Who dare say to the contrary? Not I!

Again, "Thou shalt love the Lord thy God with all thy heart, with all thy strength, and all thy might" said Christ to the young lawyer. Where is the seat of love? In the heart. I love you with all my heart. But that's not all.

Prov. 3: 5, Solomon said; "Son, trust in the Lord with all thine heart." Now look at it. What does the heart do? It desires, yearns, longs for a thing. What else about it? It loves, and it is the seat of affection. Well, what further? It trusts, confides, reposes. What do men call that? Our Emotional nature. Friends, look at it. God says the heart is that part that thinks, that reasons, that understands, that believes. Man says Intellect. God says the heart intends, purposes, executes. Man says the Will. God says the heart is that part that desires, that loves, that trusts. Man says the Emotion. Friends, into how many departments is man divided according to our psychologists? Into three. What are they? *Intellect,* the power to know; *Will,* the power to do; *Emotion,* the power to feel. Now there's the man, as God made him. That's the thing that God wants converted. He wants my thinking turned in the right direction; my reasoning after God's pattern; my understanding changed to the right, my faith centered in Jesus Christ our Lord. He wants my intentions to be to do His will, and my purpose to walk in His footsteps, and my determination to be to execute that which I have decided to be the will of God. And after that, then what? There is that desire for better things, based upon a splendid promise. There is a love that grows brighter day by day, and ultimately casts out all fear, and there is that thought that wheresoever He lead me, I will gladly follow. I can do all things through Christ, who strengtheneth me. Friends, that's Man. Well, all right. God made him—now hold that in mind—his Intellect, his Will, his Emotion.

Now, let's study the gospel. First, what is the gospel? The gospel is something that God wants preached to every creature in all the world. Now, I know that much about it. Second, "Though I preach the gospel, I have nothing to glory of, yea necessity is laid upon me, woe is unto me if I preach not the gospel." 1 Cor. 9: 16. I know that much about it. Well again. Gal. 1: 8, 9. "Though we, or an angel from heaven, preach any other gospel unto you than that which you have received, let him be accursed." "And as we said before, so say I again, if any man preach any other gospel unto you than that which you have received, let him be accursed. And I marvel that you are so soon removed from the gospel." I know that about it. Now, what else?

Here's another—2 Thess. 1: 6, 7, 8. "God will recompense tribulation unto them that trouble you, and unto you who are troubled, God will recompense rest with us, when the Lord Jesus Christ shall be revealed from heaven with his mighty angels," now watch it—"taking vengeance upon them that know not God, and that obey not the gospel of His Son, who shall be punished with everlasting destruction from the presence of God, and from the glory of His power." Now I know that much about it. It's something that must be obeyed.

Well, again, "Moreover, brethren, I declare unto you the gospel which I preached unto you, which also ye have received, wherein ye stand, and by which also ye are saved." Now look at it—just those things you have learned thus far: The gospel is something God wants preached to all men; woe is unto the man who does not preach; it must not be perverted, and cannot be with impunity; it is that which man must obey, or else be punished with everlasting destruction from the presence of God and the glory of His power; it is that wherein Christians stand, by which they are saved, if they keep in memory what has been preached, unless they have believed in vain. Now, I know that much about it. But that is not all. Hear Paul further: (1 Cor. 15: 1-4) "Moreover, brethren, I declare unto you the gospel which I preached unto you, which also you have received, and wherein you stand; by which also you are saved, if you keep in memory what I preached unto you, unless you have believed in vain." Now mark it: "For I delivered unto you first all that which I also received, how that Christ died for our sins according to the scriptures; and that he was buried, and that he rose again the third day according to the scriptures." Christ died—that is fact number one; he was buried, fact number two; he rose again, fact number three. Now what do you have? Three fundamental facts of the gospel of God's Son, by which all men are to be saved, and of which Paul said "I am not ashamed of the gospel for it is God's power unto salvation" unto everyone that believes. And therein—not thereout, but therein—in the gospel is the righteousness of God revealed from faith unto faith.

Friends, that's not nearly it—that's it! And that's God word for it.

So, then, the gospel tonight, friends, is composed of three facts—what are they? That Christ died for our sins, according to the scriptures; that he was buried; and that he burst the bars and came forth triumphant on the morning of the third day according to the scriptures. Those are the three piers on which the bridge that connects the shores of time with the shores of eternity must forever rest. Upon what do you propose to make the transition? Upon that great bridge, may I say, that rests upon three solid pillars, deeply founded and correctly set. Here they are. The fact that Christ tasted death for every man; that he was buried in a borrowed tomb; that he burst the bars and came forth triumphant over the powers of the Hadean world—all of which constitute the fundamental facts of gospel truth.

But is that all? No, the gospel is not only made up of facts, but it is made up also of commandments that challenge the attention of mankind. What are they? As the facts are three in number, likewise are the commands. Faith in Jesus Christ, our Lord; a genuine repentance of every sin; and a burial into the name of the Father, Son, and Holy Spirit, upon a confession of that faith. Those are the commandments of the gospel. Well, is *that* all? No. There is something else yet. As there are three fundamental facts—death, burial, and resurrection of Christ; as there are three commands—faith, repentance, and baptism upon an acknowledgment of that faith; likewise there are three great and exceeding precious promises. You ask, what are they? First, forgiveness of every sin. Secondly, the gift of God's Spirit to comfort and console us, as on down life's way we journey; then when we come to the end of the road, he promises eternal life. Now then, mark it—the *gospel* is made up of Facts, Commands, and Promises. Well, what's *man* made up of? An Intellect, a Will, and an Emotional nature. Now then, what part of the gospel is adapted to the intelligence of man, to his thinking, reasoning, understanding, believing? I submit to you, friends, the wonderful harmony, the absolute fitness in all things divine—the facts of the gospel challenge the intellect of man! What can I do with the facts? Someone said, "Obey them." No! I never obeyed a fact in my life. Well, someone said, "Enjoy those facts." Not that. To what part of my nature do the facts of the gospel appeal? They challenge me to think on the tragic story of the cross, to reason whether or not it be out of line for God to raise the dead. Do you think it incredible that God should do it? And further, that Jesus came forth triumphant by the power of God Almighty, which was wrought in Christ Jesus our Lord? Friends, what can I do with those facts? I can think about them, reason about them, try to understand just how the facts came to pass, even if I do not understand the method by which they were wrought, and finally, thank God, I can believe those facts without any hesitancy whatsoever. Therefore, my intellect is satisfied by the facts of the gospel. I think about the facts, I reason regarding them, I try to understand them, I believe them, hence, that part of my nature is conplemented by the gospel of God's Son.

Well, the next part: What may I do with the commands of the gospel of Christ? To what part of my nature do they appeal and apply? May I ask: what's a command for? It's a challenge, always, to our will power. No father, mother, teacher, or anybody else, ever gave an order in the form of a command, but it meant to call on someone's will-power. And to that part of his nature it appeals. It isn't a question of whether you believe it or not; it is not a matter to reason about; but rather, do you intend to do it; do you purpose in your heart to carry it out; will you walk in obedience, and execute the same? Hence, the commands of the gospel challenge man's will-power. I can form intentions and purposes regarding them. I can make plans and purposes respecting them. Finally, I can walk out and obey the same, and that's exactly the adaptability of the one to the other. Well all right, my intellect is satisfied by the facts of the gospel challenge; my will-power is complemented by the commands of the gospel. Now then, what? There is my emotional nature whereby I delight to revel in fancy's vision of the glories I anticipate on the other

shore. What part of the gospel now is fitted to that? Thank God, I can look back and say, though my hands were stained in sin, and my heart was blurred and blackened by it, there is a fountain filled with blood that can cleanse the soul of every stain. I have forgiveness of sins in that I have obeyed from the heart that form of doctrine, and have been delivered from sin and become a servant of Christ Jesus our Lord. And I revel in the splendid promises contained in his word. Friends, I want to ask you, what's lacking? Wherein is there need for supernatural power? Why not all brethren stand as did those of the Restoration, and preach as did the apostles, the adequacy, the all-sufficiency of the gospel of Christ, God's power unto salvation? Why not blend together, with all opinion in the background, and all matters disturbing the peace, tranquillity, and harmony of the Church of the Lord, laid aside? Then recognizing the tremendous fight of Satan and his mighty forces, why not marshal all of our strength against him and as a solid phalanx, march together underneath the banner of Him who has never yet lost a conflict?

It makes the heart of a real Christian bleed tonight to think of the divided condition among those who profess to believe just what I have preached. Under other conditions they would endorse it 100 per cent, and yet, because of some matters which even they recognize as non-essential, they would mar the happiness and the unity of all efforts earnestly put forth. I pray God that the time may come when such will not be, when all will rally around the truth of God and will stand four-square for the gospel as "God's power unto salvation," against all who teach the necessity of supernatural, "separate and apart and distinct" action in the conversion of men.

If there is present tonight a soul who recognizes the need of salvation, I want you to enter into the service of God, I want you to say deep down in your heart, "I believe the facts of the gospel; I will obey its commands and trust God for the promises. Come while you can.

UNITY AMONG BRETHREN

I want to join Bro. Boles and others in expressing appreciation of the presence of such a splendid audience on this Thursday night.

I am reading to you from the first part of the fourth chapter of Ephesians, "I, therefore, the prisoner of the Lord, beseech you that ye walk worthy of the vocation wherewith ye are called, with all lowliness and meekness, with longsuffering, forbearing one another in love." The word forbearing means over-reaching, as if to cover and take under protection, like the eaves of a house extending over the walls to protect the same. "I beseech you, therefore, brethren, that you walk worthy of the vocation wherewith ye are called, with all lowliness and meekness, with longsuffering, forbearing one another in love; endeavoring to keep the unity of the Spirit in the bond of peace. There is one body, and one Spirit, even as ye are called in one hope of your calling; one Lord, one faith, one baptism, one God and Father of all, who is above all, and through all, and in you all." I read that to introduce to you the topic for discussion tonight, namely, "Unity Among Brethren." The Ephesian church had it. Paul urged them to preserve it. Unfortunately, we do not have it, but are striving to bring it about. In connection with that, I am reading the 133rd Psalm, "Behold, how good and how pleasant it is for brethren to dwell together in unity! It is like the precious ointment upon the head, that ran down upon the beard, even Aaron's beard; that went down to the skirts of his garments; as the dew of Hermon, and as the dew that descended upon the mountains of Zion; for there the Lord commanded the blessing, even life for evermore."

I am wonderfully conscious of the responsibility that I assume tonight in discussing a matter of this kind, but I am also wonderfully impressed with the superlative importance of our studying matters of this sort. There's no one here that doubts the truth of the text. "Behold, how good and how pleasant it is for brethren to dwell together in unity!" There have been more heartaches, more tears, and broken spirits, over division in religious bodies, than almost anything else. I think I know the value of this text in the home. How good and pleasant for members of the family to dwell together in unity. I have been connected with a school practically all of my days. How good and how pleasant it is for all parties connected with it to dwell together in unity. Our state, our nation, the nations of the earth are, tonight, torn asunder and driven into various parties, with war clouds rumbling, and the lightning of the same flashing across the vaulted sky, threatening to disturb the peace and the tranquillity that men enjoy. It's good to dwell together in unity. But if that be true in the home, in the schoolroom, in our civil relationships of life, how far transcendent is the importance of it in the church of the living God. But due to the weaknesses, and to the frailties, and imperfections of humanity, there is scarcely a religious body upon earth tonight, but is suffering from the evil of division. There is no outside power that can harm the church of the living God. There are not enough demons in hell, nor representatives on earth, to mar the progress of the cause that Christ died to establish upon this earth. The danger is from *within*, and when that is brought about, a pall of darkness spreads over the land, and blights many a hope, discourages many an honest character, causes him to linger by the wayside, and ultimately, to die and land in hell, because of religious division.

There are lots of mottoes that I think quite applicable: "United we stand, divided we fall." The old father, pictured in one of McGuffey's readers, demonstrated to his seven sons a lesson that has been impressed upon me since I passed the fourth grade. He handed each of them a stick and asked him to break it. They did it with all ease and rather disdainfully. Then he bound seven sticks, just like those, together with a strong cord and handed it to the eldest, and on down the line, saying, "Boys, try your hand on that." With all the power of their being, they struggled and bore down upon it, but their effort resulted in failure. Why? Because of the united relation that one stick bore to the other. That's a wonderful lesson. There are enough Christian people in Nashville, Tennessee, to make it as it has been called in days gone by, The Jerusalem of America. Your strength has been heralded abroad, most especially, since you found out how great it was back in 1922, when we had our first meeting in this auditorium. History has been making, all through the years, and continues tonight. With eager eyes and anxious ears, they are listening from the four quarters of the earth. This audience knows full well that Jesus Christ, in the very shadow of the cross, lifted his voice to the Father and prayed that all those who believe on Him through the words of the apostles might be one. That's the way our faith comes. I believe, tonight, on Jesus Christ through the words that have come from the apostles. Hence, incorporated are we in that prayer, that we all might be one—not two hundred, not fifty, not torn asunder—but that we might be *one* in this sense, "As thou, Father, art in me, and I in thee. May they be one in us," now watch the purport, "that the world might believe that thou hast sent me." Christ recognized that division was the most fruitful field of infidelity that this world could ever know, hence, the closing of his career was characterized by that wonderful prayer for the unity of all who believe on him, based upon the testimony of the apostles.

But there are those, possibly, among us that are now thinking, "It's impossible for us to be united." Well, Paul didn't think so, for he said in 1 Cor. 1: 10, "Brethren, I beseech you in the name of the Lord Jesus Christ that you all speak the same thing, that there be no divisions among you, but that you be perfectly joined together in the same mind and the same judgment." Was that an idle exhortation? Did not Paul know that such was impossible? No, he thought it was possible and, my friends, indeed, it is. If I be responsible for the failure of that verse to prevail among brethren, "woe is unto me." You can see how simple that is. If I speak wholly those things that are in this

Book; if I speak as the oracles of God direct, and every other believer on this earth does likewise, there can be no difference among us. But when I give expressions of my opinions and foster my theories or any kind of fancied philosophies, then what? I destroy the unity that ought to prevail in the body of Christ. There are hundreds, yea, thousands of souls that will land in hell as the result of religious division.

I have gone into homes, as an invited guest of the husband, who believes the things that I do, but he is careful to tell me, "Bro. Hardeman, my wife is not a member of the church of the Bible." Well, I know what he means, "Don't you, Bro. Hardeman, dare discuss religious matters at our house. We can't stand for that." Well, all right, I've caught on. And then maybe the wife and mother wants to be kindly disposed, and says: "Bro. Hardeman, I would like to have you over for dinner with us." Well, I am glad to go, and she very diplomatically but with embarrassment says: "Bro. Hardeman, my husband is not in sympathy with the belief to which I subscribe." What does that spell? "Don't you open your mouth about religion at our house." Now, why not? Because of a divided condition, Christ is driven out of that home; the Bible cannot be discussed; and religious matters are never mentioned. Well, look again. There's a son in that home, who is growing up to manhood; he's mama's boy—mama's darling, and one day she says: "Son, I wish you would go with me to mama's church, I'd love to have you with me." Well, that's a very strong appeal, and he thinks about it, but he says to himself, "Now, if I do that, Dad won't like it. He'll feel that I am against him, and I'm not. So I just can't afford to do that." And then one day he and his father are off as pals together, and the father says: "Son, I wish you could see it to become a member of the church with me, and let us be together." And he possibly says, "WELL, Dad, I would like to, but, you know, that would offend Mother, and what would she think about it." Now, here's the result of that—the boy may be religiously inclined; he perhaps would like to evidence some interest along that line, but he reasons,

"If I go with Father, Mother will feel slighted, and that I am not as favorable toward her as I should be. I can't do that. If I go with her, the reverse is true." Now what's the only sensible thing for that boy to do with reference to his parents? Here it is—remain neutral! What does that mean? "I'll become a member of neither one." Hence, he goes out in life, is hardened by the affairs of the world, grows cold and indifferent to things sacred and religious, and ultimately dies and goes to hell! Why? Because father and mother, who loved him so dearly, were divided. They sent him to hell. Now, if you think that's not so, I'm from Missouri! I believe I can find you boys and girls that will tell you, precisely and exactly, this same story.

You talk about the spirit of the Master prevailing when conditions of that kind are abroad in the land! Let me say to you, friends, this world is not divided over what's in the Bible. Had you ever stopped to think of it? Where are the things concerning which we are divided? Without being tedious tonight, and specific along that line, I think maybe, a hint will suffice. Let us see about some things. Are we divided over the fact that Christ wants all men to become Christians? No! You couldn't get division about that. But someone said, "I think they ought to be Mormons." Look out! That will bring division. Does God say anything about that? No, that's outside the Bible. I think all men ought to become a member of the church that you read about in the Bible. Nobody will disagree on that. "But I think some church that God never heard of will do just as well." No, that'll bring division. Can you see that? And thus it goes, on and on, endless in multiplicities of theories, guesses, fancies, varied philosophies all over the land. How good and how pleasant it is to dwell together in unity and to be at rest with kindred heart and congenial spirits!

Now, when I come to study David's statement rather carefully, I know that there are lots of things that are good, but they are not pleasant. I never have had to take very much medicine; it rarely dawns on me that such a thing is necessary, but I never saw any of the stuff in my life that I thought was good. I can remember that as a boy I had chills, and I know old Groves put out what he called Tasteless Chill Tonic, but I can still taste it. I think it is good for malaria but he surely misrepresented it when he said it was tasteless. Well, if I had something physically the matter, of course I'd go to a surgeon, and if necessary, submit to an operation, on the ground, it's good for me. But it isn't pleasant until after it's all over and you get well, and then at a social gathering you get to tell your experience. Then on the other hand, there are some things that are pleasant that are not good. It's a pleasure to turn loose and yield to the lusts of the flesh, and to gratify our desires, but no man of good sense thinks that's good for us. I can revel in sin, abuse myself, and bring my body to a premature debility, but it wouldn't be good for me. But here is a thing that is both good and pleasant, viz: "For brethren to dwell together in unity." There's the combination of goodness and pleasantness. Now to be specific about this text, I would say this further, as David did, "It is like precious ointment," what is? For brethren to dwell together in unity, "That runs down from the head, even upon the beard of Aaron, and down to the skirts of his garments." In Palestine, from April until November, there's no rain; the sun beats down exceeding hot in the daytime, and if you are unprotected, you'll find that your nose, ears, cheeks, and neck will be blistered. How do you prevent that? In David's day they had precious ointment; they put that all over their faces, as some do cold cream, or maybe vaseline, and it kept back the evil effects of the burning rays of the sun. For brethren to dwell together in unity, is a protection against the bitterness, the sadness, and the unpleasantness that otherwise follows. It's like the dew of Hermon, or the dews of the mountains of Zion. In that sacred land drought prevails, but round about Zion there is heavy dew, and in the morning vegetation is, for a time, revived. Division among brethren brings drought and distress. Just think what a good shower does when the land is parched and the vegetation is drying. All things revive. David said, in effect, "For brethren to get together in unity is like a splendid shower, breaking a long drought which gives spirit, encouragement, vigor, and life." Friends, fancy how that would be to the brotherhood of the church of Christ, not only in Nashville, but in almost every other part of our land. There are sufferings; there are heartaches; there's the lack of doing things; there's a drought on, and things are not as they otherwise would be. Suppose that all our bickering, and back-biting, and differences, were wiped out and tomorrow morning we should see things spring up with new determination and with a united brotherhood. There would be a scene worthy of heaven's benedictions! I stop to meditate upon these things and wonder what it's all about.

I came to you folks of Nashville and brethren in March, 1922, as a stranger very largely, but with a solid backing, so far as I knew, or know now, of all the congregations of this city and surrounding the corporate limits. I preached to you, the very best I could, what I thought to be God's word and will. It met with a hearty approval, and to the principles enunciated, brethren subscribed. After 16 years, I have come back to you. I believe, brethren, the same thing tonight that I did then. I stand for the very same thing now that I did then. I preach the very same thing now as then. Question: Why are there differences and the bitternesses through which we are so unfortunately passing? I stop to examine myself! Am I preaching another gospel? No! Am I preaching it in another way? No! Have I adopted something contrary to what I then proclaimed? No! Why not then the same 100 per cent of backing and of endorsement? Well, there are things that have come to pass that disturb the peace and the harmony of various congregations. It's no special surprise. Paul warned the elders at Ephesus by saying, "I know this, that after my departure shall grievous wolves enter in among you, not sparing the flock." That's bad, for somebody on the outside to enter in and break the harmony, and disturb the peace. But he said something worse than that. "Also of your own selves shall men arise to draw away disciples after them. Watch, therefore, and remember that by the space of three years I ceased not to warn everyone night and day with tears." Human nature has run in about the same channel since the days of Adam. Back in Paul's day, there were the same things through which we are passing, in principle. He makes mention of two young preachers who were doubtless fine young men. I know they had splendid influence, at least, they were influential, and had a following. Of them Paul had somewhat to say. May I call your attention to 2 Timothy the second chapter, "Study to shew thyself approved unto God, a workman that needeth not to be ashamed, rightly dividing the word of truth. But shun profane and vain babblings; for they will increase unto more ungodliness. And their word will eat as doth a canker" (and he said, "I'll give you a concrete example"), "of whom is Hymenæus and Philetus." Now there were young preachers in Paul's day, in the church of the Lord, and Paul said, "their words were eating as doth a gangrene." And here they are, Hymenæus and Philetus, who, concerning the truth, have erred. Well, in what was their error? "Saying the resurrection is already past." Now mark it—They did not deny that there was such a thing as a resurrection; to that they subscribed, but they said, "It's already past; it's a thing of days gone by." Now that is their error. They subscribed to the doctrine of the resurrection; they did not deny that; they said there was such a thing, but it's all over, and a thing of the past. Now watch the result—"And they overthrew the faith of some." These were not outsiders, but insiders—preachers, influential and with a following. They had a theory respecting the resurrection as to time. Well, what was it? It's already past; it's an historic background. Their influence was such that brethren's faith was overthrown. Well, do you know what Paul said about them further? "I have delivered," said he, "Hymenæus and Alexander," another of that bunch, "unto Satan that they might learn not to blaspheme." Well, wait a minute—what had they done? They had subscribed to a theory regarding the resurrection. "It's already past." Paul called that blaspheming. You can't get any other analysis of that text. Therefore, said equally as pious as Hymenæus and Philetus. They are disturbers of the brotherhood. They have overthrown the faith of some; they've had a theory, and in that theory they were wrong, therefore, their influence has been to mar the peace of the congregation and to disturb the tranquillity that previously had prevailed. May I suggest to you, cautiously, but candidly, that there is a theory extant tonight, known as pre-millennialism, that has disturbed, not only the church of the Lord, but various denominations of this land. There are advocates of it among preachers who are equally as pious as Hymenæus and Philetus. They are teaching a theory regarding the kingdom. Oh, they say, "There is such a thing. We are not denying the kingdom. To that idea we subscribe, but it hasn't yet come." Thereby, the faith, as has come down from the pioneer days, of some has been overthrown, and of it, there has been made shipwreck regarding the establishment of the kingdom of God on the first Pentecost after the resurrection of Christ. I know the influence of that; I know the evil that has followed. The faith of brethren who one time stood behind gospel preachers in public discussion as they earnestly contended for the establishment of the church or the kingdom of God on the day of Pentecost, has been overthrown. Such men say: "There is a kingdom." Well, Hymenæus and Philetus said, "There is a resurrection." But what about that resurrection? It's already past. What about the kingdom? "There is one, but it hasn't yet come." It just seems to me that about the only difference in this whole matter is that one was *past* and the other is *future*. And I know that there is disturbance tonight over that very philosophy and theory which is new in the church of the Lord Jesus Christ.

I need to stop and take my bearing. In Col. 1: 13, Paul said this, and I want you to see the harmony, "God has delivered us from the power of darkness, and has *translated*, what does that mean? Trans—"across," and lated means "to bear." He has "delivered us from the power of darkness," and has borne us across, out of the one into the kingdom of God's dear son. Paul, where are we, the Colossians?

In the kingdom of God, but the same Hymanæus says, that thing is in existence only by right—not in fact. What's the result? The faith of good brethren has been disturbed. My heart bleeds tonight over the condition that is prevalent in our land because of such teaching. It destroys the principles of the restoration. It is contrary, I verily believe, to God's word; it is fraught with danger; it brings into the family of God a divided sentiment and a general spirit of unrest, which nobody delights to see, except the devil and his representatives upon this earth. It has been a principle, brethren (and to you I am appealing most especially), fundamental, absolutely basic, that in all matters of faith, we speak the same thing and be perfectly joined together—that in matters of opinion, there be liberty, and in all things there be charity. To that very principle, I most heartily subscribe. I pass, therefore, out of this place into different parts of the land, meet with brethren of various conceptions, and I raise the point: Is it essential to salvation to believe the pre-millennial theory? Now what's the answer? No! All right, it's not essential. Can I worship God acceptably, and not subscribe to that theory? "Yes, you can." Then brethren, in heaven's name, why encourage a thought of that kind and continue it to the disturbance of the body of Christ?

Now let me go back and say some other things. From the beginning of the nineteenth century, or thereabout, the great Restoration of primitive affairs was proclaimed throughout our land. It shook this old earth from center to circumference. When those principles were announced clearly, unmistakably, and without modification or apology, the world sat and trembled at the very thought that it had been in error so long regarding God's word. Men from human denominations rushed to accept a gospel restored. Together a happy brotherhood marched on down the line. It was a solid body. It had one common objective, and every heart beat in perfect unison with the others. But, what happened? That peace and tranquillity was not for long. In 1849, in the city of Cincinnati, there was organized a human society for the making known of the wisdom of God to the world. What was that? A contravening of God's statement that by the church, God's wisdom was to be made known and that according to the eternal purpose, which He purposed in Christ Jesus our Lord. What do you find? That peace among the brotherhood was now disturbed by the organization of a human society. That's it. Then in 1859, up here at Midway, Kentucky, they brought in a little melodeon, wherewith to worship and praise God. And again, division was made to appear. And then further, in 1869, in Olive Street church house in St. Louis, an organ was brought in, and what was the result? An open rupture and a division in the body of Christ. Now, I want to ask, who's responsible for that? And I answer in concert with you all, the man that organizes a thing untaught to the Bible; the man who brought into the worship that which the Bible does not authorize. Years went by and division appeared in Nashville. It came into this city, at Vine Street, Woodland Street, and other places, and it went throughout the region of Tennessee, and other states, until within the lifetime of some of us, we have seen the body of Christ torn asunder with open rupture, and each one going his separate way. When I oppose these divisive innovations, their proponents say: "Hardeman, don't say anything against it. You'll cause a fuss." Now isn't that ridiculous! *You'll* cause the fuss, "and you'll divide the body, if you don't keep quiet." Well, I didn't keep quiet about such things. I contended earnestly for that faith once for all delivered unto the saints, and I declare again tonight that the responsibility for the division that followed rests heavily upon those brethren who introduced into the church these unscriptural things. I am neither afraid nor ashamed to declare such in the presence of any living man. After this unfortunate experience, brethren sought to cleanse the temple of God and once more worship Him as it is written. The church then had rest for several years. But alas! Within the last ten or fifteen years, pre-millennialism has sprung up, and again, we are going through the same experience as we did with mechanical devices, and human organizations. The proponents of societies were not out open and above board declaring it, but in a secret, sinister, clever manner, they went from house to house seeking whom they might devour. Finally, they got possession of the elders and then, with the legal background, they said, "If you don't like it, get out." Now you know that's the story, and I am one preacher who will tell you about it and not go behind the door to do it. I know those are facts. They can be attested by brethren all over this land.

This pre-millennial theory is a duplicate, in principle, to the music and society disturbance. Its apologists admit it neither essential to salvation nor to Christian living, and yet there is that continued agitation and eternal talk about these things. This is not so much in public but rather from house to house. Pre-millennialists say: The Church of God was "a spiritual contingent"—a mere accident; the kingdom of heaven has not yet been established upon this earth; we are not citizens of it; Jesus Christ is not reigning on David's throne tonight; and he will not be, in fact, until he comes back and all Jews are physically gathered to Jerusalem and the old Davidic temple rebuilt. Friends, let me say that sympathy for this theory is expressed by finding fault, by circulating slanderous reports and by sending anonymous letters over the land. Those responsible for such nefarious doings never come out in the open, but in a cowardly manner and with a pious air, they, too, seek whom they may devour. They cry: "Don't oppose—you'll hurt the church." Brethren, those are digressive tactics to a fare-you-well but I, for one, am not easily intimidated along lines of that kind. I am amenable only to God. I don't have to answer to any synod, conference, association or convention. I propose to announce these matters with an earnest, fervent prayer that we may cease the promulgating of those things that are causing unrest, dissatisfaction, faultfinding, and criticism among brethren over matters admittedly non-essential. Now, I am perfectly willing to say this: if there is a man in the brotherhood who has, in all sincerity, believed the gospel of God's Son, genuinely and truly repented of his sins, publicly confessed the Christ, and has been buried into the name of the Father, Son, and Holy Spirit, he is a Christian. If that man has an opinion as to what Christ will do when he comes again and how we shall be, and will hold that opinion to himself, I'll fellowship him. That's the principle. I know that John said, "Beloved, it does not yet appear how we shall be." I haven't heard from heaven since John wrote, but there are brethren who speak as if they have heard later messages. They think they know how it is going to be. John said, "We do not know, but one thing is certain, we know that we will be like him." Friends, that ought to be sufficient. Now, if any brother will keep his opinion to himself and advise all others so to do, all criticisms will cease. But if you continue to advocate and push that which is but a theory, you ought not to expect men who believe God's word to be silent and cease not to warn brethren night and day, even with tears, regarding the baneful results that follow. Friends, there's the ground of unity. In all matters, let us speak as God's Book speaks, believe what is clearly stated therein, practice only that as a matter of faith, hold all things else that are not wrong in themselves, as matters of private opinion, and let love prevail among us. The result will be that unity, that wonderful harmony, and that strength of which every child of God might be justly proud. How good and how pleasant it is for brethren to dwell together in unity!

There has been much said regarding the purpose of this meeting. I wrote a letter last July to every church in Nashville stating that I had been invited to hold a meeting among them at the Ryman Auditorium and that I had accepted the invitation. I said that my purpose in coming was not to discuss personal matters, but to the best of my ability, I would preach the "old-time" gospel of Christ, with the hope of bettering conditions and bringing together upon a common platform, all interests of brethren in Nashville. Against no living man do I have an unkind feeling. I regret that there are people who cannot differ with you about a matter without making it personal. I thank God for some experiences. I have had a number of religious discussions, some of which have waxed exceedingly warm, but I have never yet allowed such discussions to become personal. I have some brethren, however, whose teaching I cannot criticize without their exclaiming: "Oh, Bro. Hardeman has got it in for me, personally." God forbid, that I should ever become so little as to have a conception of that kind. I just want to say it once and for all. There is no man anywhere against whom I have a personal feeling. I want to so live and carry on, that when I come to the end of the way, no one can truly say, "I have lost an enemy." You'll not lose an enemy when N. B. Hardeman crosses to the other world. I am sincere, earnest, candid. I want to go to heaven when I die. When life's dream is over and its fitful fever is passed, I want to plume my pinions for eternal habitation on the other shore. I realize that "woe is unto me if I preach not the gospel." Is there one in this audience not a member of the body of Christ? Do you understand what the will of the Lord is? And would you like to have fellowship in the greatest organization known to men? If so, put your trust in Him and from every sin turn away; render obedience to His will; walk in His counsel the remnant of your days and Heaven will be yours at the close. Shall we stand together for the invitation.

COST OF DISCIPLESHIP

I am reading tonight from the latter part of the ninth chapter of Luke. I bid you watch closely the reading, because the talk will be based upon this paragraph. "It came to pass, when the time was come that he should be received up, he stedfastly set his face to go to Jerusalem, and sent messengers before his face; and they went, and entered into a village of the Samaritans, to make ready for him. And they did not receive him, because his face was as though he would go to Jerusalem. And when his disciples James and John saw this, they said, Lord, wilt thou that we call down fire from heaven, and consume them, as Elias did? And he turned, and rebuked them, and said unto them, Ye know not what manner of spirit ye are of. For the Son of man is not come to destroy men's lives, but to save them. And they went to another village. And it came to pass as they went in the way, a certain man said unto him, Lord, I will follow thee whithersoever thou goest. And Jesus said unto him, Foxes have holes, and birds of the air have nests; but the Son of man hath not where to lay his head. And he said to another, Follow me. But he said, Lord, suffer me first to go and bury my father. Jesus said unto him, Let the dead bury their dead; but go thou and preach the kingdom of God. And another also said, Lord, I will follow thee; but let me first go bid them farewell, which are at my home and at my house. And Jesus said unto him, No man, having put his hand to the plough, and looking back, is fit for the kingdom of God."

My friends, that's an account of the last journey that Jesus ever made to Jerusalem. It was fraught with sadness on his part, and, of course, to all the disciples, who understood what it meant. From the beginning there were those who sought to obstruct his path; to divert his steps, and to turn him from his purpose. In the study of the life of Christ, that very element of hindrance was prominent from first to last. While standing on the banks of the river Jordan, yet dripping from the baptismal act, ready to launch his campaign of publicity, there was the devil seeking to destroy his purpose and to turn him aside. His own brethren, misunderstanding his mission, sought to upset his plans and to carry their will into effect. You know that all the Jews expected Christ to come to this earth and establish an earthly kingdom. Their hearts were set upon that. Such a thing as a spiritual realm, over which he should reign at God's right hand, had not dawned upon them. Their idea was physical, temporal, earthly in nature. And one time, when he was not carrying out their ideas and making headway toward their purpose, they had in mind to take him by force and set him on a throne; but he escaped from their presence. Isn't it strange, brethren, in the light of the mistake that the Jews made and the idea they had respecting the nature of Christ's kingdom, that there are brethren running loose all around, that have not profited by that, and are following in the same mistaken steps of the Jews? For what are they contending and preaching to the hurt of the body of Christ? That Jesus must have an earthly kingdom. They know the fact that Christ said, "My kingdom is not of this world," but such passages amount to nothing. Their theory must prevail. That very hindrance to the purpose of Christ in carrying out that for which he came to this earth, has ever been characteristic of those who have marred the progress and obstructed the onward march of the cause of our Lord upon the earth. Here near the close of his earthly career he started, and stedfastly set his face to go to Jerusalem. And he sent messages on before him to make ready, and those messengers entered into a village of the Samaritans, but the Samaritans rejected them. That brings up another sad story.

The woman at the well, John the fourth chapter, very truly said, "the Jews and the Samaritans have no dealings one with the other." Trace back for just a moment in your knowledge of the Bible, and review the origin of the Samaritans. You'll find that the ten tribes which went off into error after Jeroboam got so broad-gauged and liberal that the Assyrians took them in. They then repopulated Jerusalem with foreigners, who mixed and mingled with the remnant left behind, and from that mingling, there came forth a posterity embittered toward the Jews, and the hatred was quite mutual. That's the foundation of the Samaritans. The Jews who were faithful to God had no use for them, and why? Once, all marched together under Saul, David, and Solomon, then the ten tribes began to worship like the nations around them. They copied from the denominations and the varied religions of the land, until so corrupted, that they were absorbed and absolutely lost in identity. With such the Jews had no contact, no relation whatsoever. Hence, the Samaritans rejected the coming of the Christ through their territory. And be it remembered, that in going from Galilee to Judea, or Jerusalem, one must needs pass through Samaria. Now I think you can appreciate the feelings that Christ, or rather the disciples, James and John, must have had, if you can imagine an experience of that kind. In traveling south from Nashville, to Columbia, for instance, you'd have to pass ordinarily through Williamson County. Suppose some were to meet you at the border and forbid your passing. You'd, doubtless, argue the question with them. You might say: "I am not seeking to harm your country, nor to do any damage; I just want to pass through." But their forbidding you to do it would bring forth all the animosity within your soul. When refused, James and John rose up and they said, "Lord, wilt thou that we command fire to come down from heaven and consume them." I can just imagine how James and John felt about it. The idea of you people forbidding our passing, quietly and harmlessly, through your lands, shows hatred of the bitterest sort. Now they felt like just mopping up with them, but then Christ reproved them severely, and said, "James and John, you know not what manner of spirit you are of." "Is it possible that you've been students of mine for these months and years, and yet have not caught the right spirit, and the proper relation toward your fellows? And now disciples, get it: the Son of man is not come to destroy men's lives; that's not my purpose, and away with your idea. Although they have insulted you, they are human, endued with all the frailties and imperfections and weaknesses that characterize mankind. Let's not destroy them; that's not my mission. I have come to save them, rather than destroy them." Now, you brethren and friends present have no more of the human about you than I have. Sometimes when people seek to do us injury of any kind, our first impulse is not to turn the other cheek. Well, that's not the spirit that ought to prevail, and it is much more an act of cowardice than of real courage. Christ said, "James and John, we'll not call down fire from heaven; we'll not destroy the Samaritans; let's save them." Now that's the spirit of Christianity. "Pray for them that curse you and despitefully use you, and be longsuffering, forbearing one another in love." That's the spirit. And as we grow older, and imbibe more and more of the teaching of the Lord, the less disposed we'll come to be to want to take it out and say, "Lord, I know you said that vengeance is yours, but I am just scared you won't do a good job. Step down off the throne and let me 'tend to this fellow. I just want to clean up with him." Jesus said, "I am not come to destroy men's lives, but come to save them." That's the first part of this paragraph, and then the next. "And it came to pass as they went in the way, a certain man said unto him, Lord, I will follow thee whithersoever thou goest." I am sorry I do not know who that man was. When the Bible says "a certain man," I have found that the most uncertain person in all of my study. Who was he? A certain man. Was he a Democrat? I do not know. But that's the statement of the Bible. "A certain man said unto him, Lord, I'll follow thee whithersoever thou goest." Well, of course, he covered lots of territory, and possibly much more than he was conscious of. Many times, friends, we get worked up from different causes and make statements that, at the time, we think we mean, but when boiled down, that's not exactly the thought of it. I often wonder if humanity has ever yet learned itself. I remember how the Lord said to his disciples that he must go to Jerusalem and suffer many things of the elders and chief priests, the scribes, and be killed. Peter was surprised and shocked at such a statement, and he said, "Lord, be it far from thee." Later Jesus said: "All ye shall be offended because of me. And Peter said, "Though all men should be offended because of thee, yet will I never be offended. Now can you just see that cock-sureness, and that self-confidence? Peter was perfectly honest and absolutely sincere; he had left his fishing tackle by the sea of Galilee; had left his home, and even his mother-in-law, and had gone to follow the Christ, so he said, "Others may forsake you, Lord, but I never will even if I should die with thee." Well, I am not here to rebuke Peter; I think he was just as honest then as ever after. Christ said, "Peter, this very night the cock will not crow twice, but thou shalt deny me three times." Well, Peter thought Christ had just missed it as far as it was possible for a statement to be. He felt so sure of himself, but when he got up against that which he had never experienced before and the Idol of his heart was in the custody of the enemy, he was following afar off. When the trial was on, a damsel came to Peter and said: "You were with Jesus." Peter practically said: "I don't even known whom you are talking about." Well, that passed, and another maid said: "This fellow was with Jesus." Finally, others said: "Thou art one of them: for thy speech betrayeth thee." Then Peter began to curse and to swear, "I don't even know the man." Now, friends, from that I have learned this: I ought to be exceeding careful about making such general, broad-gauged, statements as to what I'll do. In our chapter we have a man who said, "Lord, I'll follow thee whithersoever thou goest." Peter was mistaken in himself. He didn't understand what he'd do when he got up against a new experience in life. And when somebody makes a mistake, I know how easy it is for us to land on him with both feet and to condemn him most severely and say: "I wouldn't do that." How do you know you wouldn't? Maybe you'd do ten times worse. Now I think we ought to learn something as along life's path we journey. And I have learned it this way. Instead of rising up in holy horror and in a self-righteous manner, I have tried to say, "I don't think I'd do that, even though under similar circumstances, but I might." I know others equally strong and equally as honest, who thought they would not, but they did. Peter is a concrete example of the same. This man said: "Lord, I'll follow thee whithersoever thou goest." Well, you know that's a worthy statement and a worthy ambition on the part of any man, to want to follow in the steps of the Lord. Just why he had that motive and that desire, I do not know; but I do know this, there are different motives that prompt men to follow the Saviour. In the sixth chapter of John, Christ said there were those who followed him because of the miracles which he wrought. Well, I can understand a thing of that kind. I have never seen anybody perform miracles, but I have seen magicians, sleight-of-hand performers, and, they are to me, I must confess, most interesting. I've seen Mr. Richardson, and Mr. Harold Thurston, and Mr. Blackstone, who possibly is in the city of Nashville now. I know they can't do some things, but I love to see them do them anyhow. I love to see a fellow pull up his sleeves and show me, that he hasn't a thing in the world up his sleeves or in his pockets, and then take some other fellow's hat and begin to pull out eggs, one, two, three, and a dozen, and two dozen, and three dozen, when there is not an old hen anywhere to be seen. Folks love to follow to see such tricks. I'm not surprised when Jesus said that there were some that followed him not because of trickery or magical power, but because of the real miracles that he wrought. Then there's another reason.

Christ said "there were those that were following for the loaves and the fishes." And I know that's so. Back down in my country, in the summer time, you just announce, "dinner all day and preaching on the ground," and you'll get a tremendous crowd. When all the good things of the country are cooked up and a big crowd gathers, the preacher gets up and thinks, "My! How they have come to hear me from all parts of the land." But they haven't done anything of the kind. They are there because of the "filling station" that has been announced. I know that's so. Then again, had you ever thought about it, friends? When a man is riding upon the very crest of popularity with everything going his way, it's an easy matter to get the people to follow. And let it be said that at the time of this story Christ was at the very height of his earthly career. His enemies had been put out of business; he had overcome the Pharisees; had set at naught the Sadducees, and multitudes were following all 'round about. It's such an easy matter for someone to come up and say, "Lord, I'm one of your sort." Now, I do not know about this man, but I do know that on this last journey, he came voluntarily to those along the way and said: "Lord, I'll follow you wheresoever you go." Friends, let me suggest to you: if prompted by the right spirit, that's the finest statement that any man on God's earth can make. A desire actuated by the right impulse to follow in the steps of our Lord is commendable. But I am calling especial attention now to answer that Christ made to him. See the picture. Here is a man voluntarily presenting himself, saying, "Lord, I'll follow you wherever you go." And the Lord said: "Foxes have holes." I want to know what on God's earth that's got to do with this man's following Christ. He never said anything about going fox hunting. He doubtless said: "I'm talking about following Christ." All right, "foxes have holes." Now, brethren, what's that got to do with the man's request and statement? "I'll follow you." Note the answer: "Foxes have holes." Suppose some of you preaching brethren get out on Sunday or any day and began to speak forth, and some man comes and says, "I want to follow the Lord." Then you say, "Very well, sir, foxes have holes." He'd think you were not all at home, and that the attic wasn't thoroughly furnished. Now what's that got to do with what the man wanted? "Foxes have holes" was the answer to the statement, "I'll follow wherever he leads." Well, what's the next? Not only do the foxes of the field have their holes, but "birds have their nests." Yes, I know that, but the man wasn't talking about birds. He was talking about following Christ. Friends, I think there is, in this, one of the finest lessons that I have ever had to challenge my attention. What's the point regarding it? "I'll follow thee whithersoever thou goest." Answer, "foxes have holes, birds of air have nests, but the Son of man hath not where to lay his head." What do you mean, Lord? "My dear sir, I fear that you might be prompted by the wrong incentive. I want you to understand what all this means. Don't follow me with the idea of any material gain, of any earthly reward. I want to tell you that the foxes have a place into which they go after preying upon other animals; the birds may wing their way all through the day and warble their sweetest melodies, but when twilight steals across the meadows, and the shadows lengthen, they can make their flight back to their nests, put their heads under their wings and pass into dreamland. All of that is true, but here's the Son of man; I have not where to pillow my head. Be certain that you follow me for the right purpose and not for any material, worldly, or earthly consideration." I believe, friends, that's the lesson. And I think, tonight, it ought to be impressed.

A criticism is sometimes made of me, and I think it just, and that's this: "Bro. Hardeman doesn't spend so much time in exhorting people to become Christians." I am conscious of that weakness as well as are you, but there is another thing. I have seen so many preachers that measure the success of their labors by the number of names they can get, and the number of baptisms, that it has had, possibly, the reverse effect. I think there are lots of people in the church like young watermelons, namely, they were pulled too green, and they never have yet considered what it all spells—what it's all about. I would not, ladies and gentlemen, enter into any kind of an organization nor any kind of a business unless first some fellow sat with me and explained every crook and turn and every detail. "What does this mean, and that, and the other?" and then, when I am sold on it, I want to stay sold, and not wake up afterward and regret that I have ever done it. I've never yet, therefore, tried to get anybody into the church of the Lord Jesus Christ under the spell of excitement. I do not want the great enthusiasm that might cause some boy or girl to lose his head and come to confess the Lord just because some one else did. I want converts who, first of all, understand what the will of the Lord is. I want them taught God's will and His word prior to becoming Christians. In addition to that, I want them to understand how God expects them to live, and to worship, and to practice the principles of "pure and undefiled religion." I think that's sound, correct and fundamentally true in all of its phases. Therefore, I'd rather have ten men, genuinely and truly converted, to the gospel of Christ and to the church of the Lord, than a *thousand* men who are nominally in. Many seem to say: "Because I've got a chum, or a pal, or some good friend who is a member, or because they have the nicest meeting-house, and the toniest folks in town, I believe I'll go and join in with them." Or again, somebody makes the plea to Jim, "Now don't you think you ought to be a member of the church with your wife? She's a member. Come on, and be with her, and go along with her." I want to tell you, friends, I never asked a man in my life to become a member of the church of the Lord just because his wife was. I think if that's the motive, that he will die and land in hell at last, and he might as well go from where he is. And I have never yet made any kind of appeal to some woman, by saying: "I want you to become a Christian because Jim is." That's not the motive. That's cheapening to the cause of the Lord Jesus Christ. That's bringing the church down from the high pinnacle and placing it upon a plane where it does not belong. Hear it—Men ought to become children of God because they are deeply convinced of the correctness of their step and fully aware of their dependence. Each one ought to say: "I recognize that Jesus Christ is God's Son, the Bible is His word, heaven is the home of the faithful, and when life's dream is over, I want to be among that number when the saints go marching in regardless of who the company is. I am in it because of my own conviction." If I know myself tonight, I am not a member of the church of God because you brethren are. I appreciate you in all that I should, but I am not a member of the body of Christ because anybody else is. I am a member of it because I believe that Book; I believe in Jesus Christ as the spotless Son of God, and the immaculate son of Mary; I am not following him for any earthly reward; not for prestige, or glory; not for social advantage, or financial gain, or political achievement. I am following him, I trust, actuated and prompted by a motive as pure as the driven snow. I want to dedicate all the powers of my being to his service while here I live and then lean upon his everlasting arms and be wafted home to glory when life's dream is all over. I think these sentiments are embodied in this very text. "Sir, don't you follow me because you think that, like a fox, I'll find a home for you. Don't follow me because you think I have some nests unoccupied."

Well, after that the Saviour turned to another and said to that man, "Follow me." And the man said I will—but! Now did you ever see a fellow decide to do a thing and then close out with a "but" to it? The chances are, about ten times out of nine, he won't do it. You can make a deal with a fellow, verbally, and come to terms and a thorough understanding. He will say: "Yes, *but* I want to see about it." Fare you well—you'd just well count that deal not made. And so this man said: "Lord I will, but!" Well "but" what? "Suffer me first to go and bury my father." I do not know that the man's father was dead. I am not right certain as to what he meant. Maybe he had this in mind: My father needs my attention, my care; when, perhaps, he is stricken and has died, and I am freed from that responsibility, then I will." Well, I want to tell you, if I should want a position, and were to go to some company and the head of it should say: "Hardeman, I'll give you a job." "All right, sir. I want it—*but* let me go and bury my father!" If he were to say, "No, no," I would feel like turning and saying "Why you old hardboiled rascal, I don't want to work for you anyhow. If you are that kind—won't even let me go and bury my father, I don't want to have anything to do with you." Yet that's exactly what Christ demands.

What do you want to do, sir? "I want to follow the Lord!" When? "Oh, after I finish another matter." What is it? "I want to go bury my father." Christ said "Follow me!" What is he trying to indicate? Here it is: There is absolutely no earthly excuse or alibi for a man to postpone following in the footsteps of our Lord. Neither life nor death, nor anything shall come between me and the performance of duty as it pertains to the will of the Lord. "Let the dead bury their dead!" You understand this, of course. There must be a play on the word "dead." One dead man cannot bury another, if they are both dead in the same sense. But there is a figure of speech, technically called, "paronomasia," which means this: The use of the same word close together but with different meaning. Let the dead—those who are not alive to me, uninterested in the cause, out in the world, disconnected with my work—let them bury the literally dead! Follow me! Now that's the story.

I happen to know one or two concrete demonstrations. We have a woman in school at Freed-Hardeman College, a widow, from Texas, of an exceeding fine family, a member of the church of the Lord. Her husband died on a Saturday. His body was prepared and brought to the home, where it lay in state, preparatory to the burial on Sunday afternoon. Friends gathered in with all their sympathy and kindness, as neighbors will do. Sunday morning, this woman began to arrange her attire as if she were going somewhere. Her friends asked: "What are you going to do?" She said, "I am going to church." "And your husband lying there, dead?" "Yes. There are plenty of you who would not go to church if he were not dead. Very kindly have you come, and I appreciate your sympathy and your presence. I won't be gone long, but my duty is at the house of the Lord!" She went. What would you do about it? Did she do right, or not? I've been to the town in which she grew up as a girl, married, and lived. Get it! I think she never did anything in her life to make a finer impression of her loyalty and devotion to the cause of Christ than the one act. And that was not for show, but in harmony with her practice from a girl, undisturbed until now. But there were critics on every hand. That's exactly what the Saviour said—"Let the dead bury their dead, follow me!"

And yet I know of some who sit up on the front seat every

Sunday morning and sing "I am bound for the promised land" when they ought to be singing "When the roll is called up yonder," (speaker pointed upward) "I'll be there" (pointing downward), in exactly an opposite direction. They are wonderfully devout at certain times, but a catch in the back or a crick in the neck, or some visitor come, and they'll just stay at home. Friends, that's the trouble with the church of the Lord. Jesus Christ stedfastly set his face upon the performance of duty. I have set my face toward the word of the Lord. Now, then, what am I going to let hinder? "Let the dead bury the dead"—even that is not an excuse.

Well, he said to another, "Follow me." And that second one said: "I will—but!" And he had the same idea. "There is something that I lack as yet"—what was it? "Let me first go and bid goodbye to them that are at my home and my house." Don't you think that is a reasonable request? It appears so. The man wanted to follow Christ. Jesus said: "Sir, No man having put his hand to the plow, and looking back, is fit for the kingdom of God."

I think there are wonderful lessons in these statements. Have you tonight set your hands to the gospel plow? If so, in what direction are you looking? I used to plow some. I came up back in the country on the farm. I don't want to enlarge on it as I heard Gov. Bob Taylor do once. When he said he was reared in the cornfield, brought up between two rows of corn, some old fellow called out: "I'll bet you're a pumpkin." Years ago, if a man rose early in the morning and broke up one acre of ground a day, he had done an average day's work. Well, I've tried to do that, and about three o'clock in the afternoon when the sun is coming down in a fury, it's fine to stop and rest for a while, sitting on a two-inch beam of the plow. As you sit there and look back over what you have done, the first thing you know, you'll think: "Well, I believe that is about an acre. I certainly have been stepping today. Already I've done quite a good day's work." And you can become so satisfied with what you have done, that the first thing you know you will be dropping the traces and tying up the lines ready to quit.

Just look out yonder before you! There are twenty acres to be broken, but that doesn't impress you just now. We get comfort out of what we have already done and drop the whole thing. That's the danger that lies along life's way.

Many a man and his wife, while living out in the country, helped to build the meeting-house. For thirty-five years they swept it every Sunday morning, made the fires in the winter, and, added to that, they always kept the preacher. They gave the most of the money to carry on, and after the thirty-five years of such work they move to the city or town, and he says to her: "Don't you think we've done our part?" She says "Yes, we've had a hard struggle." They agree, "Suppose we just take it easy and rest from now on." There's the danger. What is it? Looking back! Finding comfort and perfect satisfaction in what they have done. God says you cannot do that. There is no such thing as looking back! There is more territory yet to be covered. There's more ground to be broken.

Why, brethren, as young as I am, I could say to Mrs. Hardeman, "Haven't we been struggling along for thirty-five years with our noses to the grindstone?" Yes. "Have there not been many dark days with great burdens?" Yes. "Have there not been problems that it seemed could not be solved?" All true. "Now don't you think we ought to let up and take the thing easy?" Perhaps she would agree, and out of the comfort of what we have done, we might drop the handles, die, and land in hell at last. Friends, I can't do that. I know that God said the man who takes hold of the plow and looks back is not fit for the kingdom of God. Old age is likely to be deceived, in looking back, by the consolation of what it has done. Middle life is too content with the present! Youth looks out upon the future bright with hope and prospect and wants to go on. That is exactly the motive that ought to characterize everyone. Though our hairs be frosted in the service of the Lord, and our cheeks furrowed by the finger of Time, and our forms bended low, we cannot take our hands from the gospel plow and look back, for Christ says that then we are unfit for the kingdom of God.

Friends, it's no child's play to become a Christian. It's no light thing to live the Christian life. But it's a serious, solemn, sacred challenge that comes to the intelligence of every man, "Do I believe the gospel story? Do I stand like a stone wall for the eternal truth of God? Am I moved by every wind of doctrine, and swayed by every theory and new-fangled philosophy? Do I take to every speculation, to every guess, and to every new idea? Having put my hand to God's eternal plow, with His word as my guide, let me say, "Lord I never intend to give the journey o'er." That is the spirit that must prevail. That is the spirit that will conquer, that will be victorious in the end.

You ask one of the purposes of all our meetings? It is to try to arouse brethren, and stimulate them to persistency, and to continuity. I know, brethren, the pitfalls along the way, and the discouragements that confront us. I know the problems that are round about in life's affairs. I've climbed many of the hills and labored up the mountains to have great disappointments one after another, but thank God I expect to keep on, until by and by when the last rung has been climbed and the summit has been reached, in the very sunlight of His eternal presence, I can look across to the glittering crown that awaits the faithful. That is the incentive that ought to inspire and motivate every soul to become a Christian.

Is there one in this company who has never decided to follow the Christ? Don't you think it is time that you made that decision? Are there brethren who once took hold of the plow handles, but because of the enticements and allurements of the world, plus the discouragement of the divided state and bickerings in the church, have become discouraged, and have decided to quit? You can't do that. Won't you come tonight, acknowledge any delinquency, any wrong, and rededicate yourself to the cause of Christ? Brethren, roll up your sleeves and determine to fight under the leadership of him who has never yet lost a conflict. Then when it is all over, we will stand with him on the glad plains of Eternity. If there is one of that type and disposition tonight, the invitation is gladly tendered, while once again we stand together and sing.

ESSENTIALS AND NON-ESSENTIALS

I read to you two verses from the book of Acts, 3: 22 and 23. Just after Peter had delivered that second sermon on Solomon's porch to a great throng of people assembled, having announced to them that Christ, whom they crucified, had been raised from the dead, he then quotes from Moses: "Moses truly said unto the fathers, A prophet shall the Lord your God raise up unto you of your brethren, like unto me; him shall ye hear in all things whatsoever he shall say unto you. And it shall come to pass, that every soul, which will not hear that prophet, shall be destroyed from among the people."

Friends, that's a most solemn statement. It is fraught with so much meaning. The consequences connected with it are terrible. Hear it again: Moses said to the fathers 1500 years before the Christ, "A prophet shall the Lord God raise up unto you of your brethren, like unto me; him shall you hear in all things whatsoever he shall command you. And it shall come to pass that every soul that will not hear that prophet shall be destroyed from among the people." No wonder the Bible says: "It's a fearful thing to fall into the hands of the living God."

Based upon this reading tonight, I want to talk about a rather unique thing, namely; Essentials and Non-essentials, in connection with man's duty toward God. Those words are quite common among many professed Christians. Some things are Essentials, some things Non-essentials. The fact is, I came up under expressions of that kind. The implication was that God had commanded lots of things, some of them were important and obligatory upon man; others, while in the Bible, and plainly taught, were just commands. The idea was that we can be saved as well without them as with them. Hence, they are Non-essentials. I think that is the idea of the world in general now. Of course, say they, there are things mentioned in the Bible, but you don't have to respect all of them. Therefore, there are Essentials and Non-essentials. Now when I am talking about it tonight, I have no such idea in mind as that.

I believe the Bible, and what Moses said: "A prophet shall the Lord your God raise up unto you of your brethren like unto me," now watch it—"and him shall you hear in all things whatsoever he saith unto you." Now if there were nothing else at all, I'd get the idea that whatever God has said is fraught with such significance that if I will not hear it, I'll be destroyed from among the people. I hope this statement may register in our minds. There are no idle expressions nor vain commands in the book of God. There's not a syllable in the Bible applicable to man, but there is meaning attached to it, and upon our acceptance or rejection, depends our eternal destiny. So, I want to present some matters for study along those lines, and if there be any beauty in it at all, it will be in its absolute simplicity.

I am commencing, friends, with the Great Commission of our Lord Jesus Christ, the last statement ever delivered by him to the disciples, wherein he says: "Go ye therefore, and teach all nations, baptizing them in the name of the Father, and of the Son, and of the Holy Spirit; Teaching them to observe all things whatsoever I have commanded, and, lo, I am with you alway, even unto the end of the world." Now, are there any Non-essentials about those statements? Well, think of it after this fashion: God said first, "Go." That must be done. Why? Because Moses said that "Him shall you hear in all things commanded," and that's one of them. Now it isn't optional with me as to whether I go or stay. If I have the spirit of the Master and the spirit of obedience, I must "Go." This means, transition, moving about, change of status, locomotion; that's the idea in it. Now any church or any Christian, that does not have that idea of "Go" ought to take an introspective view and examine himself, "whether or not he be in the faith." To go is the very spirit of the gospel of Christ. That must be done; that's positive.

Note another thing about it: there are two ways by which

I can execute that command. I can either walk or ride, and in either way, I have fulfilled the word of the Lord. Now get this: Is it Essential to the carrying out of the will of God that I *"walk"* into the different parts of the earth? No sir! That's not Essential, but what is Essential? That I "go." Well, why isn't to walk then Essential? Because I can do what God said by *riding*, and thus the alternative and the choice is left with me. Now think on those things: two methods by which I may carry out God's commands in the first word "go." I can either walk and preach the gospel, or I can ride. Well, that's subdivided. The reason that my attention was first directed to try to get up a sermon along this line is that a good old brother once said to me, "Hardeman, you are such a contender for the Bible, why don't you ride a donkey like the apostles did when you go to preach?" I got to thinking about it. Perchance they did, and I want to do exactly what the word of the Lord says, so why don't I do that? I must *go*. That's what God said, but he never told me to ride; he never told me to walk. Then it's optional with me which way I carry out His command. If I ride, on what must it be? May I ride a mule? Yes. Would that be carrying out the Lord's will? Yes. Well, may I ride in the buggy? Yes. May I get in an automobile? Yes. On a train? Yes. On a steamboat? Yes. In a ferry boat of some kind? Yes. What about an aeroplane? Yes. Now I have done nothing more nor nothing less than what God said, when I get from one place to the other, be that method of transition as it may. Friends, I think we need to analyze matters and study things of that kind. Now, may I just add this? Of all people on earth that are anxious and particular about going according to what they think the Book teaches, I believe the church of Christ is in a class by itself. But sometimes we get cranky and become hobbyists and exceeding peculiar, when a little thought on our part would relieve us of all such. So then, I can carry out God's will either by walking or by riding, but watch this: there are the two co-ordinate ways of travel. I can't make one of those ways subordinate or an aid to the other. I can't use walking as an aid to riding. Why? They are co-ordinate. I can't use riding as an aid to walking. Why? They stand equally related and one of them is not sub-ordinate to the other. Therefore, I have to do it either one way or the other, and if God had said *walk* into all the world and preach the gospel, it would have been a willful violation of His word for me to ride. Why? That's not what he said. But since he used the generic term "Go," I can carry it out by either walking or riding; I'm at liberty to do either and still be within the realm of God's authority.

Think again, "Go ye therefore, and *teach*." Now what must be done? I must hear that prophet in all things, one of which was "*Teach*." Now that must be done. What does that mean? To instruct, to clarify, to let the light on, to banish darkness, and to impart intelligence; that has to be done. The gospel is a thing to be taught unto man. That's an Essential. Is it essential for me to carry that out before a public audience and speak orally? No sir! If I were a "slinger of ink and a maker of phrases," I could write God's word and be carrying out exactly what he said, when he declared "teach" all nations. I could also stand before my fellows, and orally do just what the Lord required. Therefore, in either case, I would be doing God's will. That's what I'm trying to get before you. The essential thing is, *teach God's word*. Someone said, "I object to a blackboard." Well, why? "God never said anything about a blackboard." I know he didn't, but what did he say? He said "Teach." If that and only that is done by use of a blackboard or a chart, you have done just what God said. The sole idea is to transmit intelligence and impart instruction.

There are brethren before whom I can go and discuss a topic to their delight. They will gladly accept what I have to say about it, but if I write out a discussion of the matter they raise an objection and candidly think such is unscriptural. Soon after I had returned from Palestine I went to Texas for a meeting. I reached the town on Saturday night and one of the brethren came to see me with a request that, since I had been to that sacred land, I might help him prepare to teach his class on Sunday morning. After telling me what the subject was, he said: "Now we don't use literature, we just use the Bible." Of course, I had heard of his kind. I tried to give the setting for his chapter, the time, place, persons etc. Then I commented on the different items mentioned. When I had finished he said: "That's fine, I'll be better prepared tomorrow to appear before my class." Then I said: "You say you're opposed to the literature?" "Oh, yes, I think it unscriptural." And I said, "Suppose I just write out what I have told you, word for word, and give each fellow in the class the same comments. Why not let them have the advantage of what I have said? If it is good for you, it might help them. He left me still opposed to written help but perfectly willing to receive oral assistance. Friends, such a disposition makes cranks, and hobbyists all over the land. They try to make a difference where there is no distinction. God said, *"preach."* If I can do that by oral demonstration, all right. If I can write it, still all right. If I can diagram it or picture it, or illustrate it, what have I done? Exactly what God said, no more, no less. Now we ought to think on these things.

Look at the next item. *Go, teach, baptize.* Who said that? The Lord did. What's the text? "A prophet shall the Lord your God raise up unto you of your brethren like unto me, him shall you hear in all things whatsoever he commands." What did he command? He commanded the *going;* he commanded the *teaching;* he commanded the *baptizing,* and he said, "It shall come to pass that every soul that will not hear, shall be cut off from the people." God said "baptize"; that's the thing that must be done. Well, what does that mean? Without going away around and coming up from some foreign angle, let me get right to the point. God said that "baptize" means to bury, and bury means to cover up. If there is anybody in this country that hasn't yet learned what "bury" means, that fellow isn't ready to be baptized. He needs to learn a lot of things, preparatory to that act. Certainly so. Now God said "go baptize." What do you mean by it? I mean buried with the

Lord in baptism. All right, that's settled. Now, let's talk about some other affairs. *Water is the element.* The Bible says that. Had you ever thought about just what temperature the water has to be to make it scriptural? What do you think about that? Is it essential that it be 98 degrees or would it do at 106? Or suppose it's down to 50 degrees—don't you see it is not Essential for the water to be at a certain temperature? That is a Non-essential in connection with the doing of God's word. Of course, I never thought of that until we got to putting furnaces in our meeting houses and running pipes through the baptistry. We used to take it straight. So, baptize in water. That's what God said. The temperature doesn't have anything to do with it. I have baptized when we broke the ice, and I have baptized when we needed ice.

Now then, I want to talk about another matter. When we baptize a man, do we have to stand him up erect and say, "now fold your arms," and baptize him backward? Does it have to be that way to make it valid? What about the posture of the character in being baptized? Someone said, "I never did see anybody baptised any way except backward." How would it do to baptize the fellow face foremost? How would it do to baptize him sidewise? I was baptizing a man in Forked Deer River once, an old gentleman, rather tottery, and just as I raised my hand to say that ceremony, he said, "Brother Hardeman, suppose I just squat." I said, "Oh no, stand up, it'll be all right," but I got to thinking about it afterward. Suppose he had squatted until he was buried? What have you brethren got to say about it? I have baptized people sitting in a chair. Was that scriptural? The Bible does not declare in what position the person to be baptized shall be, and if you baptize him face foremost, or backward, or sidewise—hear it—if you bury the man who has faith in God and who has repented of his sins, and do it in the right name, that's doing what the Bible says.

Well, now let's see again. If I baptize people in the Atlantic Ocean, what should I do? Well, here's exactly it. We would go down into the water and there I would bury him, and after that we would come up out of the water and go on our way. That's what the Bible says; I would neither add to God's word nor take from it nor substitute for it. That's it. Well, I have baptized people in the Mississippi river. Someone asks: "What'd you do there?" We went down into the water and there I buried them and then we came up out of the water. And then I have baptized people in old mill ponds. Do you know what we did? We went down into the water, there I buried them, and after that, we came up out of the water. Any objections? No. Suppose you dam up a branch and dig out a place of sufficient size and baptize a man in it. What have you done? Only that which the Bible demands. Exactly what one would do in the Atlantic Ocean or in any river. Well then, I have some kind of an artificial work to contain a sufficient amount of water that I may go down into it, bury a man and raise him up, what about it? Someone says: "I object; that's a baptistry." Friends and brethren, a failure to see that, just so long as we do only what God says, all is well, is responsible for many cranks and hobbyists among us. Let us do exactly what God said and with that be content. Now, to my way of thinking there just isn't any sense in anything other than that. Whenever I fail to carry out God's will and only that, I am subject to criticisms, but otherwise, they ought to be withheld.

Let us take some other item, for instance, the Lord's supper; there are things about that worthy of study in the light of our subject: "Essentials and Non-essentials." First, God commands the eating and by approved example, I learn the time, the first day of the week, that I must eat of the bread and drink of the fruit of the vine. I must not take cheese and substitute for the loaf; I must not add Log Cabin Syrup to the loaf. I must do just what God said, and when. That's Essential. Now let's talk about the Non-essential. Shall we pass it among the brethren and sisters or let them come up around the table and break of it there? Now do you know that the Bible doesn't say. There is one scripture governing all that, and here it is: "Let all things be done decently and in order." Now whatever good sense may suggest will fulfill that text and meet with heaven's approval. I have to observe the supper of the Lord on the first day of the week. Now, I want to raise another point. At what hour on the first day of the week? Someone says: "Ten minutes past twelve, or else it's not scriptural." Now brethren, you know that won't do. How about observing it at seven o'clock in the morning of the first day of the week? Perfectly all right. How about 10:30? Absolutely, it would meet God's requirements. What about 3:30 in the afternoon? It would do just as well. I know of one place where they wouldn't have the Lord's supper except at night. One old brother was responsible for it. And upon investigation, I found they had it at night because he said, "supper didn't mean dinner." Back where I used to live we had breakfast, dinner, and supper, and we still have it that way at our house, but I can say it the other way just as well. We become slaves to custom and find it hard to break away and admit something else. I heard of a lady who was going to have a formal 6 o'clock dinner and having invited her guests, she began coaching the black mammy who was preparing the good things to eat. She said: "Now, here's what I want you to do. After the ladies are all in the living-room and dinner is prepared, you come to the door, open it and gracefully say, 'dinner is served.'" The cook knew it was nearly night and such talk didn't sound right, but she wanted to do as told. So she fixed everything in order and opened the door. With a happy smile she said to the ladies, "Dinner is served; all of you come out to supper." She was just determined to have supper in it no matter what about the dinner business. When John Sharpe Williams retired from the United States Senate he said he was glad to get back down in Mississippi where he could have dinner at 12 o'clock. So this old brother, said, "It is the Lord's supper; it isn't the Lord's dinner." He had been told time and again by men who knew, that the word for supper did not of necessity imply the time it was eaten. But he had a theory and intended to have things go according to it, regardless of how ridiculous it made him appear. Such is our trouble by brethren who have a zeal for God, but not according to knowledge.

I have been asked about holding the supper until the night service, so that those absent in the morning might be served. Let's see about that. When I go to church at the usual time, I have five items in mind, viz: To teach or have part in it; To pray with and for the brethren; To eat the Lord's Supper; To contribute of my means, and to sing His praise. I return for the night with only three items before me as regards the worship. Those who were absent in the morning have the same purpose at night as I had in the forenoon. Why object to their worship then?

Some say they should not miss the morning service. This may be so, but the argument, in that case, would turn to another matter. Men will also argue over when the first day of the week should begin and end. With our change of calendars and our methods of counting time, it is next to impossible to be sure of the day counted the first in New Testament time. If one insists that the first day begins at 6:00 P.M. Saturday and goes to 6:00 P.M. Sunday, he would find that while we are eating the Lord's Supper in Nashville at 12:15 P.M. it has passed into Monday in Jerusalem. The sensible thing is to recognize the first day as determined in the country where you chance to be.

Again, when it comes to the contributing of our means, God said, on the first day of the week for every one of you to give according to ability. There you have God's word. That must be done. Now shall we put it in a hat, or in a basket, or walk around and lay it on the table? Do you know that the Bible doesn't say a word on earth about that? Now that's the Non-essential part, but the thing that God commands must be done. I trust a little outline of this kind, on this Saturday night, will provoke you to study that you may analyze and distinguish between things Essential and things Non-essential with reference to obedience to the word of God. What about obeying God? That must be done. Well, must it be done tonight? This is the best time on the face of God's earth, and may be the only time, but possibly tomorrow would do; maybe next week might do, but of that you know there is no certainty. The Essential thing is to obey the Lord. If a man, therefore, will hear the word of the Lord; believe in Jesus Christ as God's son and his Saviour; genuinely and truly repent of every sin; publicly confess faith in Christ; walk down into the water and there, in the name of the Sacred Three, be buried, and then rise to walk a new life, he will become a Christian. If he will then live as he ought to live and remain faithful unto death, God will give him a blissful crown in that land of unclouded day. My friends, don't let the opportunity pass, but come while you can. Let us stand, while we sing.

"THE SPIRIT OF CHRIST"

In looking over this great audience assembled, I am reminded of days gone by. There is genuine appreciation in the heart of every one who loves the truth, because of the wonderful opportunities that are to us granted. I want to join Bro. Cullom in expressing appreciation of the presence of so many delegations from the various parts of our land. I want to thank, especially, our colored brethren for coming in a body this afternoon. To all of these services, you are most cordially invited. Unto God be all the praise and to us the encouragement. I think you ought to know that any man, appearing before an audience of this kind, is deeply impressed with the great responsibility resting upon him. I know that impressions are going to be made. God forbid that anything shall be said or done other than that which is in harmony with His will. I beg of you to study carefully and to consider thoughtfully all that may be said at this service.

The text of the afternoon is found in Romans the eighth chapter, verse 9. Hear it—"If any man have not the Spirit of Christ, he is none of his." Let's all say that to ourselves. Let it register upon our minds. "If any man have not the Spirit of Christ, he is none of his." This is a universal statement; there are no classes of men excepted. Our respective stations in life enter not into consideration of this broad, sweeping statement, which is not only universal, but is quite positive in its declaration. No matter, friends, what other things might be true of me, or of you—if neither of us has the Spirit of Christ, all things else amount to nothing. In the light of such a sweeping statement with such consequences announced as are incorporated in it, don't you think it worth our while to study, first of all, what we mean by the Spirit of Christ, and then to check up as to whether or not we possess it? There is so much said about it that I am impressed with the need of a thorough study of the matter. By the Spirit of Christ, I am constrained to believe that Paul not only meant the Holy Spirit which dwells in every Christian, but likewise the mind of Christ, the attitude of our Lord, and the disposition of God's Son in his relationship to the various affairs that confront humanity. In all of my contact with the world, I must have and manifest the Spirit of Christ or else it's already proclaimed, I'm none of His. But what does it mean? We frequently talk, with reference to men, and say they are public-spirited. Just what do we mean by that? Well, we mean their attitude toward matters of public nature. You hear it said, "There's a man with a spirit of vengeance." What do you mean by that? That he harbors retaliation in his heart, and seeks revenge upon some of his fellows. Then we talk about a sweet-spirited man, and in all of this, we have the same idea as when we speak of the Spirit, i. e., the mind, disposition, attitude, of our Lord Jesus Christ. I know that's the truth, for Paul said in Phil. 2: 5, "Let this mind be in you, which was also in Christ Jesus our Lord." Now, I want to make application. Friends, what was the Spirit that Jesus Christ manifested toward his Heavenly Father? I think you know, without a long recitation. I am just quoting one or two passages, bearing on that very idea. In Hebrews 5, verses 8 and 9, "Though he were a Son, yet learned he obedience by the things which he suffered; And being made perfect, he became the author of eternal salvation unto all them that obey him." Again, "Let this mind be in you which was in Christ Jesus our Lord, who, being in the form of God, thought it not robbery to be equal with God; but made himself of no reputation, and took upon him the form of a servant, and was made in the likeness of sinful men; and being found in fashion as a man, he humbled himself, and became obedient unto death, even the death of the cross. Wherefore God also hath exalted him, and given him a name which is above every name." Now what was the attitude of our Lord toward his Heavenly Father? That of humiliation, that of perfect submission, that of rendering absolute obedience, even though death was the result. Friends, I must have that Spirit toward my Heavenly

Father, or else I am none of His. Let me close that phase of it by the quotation respecting the attitude of Christ in the last trial and tribulation through which he passed. In the lonely garden of Gethsemane, Jesus prayed and said, "Father, if it be possible, let this cup (the suffering, and the sighing) pass from me, nevertheless, not my will, but Thine be done." I must needs have that kind of a spirit, and that kind of an attitude toward my Heavenly Father or else, Paul said, "Hardeman, you are none of His."

Well, passing from that phase of it, I want to ask this audience: What was the attitude, or the spirit, or the mind of Christ toward his earthly parents? When he was 12, his father and mother let him go along with them to Jerusalem to attend the annual feast. After that was over, they left him and parted from him a day's journey. In the evening his mother began looking for her boy, only to find he was not in her company. She thought possibly, that "since he's not in our camp, he's over there with our kinfolks," but, upon investigation, she found he wasn't there. Then she had some very fine acquaintances—the very best people of the earth—and she, perchance, thought he might be with them, but she found he wasn't there, and had never been in their company. Finally, she turned back to Jerusalem, and there she found him. Well, after her reproof and his reply, he left Jerusalem and went with his parents down to Nazareth and was subject unto them. There isn't a boy or a girl on earth, but may gather a wonderful lesson by observing the Spirit of Christ, that of subjection, respect, and obedience to earthly parents.

Now, may I ask: What was the mind or the Spirit of Christ toward governmental affairs? "Let every soul," said Paul, "be subject to the powers that be." When Peter was discussing matters regarding the paying of taxes, Jesus anticipating him, said, "Of whom do kings of the earth take customs? Of their children or of strangers?" Peter answered correctly, "Of strangers." Christ said, "Lest they be offended, Peter, you go fishing, and when you cast the hook, the first fish that cometh up, look in his mouth and there you'll find a piece of money; take that, and pay your taxes and mine." Friends, what is the Spirit of Christ toward our Heavenly Father? That of absolute and implicit obedience. Toward earthly parents? He was subject unto his, and thus left us an example. What spirit was his regarding the world about him? That of respecting the government of which he was a part, and to which men look for protection.

Well, I want to pass to the next thought, and that's this: "What attitude did Christ have toward his personal enemies, those who mistreated him, slandered him, told untrue things about him? Well, here is the answer: "When he was reviled, he reviled not again; when he suffered he threatened not, but committed himself unto him who judgeth righteously." Do you get that idea? If your enemy smite you on one cheek, turn the other; if he take your coat, give him also your cloak; if he force you to go a mile, double it, and go your way. All of this, my friends, suggests the Christ represented as the Lamb of God. I want you to think about the characteristics of a lamb. It's the humblest, and the meekest, and the most submissive of all animals on the earth. "He was led as a sheep to the slaughter; and like a lamb dumb before his shearer, so opened he not his mouth; In his humiliation his judgment was taken away; and who shall declare his generation? for his life is taken from the earth." That's Christ with reference to matters personal held against him. You can't find in all the Bible where Jesus ever retaliated with reference to personal injury, personal insult, slanderous reports, or anything of the kind. "If a man hath not the spirit of Christ, he is none of his." But friends, I think the tragedy of today in the church of the Lord is this, namely: brethren have never learned that there are two sides to the Son of God. They think that only the characteristics of a lamb ought to be evidenced in order to have the spirit of the Master, and that he is some little negative kind of fellow, rather sissy, without backbone, with no courage, and that he doesn't have any combative spirit about him. Now that's the common idea that the world has. Brethren, you are making a fatal mistake, and that mistake is, possibly, more responsible for the sad condition and the lack of harmony in the church of our Lord, than any other thing upon which you could put your finger at this hour. Lots of men in business affairs adopt a principle which, with their imperfect organizations, may be satisfactory and may prove worth considering, and it is this, namely: "Knockers don't win, winners don't knock." In material affairs, earthly business relationships, and imperfect human organizations that may be a good slogan, but I want to say to you, friends, that such a sentiment transferred into religion and applied to the church of the Lord, is more responsible for the sad plight in which we are found in Nashville, and other cities, than any other principle of which I can think. Brethren, I bid you go back to the days of the Restoration and recount the battles that had to be fought in every city and throughout the country. Imagine the Stones, Campbells, Johnsons and Smiths adopting the slogan and saying one to another: "Now brethren, be careful. Remember that 'winners don't knock.'" Had such been their idea, there never would have been a church of our Lord in this land. I think that brethren of the present are wholly unmindful of this one fact, namely: the denominational world has never opened wide a door for a gospel message. Never! Every inch of ground that we occupy, every position that has been made prominent, has been the result of a battle and of a combat on the part of those who believe the old Book. But for that spirit characterizing earlier days, there would have been no congregations like these to assemble. Someone thinks, "That's not the spirit of Christ." Now mark it—instead of Jesus Christ's being some little negative nothing who was afraid of his shadow, I want you to understand full well that the same Bible which says that he's the Lamb of God, also says, "He is the Lion of the tribe of Judah." Now I would have you stop a minute and study the nature of a lion. John said that Christ is a lion. Well, what is a lion? He is the king of all beasts. He walks out into a company of animals, wags his tail, shakes his shaggy mane, and gives a roar that might be heard from Dan to Beersheba. How do you brethren account for the idea that Christ is a lion? Well, let me give it to you. With reference to personal defense he is a lamb. But whenever the doctrine that he proclaimed was attacked and opposed, and men acted the hypocrite and violated the principles of righteousness in their lives Jesus Christ never offered one element of compromise; he showed no disposition to yield one inch, but he stood like the lion against every foe. Jesus Christ is a Lamb, and a Lion of the tribe of Judah. Well, with reference to what? A lamb with regard to personal matters, a lion with regard to error both in doctrine and practice, and to things contrary to his teaching. Now if I don't demonstrate that, I'll admit publicly, and in the presence of this company, that I know nothing about the Book of God from beginning to end. I read you some things along that line. I am calling your attention first to the story of Stephen, in the sixth chapter of Acts. Stephen was one of the seven selected to look after the affairs to which the apostles' attention had been brought. The Bible says this: that he was a man of honest report, full of the Holy Spirit and of wisdom. Now let's see our man. Stephen, who are you? "I am a man of good report; I am a man that has wisdom; I am filled with the Holy Spirit." There's the man that I introduce to you. In the course of time, Stephen brought accusation against the error of his day, and afterward the enemy suborned men who said, "We have heard him speak blasphemous words against Moses and against God." That was a lie. They never heard Stephen say anything of the kind, but in order to down his influence, and to obstruct his onward march, they falsified by their slanderous report; "and they stirred up the people and the elders, and the scribes, and came upon him, and caught him and brought him unto the council and set up false witnesses who said: This man ceaseth not to speak blasphemous words against this holy place, and the law." There's God's man, full of wisdom, full of the Holy Ghost, and of good report. Stephen turned on them and said, "Ye stiffnecked and uncircumcised in heart and ears, ye do always resist the Holy Ghost; as your fathers did, so do ye. Which of the prophets have not your fathers persecuted? And they have slain them which shewed before of the coming of the Just One; of whom ye have been now the betrayers and murderers." I have some weak-kneed brethren who would have stood there and said: "Stephen, wait a minute, knockers don't win." Now I just want to ask you: Did Stephen have the Spirit of Christ when he said, "Ye stiffnecked and uncircumcised in heart and ears . . . you are betrayers and murderers"? Someone says, "I don't think he ought to have said that; that's not nice, and he might offend them. That's not the Spirit of Christ." The man who makes that statement wouldn't know the Spirit of Christ if he were to meet it down on Broadway. He would be an absolute stranger to His Spirit. Should Stephen have said: "Now gentlemen, I don't think you ought to do that, but I'll recognize you, and one of you brethren will please come around and lead us in prayer"? Stephen had the Spirit of Christ and evidenced it to these betrayers and murderers.

Well, again, I turn to the 13th chapter of Acts, where we have a record of the first missionary journey of Paul and Barnabas. They left Antioch in Syria, went down to Seleucia, on the seacoast, took a boat to the island of Cyprus, went to Salamis and on through the island until they came to Paphos, and there they found a Jew by the name of Bar-jesus, and he was with the deputy of the country named Sergius Paulus whom the Bible says, was "a prudent man." Well, what does that mean, Luke? That means this: Sergius Paulus was a man of good sense but Bar-jesus was wicked. Then this prudent man called for Barnabas and Saul, and desired to hear the word of God. He was an honest, sincere man. He saw that these men were preaching something of great importance and he wanted to hear them. "But Elymas, the sorcerer, withstood them, seeking to turn away the deputy from the faith." Well, I'm sorry that all of that kind are not dead yet. There are plenty of characters like Elymas that would like to turn men away from hearing the gospel of God's Son, and they would pull off any kind of an entertainment to lure them away. Now note: Paul has somewhat to say but may I ask: Does Paul have the Spirit of Christ or not? Well, let's see the Spirit of Christ in action. Let's see a lion turned loose. Paul said to him, "O thou full of all subtilty and of all evil, thou child of the devil, thou enemy of all righteousness, wilt thou not cease to pervert the right ways of the Lord"? Paul, don't you knock; that won't get anywhere; you be soft and sweet-spirited. Paul said: "Thou child of the devil, thou enemy of all righteousness," why don't you quit perverting God's word? Friends, I stand in the presence of God Almighty, certain of the fact that to condemn, rebuke and refute error is either the spirit of Christ, or that Paul, the peerless apostle, was wholly out of line with the Spirit of his Master. Now what do you say about it? Did Paul have the Spirit of Christ when he said to Elymas, "You're a child of the devil; you're full of all subtilty and of all evil; why don't you stop your opposition to God's word"? Brethren, what do you say about it? Someone replies that Paul was denouncing a sinner, but "I don't think you ought to do that way toward brethren." Well, fortunately, the Bible is a complete Book. I am reading now from the second chapter of Galatians. "But when Peter was come to Antioch, I withstood him to the face, because he was to be blamed. For before that certain came from James, he did eat with the Gentiles: but when they were come, he withdrew and separated himself, fearing them which were of the circumcision. And the other Jews dissembled likewise with him; insomuch that Barnabas also was carried away with their dissimulation. But when I saw that they walked not uprightly according to the truth of the gospel, I said unto Peter before them all, If thou, being a Jew, livest after the manner of Gentiles, and not as do the Jews, why compellest thou the Gentiles to live as do the Jews?" Here Paul comes face to face with Peter and blames him. He accuses Peter of being a hypocrite and a coward. This he does before them all. I now want to ask: Did Paul have the Spirit of Christ? What do you brethren say about it? Now then, when I tell some brethren they are wrong and are not standing four-square, what's the retort? "Brother Hardeman doesn't have the Spirit of Christ. He's a scrapper." Thank God I am, when it comes to the doctrine of our Lord and Saviour Jesus Christ. I allow no man to preach error and get away with it if I have the opportunity to stand and uphold the banner of the Lord, and proclaim the truth. Because of that, I want to say to you humbly, that I command the respect of even my opponents. It is the spirit of Christ to stand for God's word.

I now turn to Jesus Christ himself. I want to see what spirit he had toward all kinds and degrees of error that confronted him. In Matthew 21, verse 12, hear it!—"And Jesus went into the temple of God, and cast out all them that sold and bought in the temple, and overthrew the tables of the moneychangers, and the seats of them that sold doves." Imagine his saying to them, "Gentlemen, I hate to say anything about it, but I wish you wouldn't do that." Now, that sounds like some modern preacher trying to hold his job. Let's hear the Christ; he said to them: "It is written, My house shall be called the house of prayer; but ye have made it a den of thieves." Let me ask: Is that the Spirit of Christ? Brethren, that's Christ himself. Jesus said: "My house shall be called the house of prayer—but you thieves have taken possession of it. Get out." Some weakling might say: "I wouldn't treat anybody that way." Maybe that kind wouldn't, but Jesus Christ did. Brethren, who has the Spirit of Christ? Is it some of these over-pious fellows who haven't a backbone, who will let the truth of God suffer because of personal ties? My friends, we need to study the Bible again. That weak, negative, apologetic type of preaching is responsible today for a state that exists among us. Whenever the people of God get the spirit of the apostles; whenever they imbibe the Spirit of the Master; whenever they recognize the spirit that characterized the Restoration; whenever they decide to endorse only a positive gospel sermon and stand by those who will expose error; then and not till then will the cause prosper as in the days of the Apostles and Restorers.

But again, I read in the last speech that the Son of God ever made where Jesus spake to the disciples, saying: "The scribes and the Pharisees sit in Moses' seat; All therefore, whatsoever they bid you observe, that observe and do; but do not ye after their works: for they say, and do not. For they bind heavy burdens and grievous to be borne, and lay them on men's shoulders; but they themselves will not move them with one of their fingers. But all their works they do for to be seen of men; they make broad their phylacteries, and enlarge the borders of their garments, they love the uppermost room at feasts, and the chief seats in the synagogues, and greetings in the markets, and to be called of men, Rabbi, Rabbi. But be not ye called Rabbi, for one is your Master, even Christ; and all ye are brethren." Now note, "And call no man your father upon the earth." Brethren, don't let your regard for man cause you to violate this statement. The man who does shows that he loves the praise of men more than he does the praise of God.

Again, "Woe unto you, scribes and Pharisees, hypocrites!" Who is this talking, anyhow? That's Jesus Christ, the Son of God. Who are the Pharisees? They were the leading denomination of Christ's day. They represented the very best element in society, in business, in politics. They had their organization to the very highest point, and they loved to cater to the ways of the world, and to be prominent. Lord, what are you saying about them? Jesus Christ said: "Woe unto you, scribes and Pharisees, hypocrites!" Did he have the Spirit of Christ? "Now, Lord, don't you knock. You should know that knockers don't win. Just go on and preach the truth and let them alone. Say nothing about them." It's a pity that the Lord didn't have some sweet-spirited "pastor" to tell him how to preach. Christ said: "You're hypocrites." Well, why? "Ye devour widows' houses, and for a pretense make long prayer: therefore you shall receive the greater damnation." Whom is he talking about? Nobody. He's talking *to* the leading denomination of his day. What did he say to them? Lord, what else about them? "Woe unto you, scribes and Pharisees, hypocrites! For ye compass sea and land to make one proselyte, and when he is made, ye make him twofold more the child of hell than yourselves." Now Lord, what are they? Children of hell. Well, what about their converts? They are twofold more so. I leave the matter with you, friends. Is that the Spirit of Christ or not? What do you say about it? Does that look like a lion? Doesn't that demonstrate that "every plant which my heavenly Father hath not planted shall be rooted up"? I want to ask you, in what kind of business was Christ engaged other than in rooting up error and in teaching the truth?

But hear him further, "Woe unto you, scribes and Pharisees, hypocrites! for ye make clean the outside of the cup and of the platter, but within they are full of extortion and excess. Ye are like unto whited sepulchres, which indeed appear beautiful outward, but are within, full of dead men's bones, and of all uncleanness." Friends, that's the language of Jesus Christ in the last address that he ever made on the face of God's earth.

What's the next thought? "Ye serpents, ye generation of vipers, how can ye escape the damnation of hell?" Friends, those are but extracts and samples found in the Book of God by those who were filled with God's spirit. Now mark it—with reference to personal attack, personal insult, personal slander, and varied ugly reports, what about him? He was a Lamb. When reviled, he reviled not again; when suffering, he threatened not.

Now what's the last part? "He's the Lion of the tribe of Judah." Well, how? With reference to all error, with reference to all opposition to the truth. He stood, therefore, like a stone wall against the forces of opposition. Friends, let me tell you one thing. I have heard my own brethren, I think, sometimes preach what I doubt to be correct, and that's this: that because Jesus Christ preached the truth, "he was led as a sheep to the slaughter." Now, that's not so. If Jesus Christ had but preached the truth, he would have been living till this very hour, all other things being equal. Let me tell you the fact: because Jesus Christ condemned error and exposed the wrong, those very chief priests, scribes and Pharisees whom he had denounced went to old Caiaphas and said: "That man must be killed." Jesus Christ suffered on the tree of the cross, not for preaching the truth, but for exposing and condemning error.

I want that idea to register. The opposition of the religious world is not aroused by some one's preaching the truth. But when you expose their doctrine, they first seek to ignore you. Next, they'll want to debate the issues, and finally they'll want to put you to death. Be it remembered, the peerless apostle to the Gentiles was not executed simply because he preached the truth; but because he exposed the error of his day, they beheaded him in the city of Rome. Let me read about that just a little bit. In 2 Timothy 4: we have this statement. "Alexander the coppersmith did me much evil; the Lord reward him according to his works; of whom be thou ware also; for he hath greatly withstood our words." Did you ever see somebody trying to withstand the preaching of the gospel, and be in direct opposition to it like old Elymas, who tried to keep men from hearing it? Paul could say: "Brethren, I had that kind." Who's one of them? "Alexander the coppersmith." Paul, what did you do with him? In 1 Timothy 1: 20, Paul said, "Of whom is Hymenaeus and Alexander; whom I have delivered unto Satan, that they may learn not to blaspheme." That's what Paul said about him. Now I ask: did Paul have the right spirit? Well, that's up to you now to decide whether he did or not. Friends, I leave this thought with you: I believe confidently that the failure to demonstrate the Spirit of Christ is more responsible for the weak and the compromising air in the church than any other one thing. I am appealing to my brethren everywhere. I believe we have the truth; there's not a plank in our foundation but absolutely rings clear. I stand ready to defend every single, solitary plank in the platform upon which I have launched my campaign for eternity. In view of that, it's little enough that I should unfold the banner of our Lord and let it wave in the breezes of high heaven while I unshield the sword of the Spirit, and fight the good fight until time's knell is sounded and the ransomed of earth are gathered home. That's the spirit that I believe must prevail. With all of this, so far as personal relationship toward my fellows is concerned, I am not conscious of being any enemy to any man that lives on God's earth. There is no man against whom I would do anything destructive to his fair name or to retard his influence. I pray God that I may not be filled with envy and with jealousy that will make me see things other than the truth demands. With the Spirit of Christ paramount, I stand against error, from whatsoever source it may spring. With due deference to the feelings of my fellows, I cannot yield one-tenth of an inch. There is no compromise in the church of the Lord. There's not a single doctrine taught by Christ or the apostles that I have a right to modify or to minimize in the least. I believe that Jesus Christ said "Go into all the world and preach the gospel to every creature; He that believeth and is baptized shall be saved." I look upon the man who fulfills that as a Christian. I am ready to fellowship and to recognize him; but however much I may think of any of you, brethren or friends, personally, if you have not obeyed the gospel of Christ, as I believe it is, I am not recognizing you, nor playing "buddy" with you; nor am I calling upon you to invoke God's blessings upon what you don't believe. I cannot invite you to pray for me when you don't believe what I teach. Friends, that's getting down to brass tacks, but that's right where we live. Now the unfortunate thing is this: There are brethren who, if I file a criticism against their teaching, fly up in the air and say: "Hardeman's got it in for me personally." God knows I'd hate to be that little. I'd just hate to be so small that I could not distinguish between personal attacks and attacks where principle is involved. I contend for the truth, as I see it, against the claims of all persons who oppose it, but for any man, personally, I have but the kindest of feelings.

Now, from a talk of this kind, possibly no one could lèarn what to do to become a Christian; I realized that before I started, but if from other talks or from other information, there be those in this audience who understand what the will of the Lord is, and are disposed in heart and mind to accept it, the invitation is tendered as we stand together and sing the song.

THE BLOOD-BOUGHT INSTITUTION OF THE NEW TESTAMENT

It occurs to me, friends, that the fellowship and the social relationship that characterize such a splendid assembly are mighty well worth the time here spent. I join Brother Acuff in expressing appreciation of these gospel songs. They are inspiring and encouraging. I am sure that you know that we are making no effort to entertain you, other than to appeal to your good judgment by trying, most earnestly, to proclaim His word. I want no better opportunity than is afforded by the gospel of Christ to reach men and to attract their attention.

This meeting is somewhat unique in various ways. It was not intended, on my part, to be primarily an effort to have a large number of additions. Brother Tant would doubtless say we have too many now, of a certain kind. I have understood full well the sentiment prevalent among brethren, because I go from place to place and the very same conditions are found in various parts of our country. The church of the Lord is passing through a crisis, and I am hoping and praying most earnestly, that we may stay in the old paths and come through the present excitement solidly bound, and that we may be able to sing: "Blest Be the Tie that Binds." My friends, I decided, when invited to hold this meeting, that if the preaching of the gospel of Christ failed to pacify varied interests and to crystallize a sentiment of old-time unity, that I would and could have no other remedy in mind, no other panacea for any of our troubles. I believe that all appreciate the gospel. We have been viewing it from different angles. We have our respective ideas of how it ought to be preached. Herein lies the chief difference among us. Let us hope that ere long we may all speak the same thing, and be of the same mind, and of the same judgment, and that there be no division among us. In matters of faith there should be absolute unity; in matters of opinion, liberty, and in all things, charity. That's the platform that will bring to us that peace for which every child of God most earnestly sighs.

I am talking to you tonight about that heaven-born, blood-bought, and spirit-filled institution revealed in the Bible. There are some things about it, that on the surface are a little bit confusing, and yet when clarified, they present a beauty and an appreciation that otherwise would not result. Sometimes that institution is referred to in God's book as the "kingdom of God," or the "kingdom of heaven," or the "kingdom of Christ." Then the same thing is referred to as the "body" of our Lord, with Christ the head, the Spirit the life, and Christians the members. Well, that same thing is referred to as the "church of the living God," the "church of the Lord," the "house of God," the pillar and ground of Truth." Now then, I raise the point: Why does the same thing have different names; Kingdom, Body, Church? Instead of there being confusion, anything other than that is true of it, when correctly understood. Well, do the words "kingdom" and "body" mean the same thing? No, not necessarily. How then can two different names apply to the same thing? Do these terms and the church mean exactly the same thing always? No, they do not. Now that I may get that before you, just as simply as possible, suppose that I make this kind of an illustration: There sits a man before me. You ask "Who is that man, and what is he?" I'd say, "There is a white man." Well, I think nobody would misunderstand it. And then in a moment somebody asks "Who is that?" I'd say, "There's a Democrat." Well, do the words "Democrat" and "white man" mean the same? South of Mason and Dixon line there are some who think so, but I guess they are wrong about that. Can a person be a white man and not a Democrat? Yes. Well, can he be a Democrat and not a white man? Yes. Then how can I refer correctly to the same man as first, a white man, and second, a Democrat? Well, I can; I did; but a third man raises a point and asks me, "What is he?" And I say, "There's a merchant." Well, does the man have to be white to be a merchant? No. Does he have to be a Democrat in order to be a merchant? No. Do these terms mean the same thing? They do not. How then can that man be all three of them, when they are different? Well, he can't, if viewed from the same angle and approached with the same idea in mind. But you don't have any trouble about understanding that. When I said there was a white man, I had one thought paramount; I was thinking about the race to which he belonged, the color of his skin, and the complexion. And from that point of view, with that thought to be emphasized, I said he was a "white man." Well, all right. When you asked again, and I said, "He's a merchant," I had made subordinate the idea of his color, and now emphasized his occupation and his business, and from that angle, what about him? He's a merchant. Well, changing from that, I turn again and view him with reference to his political alignment and his relationship from a party point of view. Now what is he? The word "merchant" doesn't apply, and the words "white man" wouldn't answer, but the answer now is, "He's a Democrat." Don't you see how he can be all three of them at the same time: a white man, a Democrat, and a merchant, and nobody ever did get bothered about a matter of that kind? But when you take the institution in the Bible and sometimes call it the "church" and sometimes the "body," and sometimes the "kingdom," we get all "balled up" and confused. Friends, why not just quiet down and study things as they are? God, in the New Testament, views that institution from different angles and from different considerations. Now, if you are thinking about that institution with reference to its governmental feature, then what? It's not a democracy. Just put that down. It is not a republican form of government. Don't you see that? It is a kingdom. What does that mean? Simply this, that all the powers of government are vested in one character, who makes the laws, judges them, and executes them. But, let's think about that a minute. There are two kinds of government and they are directly opposite. One is a kingdom, or a monarchy; the other is a democracy. These are quite different in nature. The same functions are embodied in each of them, namely, legislative, judicial, and executive, but the method by which these functions are carried out are contrary to each other. Now in a monarchy, or a kingdom, one man makes the laws, one man passes upon the laws, one man executes the laws, and the subject has nothing whatsoever to do with it, except he can either accept it or reject it. But so far as having a part in the making of the law, or in deciding whether or not that it has been violated, or in the execution of it, he is absolutely left out. Such is the nature of a kingdom.

Well, what is a pure democracy? Really, there is no such thing on the earth, and there cannot be. It is impractical. If the city of Nashville were a pure democracy, every man, woman and child in it would have to meet every time a law was passed; they would also have to meet to decide upon the laws, and likewise when a law was executed. So what do we have? In this country, we have what we call a representative democracy—a republican form of government. The people are supposed to rule, but they rule through representatives, through committeemen, through delegates. Now that's the way we do it. We elect the very wisest of our land, of course, and send them up here on Capitol Hill, and there they supposedly represent us—the people of Tennessee. It is presumed that we express our will through these men. So it is in national affairs; we execute our wishes through representatives.

Now then, I just want to ask you, what is the nature of that institution over which Christ reigns tonight? Here is a very vital, fundamental, primary difference between the church of the Bible, and practically all denominations which are of human origin. The average member of the various churches thinks the church is a democracy just like Tennessee, and that it must be carried on by councils, synods, associations, conferences, to which the people all over the land send their delegates; and when they get in conference, they make laws and then relay them to the people. So we have it. Now that's the common idea. Therefore, denominationalism is based upon the idea that the church of the Bible is a democracy, a representative form of government. But the Bible is a stranger to any such a conception as that.

There is not a hint, nor any intimation of anything at all in God's book, but is definitely and actually the very opposite of that sentiment. Christ said, it's a kingdom. In that kingdom there is but one man, one authority—Jesus Christ our Lord. There is no human law-making body. There's no body on God's earth clothed with the right to make a creed, or a discipline, or a confession of faith. That's based upon the wrong conception, and it is fundamentally contrary to the very spirit of the New Testament Church. Friends, until you can get men to understand the very nature of the church of the Bible, you can't get anywhere in converting them to New Testament Christianity. You may transfer their names to the Church of Christ record, but unless they are properly taught and get back at the little end of the tap root of what it all means, you do not have a converted and dependable membership. So, I want to insist that in the church of the Bible, Jesus Christ has made all the laws; he has passed upon all the laws; and it will be his to judge at the last great day. Therefore, in the church of the Lord, there is no voting on what shall be the rule, the doctrine, or the polity. Either I can submit to the monarch and to the chief sovereign's decree and rest upon his promise, or I can reject it and subject myself to the consequences. I have no other alternative. What is your idea about the church of the Bible with reference to government? Now I said to you that this was practically the difference between the church that you read about in God's book and all human denominations. Let's see about that for a minute.

When some denomination wants to have some point of doctrine incorporated in its creed or some doctrine or practice changed, how does it go about it? First of all, there is a council, or a conference, or a synod called in session to discuss the matter. Very well. Different churches of that faith, all over the country, meet and select their delegates. These delegates meet at Nashville or somewhere, and they are called in session. This assembly is characterized by much gravity and great piety. The chairman calls the meeting to order and somebody suggests a change in the doctrine or the polity—a change in our Discipline, or Confession of

Faith, or in whatever booklet is adopted by that denomination. That change is then taken up and discussed back and forth. Heated arguments are many times in evidence. Finally, the question is put before the body and the ballots counted. A majority have voted for the change. Now look what they have done. The delegates have fastened upon that church a doctrine of which the members back home as yet know nothing. After the meeting is all over, they go back to their respective places and announce to the individual congregations what they must believe from now on. And being loyal partisans under the crack of the denominational whip, they say, "Well, I'm a loyal member, and I now believe what the conference decided upon." Who did that? That crowd assembled, in a legislative capacity, by a majority vote. Friends, there is not anything in God's Book that looks like a distant relative of a thing of that kind. Men ought to know that, and I'm your friend to tell you these things. But some one might say: "That's not the way it is?" Yes it is!

Let me tell you, our Catholic friends have a Pope; then they have their cardinals; they have their sessions, which are called councils. Now note: back in 1311 there was a council of the Catholic church called at Ravenna, Italy, for the purpose of discussing the question of baptism. It had been agitating the Western branch of the Catholic Church for quite a while. When that council was called and order had prevailed, the question was put: shall we recognize sprinkling as the equivalent of and upon a parity with immersion? Well, there were those who fought it while others favored it; they argued back and forth, and finally, by a small majority, it was voted into and upon the Western branch of the Catholic Church. Now there isn't any Catholic in Nashville who will deny that. They had not recognized sprinkling until 1311. That, ladies and gentlemen, is the way that sprinkling was brought into the Catholic Church, and varied denominations have borrowed it, not from the Bible, but from the Roman Catholics. Be it known that the Greek Catholics practice only immersion. The error of the Roman church and of her daughters and granddaughters is a misconception of the nature of the church. Had they caught the idea that the church of God is a *kingdom,* no such fallacies and doctrines contrary to God's word would be recognized tonight. That's not *nearly* it. That's it.

Now, in referring to the Catholic body, I have no intention to reflect upon anyone who is a member of that church, not in the least.

Again, the Methodist Church of our country is an honorable body. It is made up of fine people, good citizens, good neighbors, good politicians. The Methodist Church started in 1729. In 1784 it adopted its creed. In that creed is the statement that "all men are conceived and born in sin." Now you can't get back of that. That's putting it down unmistakably. "All men are conceived and born in sin." That was a doctrine of the Methodist Church from 1784 until 1910. In 1910, when the great Methodist Church met in its ecumenical council over at Asheville, North Carolina, a delegate argued that such a statement was untrue and that it should be changed. A heated debate followed, but finally, when the delegates cast their ballots, it was found that a majority did not believe their discipline, and so, another statement wholly different came out in their next edition. Since 1910, according to Methodist doctrine, no baby is born, much less conceived, in sin. Now who did that? Every Discipline since 1910 says exactly the opposite of all those so loyally accepted since 1784. But how was that change in doctrine brought about? On the principle that the Methodist Church is a democracy, just like the State of Tennessee. Delegates were selected by each congregation and when they left home, all believed that every baby was "conceived and born in sin." But when they went to Asheville and legislated on their doctrine they came back and told what they had done and the people changed their faith. Brethren, how did they come to change? Well, because they were loyal partisans, and they proposed to follow the partisan idea. The members at home were not affected by what the Bible had to say, but they were wholly influenced by what the Conference said. Methodists are loyal to their Conference. Friends, that's wrong, absolutely wrong. It's a failure to understand the very foundation of the church of the Lord. Had they the right conception, that the church of the Bible is a *kingdom,* and not a democracy, there would have been no conference over at Asheville; there would have been no delegates.

Let me tell you one thing. Friends, every departure from apostolic doctrine and practice has been brought about by a council or a conference of men, assuming to themselves legislative powers, wholly unauthorized by our King. Had there been no conferences, no assemblies, and had the people been content to take God at His word, to believe what He says, to do what He requires, and to live as He directs, there would be no confusion and no bitterness in our land tonight.

Let's see about that a little bit further. Here is an audience of—oh, I don't know how many, say 5,000 people—and all of us members of the body of Christ, worshipping God as it is written. Very well, somebody comes along and suggests: "Now brethren, we've been teaching Repentance as a cardinal doctrine of the church for, lo, these many years, and I really believe we have outlived that; folks are no longer paying much attention to it, and we can't enforce it, therefore, I make a motion, if I can get a second, that we go on record as disapproving of that old doctrine." Well, all right, it's discussed. Now then, out of 5,000 of us, suppose 4,999 vote in favor of repealing the doctrine of repentance, and I as chairman announce the vote. It's carried. I want to know if you think that has affected the gospel plan of salvation. What do you think about it? Does God recognize the cancelling of the doctrine of repentance? No sir, it's still in His word, "all men everywhere must repent." Our vote, therefore, has had the same effect as if a man should walk down to the Cumberland River, stick his finger in it, then withdraw it and look for the hole.

Suppose some one decides he wants a mechanical device in the worship, that we may be like the denominations about us. Suppose we call a great meeting of delegates from the different congregations and a motion is made to add such a device to our worship. Very well, the question is put and it carries by a big majority. Thus we bring the instrument in. Now question: Have you changed the King's law? Does God recognize your majority vote? What have you done, except to insult the authority of Jesus Christ and to repudiate the sacredness of his word? That's all. Friends, are you content with Jesus Christ as King? Are you willing to submit to his authority in all matters?

Now, let us view that Institution from another angle. It is spoken of as the "Body of Christ." Well, look at it. With reference to government, what about it? It's a kingdom. All right; as regards its organization, what is it? It's a body, and the Bible takes up this human body as the illustration most suited to convey that idea. There's never been such an organism as is the human body. This thing functions automatically in all of its parts. Much of the Bible is devoted to a presentation of this body of mine, in all of its various parts, from which there is made the spiritual application, "As we have many members in one body and all members have not the same office, so we being many, are one body in Christ." Well, now let's learn some things about this one of mine and yours. We have one head, that's all; one body, that's all; one spirit, that's all. Someone may ask: Does that fit things as they are? Yes, it fits things as they are in the Bible, but not as they are out in the world. In our own fair land of America there are more than two hundred denominations. Some wonder if they can harmonize such with the Bible statements. No, I don't think you can, but try it. Well, all right, we have just one head, Jesus Christ; all denominations recognize him as the head. Very well, how many bodies have you? Oh, there are about 200. Now look at that freak; one head and under it about 200 bodies. I think Ringling Brothers Shows are coming to Nashville next week. If I had a thing like that, my fortune would be made. I'd go around to the side-show department and say, "I've got a freak, like of which you never dreamed of in your life. I've got a thing with one head, and 200 bodies attached to it." Don't you know that won't do? Had you ever thought about trying it the other way? Suppose one says: We are all one great big body of Christians; we just have our different heads—John the Baptist, and John Calvin, and John Wesley, and so on. Just look at that picture a minute; one big body and 200 heads bobbing up. You haven't helped the thing a bit. Friends, truth cannot be trifled with. You can't get any sense whatsoever outside of one fact and that's this: "one head, one body, one spirit." Every child of God on earth is a member of that body and be he ever so humble there is a place wherein he functions. Christ talked about that. The eye cannot say to the nose, because I cannot smell, I am, therefore, not a part of it, and neither can it say to the foot, I have no need of you. Nay, our most comely parts are exceeding vital. If we all could just learn our places in the body of Christ and be content to fill them, this world would be transformed into a perfect paradise.

Now what is the next, and the most serious matter as it affects us? Friends, in this body of mine, there is not one particle of friction. There's no back-biting; there's no effort for this hand to hinder what this one wants to do, and if I were to hit that nail with a hammer, this one wouldn't bob up and say: "I knew you were going to get it; I'm glad of it; it was coming to you." Now, that never happens. If one foot gets hurt, the other just says: "I'm sorry. Put your weight on me, I'll bear it without a murmur, without a criticism." There is that great sympathetic system running through this body of mine. Therefore, if any member suffer, all the other members suffer with it. Jesus' prayer to the Heavenly Father was, that his people might be likeminded. But look round about in the cities of Nashville, Louisville, Dallas, and other parts of our land, and think of the condition of the professed body of Christ. Such a condition does not harmonize with Christianity. The spirit of Christ is lacking. Such things ought not to be and those responsible will receive their reward. Friends, let's think on those things. All of us are rapidly beating marches down to the solemn confines of the tomb. We're not as young as once we were. Since I first came to you many changes have been wrought. Silver hairs bedeck the brow of many who were not thus then. Furrowed cheeks are in evidence on the part of some of you who then had the very glow of youth. Bended forms appear now that were not then. What is our relationship one with the other? Friends, I do not want to be distinguished from any other child of God on earth. I want to assume no name that would differentiate or discriminate or align me with any kind of a partisan spirit. I would love to shake hands with every man who has been born of water and of the spirit and be one with him in the body of Christ. I wish we could all speak as the oracles of God speak and recognize that things revealed belong to man and that things unrevealed belong to God, and with that we should be content. Friends, that ought to be the spirit. If anywhere in harmony with that I am lacking —there's that much wrong with N. B. Hardeman. The church, therefore, is not only a kingdom with reference to its government, but as to its organization, it's the body of our Lord.

But I ask: what is its relationship to the world? Now does the word "kingdom" suggest that? No. Does the word "body" determine its relation? No. Well, what does? The word "church" now applies. What does that mean? The separated, the isolated, the called out. It is no part of the world, but it has been called out of the world. Friends, that's the story; that's what God teaches on all these matters. Why then can not we, as a solid body, without a dissenting voice, give a most hearty amen to such as that?

The church of the Bible, with reference to *government,* is a "kingdom." As to its *organization,* it is a "body." Jesus Christ is the head, the Holy Spirit is the life that dwells in the body, and every child of God is a member. Then as the church, let it be separate and apart, wholly distinct from the world. Let it not compromise with the world. Let not the line of demarcation be blurred, but be clear, open, and above board. Don't remove the old landmarks, but march under the leadership of Christ Jesus our Lord, who is in deadly conflict with the arch-enemy of mankind. The war is on, the battle is raging, and it will continue until time's knell is sounded. I want to be among that number who will gladly raise aloft the blood-stained banner, who will unsheathe the sword of the Spirit and fight error, wheresoever it be.

Are there those tonight appreciative of that idea? Have you accepted fully the sentiments as thus expressed? If so, I bid you march on and never give the journey over. If not, "Why Not Tonight?"

THE ESTABLISHMENT OF THE KINGDOM

My friends and brethren, I rejoice on this Monday evening to see such a splendid crowd assembled, and if last week is duplicated, the audiences will grow from night to night.

We are all here, in the presence of God, to hear all things that are commanded of the Lord. I am deeply impressed, not only with the number of people present, but with the quality of the audience assembled. I think we have no light, flippant crowd, but we have men and women, boys and girls, with serious minds, conscious of conditions and responsibilities, who are assembling from night to night to hear what may be said. I trust you will weigh everything in the light of His word.

I am discussing tonight an old theme, namely, "The Establishment of the Kingdom of God, or of the Church of the Lord." I doubt if those who have not given special attention to a study of this matter are appreciative of its importance. If you recall the story of the past, and the struggles through which the church of the Lord has come, you'll find that in most of the discussions, "The Establishment of the Church" was one of the propositions always debated. Well, why? Because so much depends upon it. It we are right in our contention that the church or kingdom was established upon Pentecost, it argues very largely that the teaching based upon that is likewise scriptural. If wrong at the beginning, though lines might be correctly run according to the guide, we would not come out as God intended. If I had to name the cardinal principle and the distinguishing feature of the church of the Lord as contrasted with all human bodies, its beginning would be one of the main points mentioned and emphasized. So I state to you that which has been contended for all down the line, namely, that the church of the New Testament was Established, Inaugurated, Set Up, Firmly Fixed, on the first Pentecost after the Resurrection of Jesus Christ from the dead. That's the statement to which efforts tonight will be directed.

But I am reading to you, from God's book, a prophecy known to all of you brethren.

In the year 606 B.C. there was a struggle between the East and the West as to which ruler should be monarch. The world was not big enough for Nebuchadnezzar of the East and Pharaoh-nechoh of the West. There was a battle away up on the Euphrates River at old Carchemish to determine which one of these rulers should have universal dominion. After the smoke of battle had cleared away, Nebuchadnezzar was victorious, and after that he swept down through the Jordan valley, subdued the people of Palestine, put them under tribute, and then, nineteen years later, he literally carried them away across the desert and beyond the Euphrates to serve him for fifty-one years more. While they were over in that land, Nebuchadnezzar had a wonderful dream, that not only bothered him but pestered him. He was greatly disturbed about it, and having made inquiry of his own wise men, only to meet with failure, he flew into a rage and sent forth a decree that all of them should be killed. Then it was that Daniel, one of God's people who was taken from Jerusalem, told him not to be hasty about the matter; that there was a God in heaven who could reveal secrets and make known what would come to pass. Upon being brought into his presence, Daniel unfolded to him just what he had dreamed, and what it meant. I now read from Daniel 2: 31-44. Hear it:

"Thou, O king, sawest, and, behold, a great image. This great image, whose brightness was excellent, stood before thee; and the form thereof was terrible. This image's head was of fine gold, his breast and his arms of silver, his belly and his thighs of brass. His legs of iron, his feet, part of iron and part of clay." Now can you just see a picture of that kind—an image after that make-up? Now hold that in mind, the head of gold, the breast and arms of silver, the belly and thighs of brass, the legs of iron, and the feet part of iron and part of clay. Now note: "Thou sawest,"

Nebuchadnezzar, "till that a stone was cut out without hands, which smote the image upon his feet that were of iron and clay, and brake them to pieces. Then was the iron, the clay, the brass, the silver, and the gold broken to pieces together, and became like the chaff of the summer threshing-floors; and the wind carried them away, that no place was found for them and the stone that smote the image became a great mountain, and filled the whole earth. This is the dream and we will tell the interpretation thereof before the king." Now friends, if God had not interpreted that, I'd be the last person, I think, in all the land to speculate and to theorize as to what it all meant, and even if I did, when I got through with my theories and guesses, nobody on earth would have right or reason to put confidence in them with assurance, but Daniel said this is the interpretation of it. Well, get it then:

"Thou, O king, art a king of kings; for the God of heaven hath given thee a kingdom, power, and strength, and glory. And wheresoever the children of men dwell, the beasts of the field and the fowls of the heaven hath he given into thine hand, and hath made thee ruler over them all." Now mark it: "Thou art this head of gold." Now, is it guesswork when I tell you that Babylon represented the head of gold? Absolutely not. God said it. Now note: "After thee shall arise another kingdom inferior to thee, and another third kingdom of brass, which shall bear rule over all the earth. And the fourth kingdom shall be strong as iron; forasmuch as iron breaketh in pieces and subdueth all things; and as iron that breaketh all these, shall it break in pieces and bruise. And whereas thou sawest the feet and toes, part of potters' clay, and part of iron, the kingdom shall be divided; but there shall be in it of the strength of the iron, forasmuch as thou sawest the iron mixed with miry clay. And as the toes of the feet were part of iron, and part of clay, so the kingdom shall be partly strong, and party broken. And whereas thou sawest iron mixed with miry clay, they shall mingle themselves with the seed of men; but they shall not cleave one to another, even as iron is not mixed with clay." Now note: "And in the days of these kings shall the God of heaven set up a kingdom which shall never be destroyed; and the kingdom shall not be left to other people, but it shall break in pieces and consume all these kingdoms, and it shall stand forever."

Now that's a rather lengthy reading from verse 31 to 44. Of that, for awhile, I want to speak to you in tones as clear and statements and sentences as simple as I possibly can. I love to preach so that folks will know what I'm talking about, and if I had all the education in the world, I think I'd still have sense enough not to try to delve into things concerning which the audience knows absolutely nothing.

Friends, this is about 600 years before Christ. God comes to Daniel, a Hebrew servant in the land of Babylonia, a captive of old king Nebuchadnezzar, and makes known to him a wonderful dream that the king has had. And after reciting the dream, Daniel tells him the interpretation of it. Now, not to be tedious, but to be clear and positive, I want you to see again. There was the great image that appeared, the form of which is terrible. Now watch the analysis of it. The head of that image was of fine gold, the breast and the arms were of silver, the belly and the thighs were of brass, the legs were of iron, and the feet were part of iron and part of clay. Now that's the scene; that's the thing that troubled Nebuchadnezzar wonderfully, and which he entirely forgot by the next morning. Daniel said: "Nebuchadnezzar, here's what that means: that dream is with reference to worldly governments and kingdoms. In the analysis of it, therefore, Nebuchadnezzar, God has given thee a kingdom, power, strength, and might. Thou art that head of gold," and so the first part of the image represented the government of Babylonia, of which Nebuchadnezzar was king. All right, now, after thee shall arise another kingdom, inferior. The second is not to be as great as was Babylonia. After that, there will be a third kingdom, represented by the belly and the thighs, and this third shall bear rule over all the earth. And after that, there will be a fourth kingdom, and then in the days of these kings, namely, the fourth kingdom's kings, then what? God is going to set up a kingdom which shall never be destroyed.

Now that's the image, and precisely and definitely is it told just what God is going to do, and just when he is going to do it. Now, let us pass to profane history and trace the fulfillment of this prophecy.

The Babylonian empire lasted until 536 B.C. It came to an end with the grandson of Nebuchadnezzar, whose name was Belshazzar. On that memorable night when he was serving tea to his friends, and having a high old time, there came a finger writing on the plaster of the walls, "MENE, MENE, TEKEL, U-PHARSIN," which means, "God hath numbered thy kingdom and finished it. Thou art weighed in the balances, and art found wanting. Thy kingdom is divided, and given to the Medes and Persians." That night, 536 B.C., Belshazzar was slain, and the Bible says that Darius, the Mede, took the throne, being three score and two years old. But the real power rested in his nephew, Cyrus of Persia. So what do you have? A government of two parts joined together, the Medes and the Persians, who were the arms of the image. "After Nebuchadnezzar, there will arise another kingdom, inferior," represented by the chest and arms of silver. Well, all right. The Medo-Persian government lasted from 536 B.C. down to 330 B.C., at which time Alexander the Great, with his father's famous phalanx, started out to conquer the entire world. Now God said that this third one should bear rule over all the earth. Then the great Macedonian, who really bore rule over all the earth, died and his government was finally divided between two characters, namely, Seleucus of the North and Ptolemy of the South. Time rolled on and finally there sprang up on the banks of the historic Tiber, Rome, the city builded upon the seven hills. In the days of Pompey, 63 B.C., the Roman Empire was extending its influence over all the face of the earth. Now mark it, there's the Babylonian, the head of gold; there's the Medo-Persian, the breast and the arms; there's the Macedonian or Grecian; and then there's the Roman Empire, swaying the scepter over all the nations of the earth. Now what did God say about it? Nebuchadnezzar, in the days of these kings—What kings? Of the Roman kings. Well, what's going to happen? The

God of heaven will set up a kingdom and that kingdom shall never be destroyed. Friends, I believe just that. That thing has been taught by the brethren of the church of the Lord for more than a hundred years, and it has remained, until quite modern times, for it ever to be questioned by those who claim membership in the body of Christ. That such is the fact in the case, I think does not admit of a shadow of doubt. Now then, mark it—I said to you that Pompey of Rome began to exercise world-wide dominion about the year 63 B.C. Then, there came the Caesars, a little bit later, who likewise extended their influence, and at the time Christ was born, Herod had been appointed king over Palestine by the Roman Emperor. Therefore, after some years passed, both John and Christ had been born upon the earth. Soon the clarion voice of John the Baptist broke the silence of the wilderness of Judea, saying unto the people: "Repent, for the kingdom of heaven is at hand." Now when was that? "In those days came John the Baptist." Now I just stop and raise the point: In what days? Well, in the days of the kings of the time. Who were then rulers? The Caesars were at Rome, the Herods were kings over Palestine, hence, "in those days," in the days of the Caesars, and of the Herods, John came announcing, as Daniel had prophesied, "the kingdom of God is at hand." Now, is that sensible? What did God say about it? There is the Babylonian; after that will be the Medo-Persian; after that will be the Macedonian; and then the Roman. In the days of the Roman kings God will set up a kingdom. Well, the Roman kings are on, they are now in authority and are ruling. What happened? "The time is fulfilled and the kingdom of God is at hand." No wonder that John thus made the announcement unto the multitudes that assembled that the kingdom of God was at hand—and that was in the days of the Roman kings, at which time God had said that he would set up a kingdom upon this earth.

To all who are not members of the body of Christ I want to apologize by saying that I have some brethren in error. They teach that the kingdom here mentioned by Daniel has not yet been established. I am sorry to have to say, that within the midst of the church of the Lord there are brethren that have risen up to deny that which has been affirmed and defended in debate and proclaimed all over this land for more than a hundred years.

Well, there are some things that I think need to be said. Our premillennialist friends argue most earnestly tonight that the kingdom predicted by God as revealed in Daniel 2 has not been established upon this earth, but that it must be established in the days of Rome. But they say Rome is gone, and you know that's so. The Roman Empire fell in 476 A.D., and passed out of existence, and there has not been anything of the kind in the physical affairs and political realms of men from that time until this. But the proponents of that premillennial theory suggest that Rome must come back and become a world empire again, and when such is done, then God will establish the kingdom. These erroneous brethren further say that Jesus Christ fully intended to establish the kingdom at the time John said, and when it was declared that in the days of the Roman kings the God of heaven would set up a kingdom, such was the intention; but when Christ came, the Jews would not accept him, therefore he postponed the kingdom and decided that until the Jewish nation, as a whole, got ready to accept him, he would establish the church instead. Therefore, we are in the church age now, and will not be in the kingdom in fact until the Jews get ready. Then Christ will come and fulfill that which he aimed to do 1900 years ago. Such is a theory that has already done much harm to the body of Christ.

I am saying, tonight, with all the power of my being and with perfect confidence of my ability to sustain myself, that the premillennialists among the churches of Christ do not believe that the kingdom of God is in existence, *in fact*, upon this earth. And yet when I announce that, some little up-spurt says: "Brother Hardeman, you don't understand it." Yes, I do understand it. Well, you ask, what's the proof of the thing? Friends, whenever a man publishes a book, that book becomes public property. I have here "The Kingdom of God," a book written by R. H. Boll, of

Louisville, Kentucky. I am reading to you on page 61, hear it: "Yet all the while, though unrecognized by men, Jesus Christ was God's king." Now you watch *how*—"as it would be put in legal language, the throne was his, *de jure et potentia,*" what does that mean? By right and by authority, "but it is not his, *de facto et actu.*" What does that mean? As a matter of fact! Now let some fellow who thinks I am misrepresenting come out in the open. There it is. How is it that the kingdom belongs to Christ and how is he king? He's king by right, but he's not king in actuality, therefore the kingdom is here by right, but not as a matter of fact. Brethren, when Paul said: "God hath delivered us from the power of darkness and hath translated us *into* the kingdom of his dear Son," that means by right and authority, but not actually. So brethren, you are in the kingdom by right. You are not in, sure enough. You just think you are in it. Now, that's the doctrine.

Well, let me read again, this time from the "Word and Work," the issue of June, 1936, from the pen of Robert H. Boll, Louisville, Kentucky. Hear it: "The Roman Empire Reappears," "Mussolini solemnly proclaimed the rebirth of the Roman Empire of the Caesars." (He quotes the *Courier-Journal.*) "After fifteen centuries, the empire has returned to the fateful hills of Rome." To the countless multitudes that thronged the public place, Il Duce addressed the question, "Will you be worthy of it?" Then there came the answer, wherein they proclaimed their fidelity. Now then, hear Brother Boll's comment: "So the Roman Empire has stirred from its long sleep and again emerges upon the world's stage, just as God's word said it would and must." Brother Boll, what are you saying? That Mussolini is the fulfillment of God's prophecy to Daniel, that the kingdom is not yet established, and Mussolini, according to God's word, has raised up and the Roman Empire has appeared. "The last of the four world-powers of Daniel's vision (Dan. 2 and 7), the Beast that was, is not, and shall come (Rev. 17: 8) has reappeared to play its final act in the drama of the world's rebellion." Now what do we have there? That in the appearance of Mussolini, God's promise to Daniel is being fulfilled, the Roman Empire is established according to God's word, and Mussolini has brought it back into existence. Well, all right! I want to raise this point regarding it: Will Brother R. H. Boll fight the government of Rome, in influence, by word or with a sword? No. Why not? That would be fighting against God. All right; if he should be a loyal citizen of the United States and, in sentiment, want to defend our flag, what about it? He would be fighting against God when Mussolini tries to exercise authority over this fair land of ours. Why? Because premillennialists say that God's agent, Mussolini, is carrying out God's word, then they must not fight the Roman Empire. And if Italian ships were to land on our eastern shores and want to plant their flag on the soil of our country, premillennialists cannot fight them. Why? That's God's order; that's God's fulfillment. Therefore, I am charging tonight that all premillennialists who believe as Brother Boll does would, of necessity, have to become traitors to the government of the United States or else fight against God.

Friends, let me ask you in all candor. Do you subscribe to a doctrine of that kind? Do you think we are not actually in the kingdom? Do you think that Jesus Christ is not now king in fact, and that he will not be until Mussolini extends the Roman Empire over all the earth? I have had brethren say: "Brother Hardeman, I don't believe a word of that." Well, I want to accept that statement, and yet, some of that type will criticize me for exposing such teaching. This is inconsistent, and it has the effect of encouraging those who thus teach. Brethren, I'm ashamed of any man on God's earth who says: "I think the doctrine is erroneous, but, Hardeman, I don't want you to fight against it. Don't mention it." Now where is your influence? You say you don't believe it. All right, whom are you criticizing? Here's the Gospel Advocate, contending for the old paths; here's the Apostolic Times; neither one of those brethren knew that I was going to say this, but they are fighting for the old principles and denouncing such erroneous doctrines as are taught, and what about it? There are some preachers over this land, criticizing all such, and they criticize N. B. Hardeman, and they criticize every other preacher who dares to raise his voice. By your silence and by your failure to endorse and stand by, what are you doing? You are lending your influence to the side of error as certain as God reigns, and here we are tonight. It behooves every child of God to uphold the hands of him who's holding aloft the banner of Christ and to see to it that error shall not prevail upon this earth. Therefore, let us contend, just as God's word declares, that we are in the kingdom tonight, *de facto et actu,* in fact and in actuality, and not simply *de jure*—by right.

Now brethren, the next time you find a sympathizer with premillennialism who says: "Oh, you don't understand it; we believe the kingdom's in existence," tell him you do understand that Christians are actually in the Kingdom of our Lord. I believe God's kingdom is actually in existence. I think that I am not in it by right; I am in it by actuality. I have literally, really, and actually been translated out of the kingdom of darkness into the kingdom of God's dear Son, therefore I can raise my voice unto the King of kings, Lord of lords tonight and plead for his mercies. That's the doctrine. That's why much of the ado; that's why much of the criticisms; and that's why I do not aim to let it alone.

Friends, thirty-five years ago, when digression raised its head in Tennessee, brethren were troubled and the result has been a division of the body of Christ. I never saw one of that crowd in my life, back there, but he said: "Oh, I don't believe in all those things; I never mention it." No, except in privacy, they would slip around from house to house and get all the converts possible. There were brethren back there who said: "Don't ever mention it; let it alone." I know what happened. We did let the thing alone until many meeting-houses all over this country, built by loyal brethren, were literally stolen by that crowd, and after all that, we came to ourselves, and the fight has been on. Now, we are getting back in line and digression is on the wane. It is scarcely found in Tennessee, except in some of the larger cities.

Brethren, a similar fight is now on. There is a great menace threatening the Church of our Lord, and it begins within our own ranks. There are those that say: "Oh, don't fight it; don't say anything about it; let it alone." If let alone, its proponents will talk it and teach it, mostly from house to house. They will assume a very pious air and deceive many good men. Finally, the church of Christ will wake up to find the old landmarks removed and the congregations of our land wholly absorbed in such an error as has not crept over the land since the generation gone by. I am wonderfully in earnest about matters of this kind. I believe with all the power of my being that the kingdom of God is in existence. I think when John said: "The kingdom of heaven is at hand," he meant exactly that, and when Christ told the disciples to pray "thy kingdom come," it was near enough for him to encourage them to look for its approach. And when he said to the disciples further: "Except you be converted and become as little children, you shall not enter into the kingdom," it was not there then, but later he said: "I will not drink of the fruit of the vine any more until I drink it anew with you in the kingdom of God," or "It is so near, brethren, that the next time we observe this, the kingdom of God will have appeared." Then further, there are "some of you" right here standing, now living, "who will not taste death until you see the kingdom of God come in power," not simply by right, but actually and genuinely, and it will surely come within the lifetime of some of you brethren. Well, how long ago has that been? Nineteen hundred years. Some say the kingdom hasn't come; I wonder where those old brethren are. You talk about Methuselah's being an old gentleman at 969. If that theory be correct, and some of those standing there were not to taste death until they see it, and it hasn't yet come, they could say to a young fellow like Methuselah: "Son, how are you coming along? When you get to be a man, 1900 years old, like we are, you'll know something." Now, isn't that a ridiculous set-up? And how any sensible brother in the church of our Lord can stand for it, and apologize for it, and criticize me for telling the truth about it, is beyond my comprehension. And brethren, I am appealing unto you, what do you hope to gain by the encouraging of things like that? You say you don't believe it, and yet you think I ought to say nothing about it. I like some of these brethren. They are fine men, and very devout. Yea, they are the most pious to be found. They always manifest a sweet spirit. But I know plenty of Methodists, Baptists, Presbyterians and Lutherans who are just as good moral men, just as good neighbors, as charitable, as philanthropic, as prayerful, and as pious as any premillennialist dare to be upon this earth. Question: Does that make Methodism right, and shall I apologize for it on the ground that they are good men? I know Baptist preachers who are wonderfully fine men. Can't I recognize and distinguish between an upright gentleman and a false doctrine? Shall I compromise God's word because I think the fellow sponsoring error is a good man morally? Not on your life. Now, that's the trouble with us tonight. There are brethren who will allow their friendship and their sympathy to cause them to put the soft pedal on error and compromise God's truth. I don't want to appear at the judgment bar of God under such a white-wash and a camouflage, and a compromising air.

Friends, I said to you some nights ago that the purpose of this meeting was not, primarily, to convert sinners, but it was for the purpose of trying to heal the breaches that are among us, to encourage brethren to put aside personal feelings, personal sympathy, personal friendship, and let God's truth override any kind of personal relationship whatsoever. I have said to you from this platform a number of times that I have nothing unkind to say about any living man. I have, I believe, no hatred in my heart toward any soul that lives on God's earth. So far as I know, there's not a man but to him I'd lend a helping hand if I could. I have for years tried to impress and to transmit to our student body the sentiment of Alice and Phoebe Carey, who said: "We make it an invariable rule to treat every person with perfect civility, no matter what garb he wears or what infirmity he bears." Friends, that's the sentiment; that's the very genius of the Christian religion.

But when it comes to the gospel of Christ and the truth of God Almighty, no man ought to come between me and the performance of duty. If I turn back to bury my dead father, Christ said: Sir, "you are not fit for the kingdom." If I turn back to bid farewell to my loved ones at home, I am unfit. What does Christ mean to say? There is absolutely nothing; there's no kind of a tie, personal, friendly, neighbourly, blood relation, marital ties, or anything, that can stand between you and the performance of God's truth and the obligations that are resting upon you.

Well, friends, Daniel prophesied that in the days of the Roman kings, the God of heaven would set up a kingdom. Now mark it—if, as the proponents of premillennialism would declare, Mussolini is but the rise of the Roman Empire destined to sweep over the face of the earth and have kings, they would not be the same ones mentioned by Daniel. Daniel pictured directly down the line Babylon, Medo-Persia, Macedonia, Rome. What Rome? Oh, not the Mussolini Rome, but the Rome that followed the footprints of the Macedonians. In the days of *those* Roman kings God would set up a kingdom. Well, 1900 years have gone by. Now suppose it were true that Mussolini is destined to become a world-wide ruler, and there should be a line of kings, and God should establish the kingdom, it would not be the same ones predicted by Daniel. But that's an extremely slim hope. I just want you to see one other thought, how wonderfully contradictory error can get, and yet folks will subscribe to it.

All of that crowd are talking about the "imminency" of the kingdom. What do you mean by that? That word means that the thing is near at hand, pending, just like a rock with the center of gravity almost beyond the support and just ready to fall at any minute. Now, that's the doctrine. The Kingdom is likely to occur any minute, and yet, it cannot occur, say they, until Rome gets world-wide dominion. I quote R. H. Boll: "A great world empire must exist before transfer of dominion to Son of God." I just ask, if you brethren think that it is quite imminent that Mussolini is liable to become world-wide ruler between now and tomorrow morning. I don't think the thing is quite that imminent. That is but a sample of the foolishness connected with the guesses of premillennialists.

But again, throughout the entire Bible from Creation down to the day of Pentecost, every prophecy and every statement regarding the kingdom points *forward;* the index finger points *down* the line, but it stops with the second chapter of Acts. You turn to the last chapter of Revelation and every statement you read regarding the kingdom points *backward* to the second chapter of Acts. Now, in this chapter, the place is revealed where God established His kingdom. In the first part of that chapter, God's Spirit had not yet come, but in the last part of the chapter, God was adding unto the church. Hence, between the first part and the last, that thing called the Church of God, or the Kingdom of Heaven, was established upon this earth.

Well, note some other things. Paul said in Heb. 3: 12: "Brethren, take heed lest there be in any of you an evil heart of unbelief in departing from the living God." To the Elders at Ephesus he said: "Take heed therefore unto yourselves, and to all the flock, over the which the Holy Ghost hath made you overseers, to feed the church of God, which he hath purchased with his own blood. For I know this, that after my departing shall grievous wolves enter in among you, not sparing the flock." Now that's bad, but here's something worse: "Also of your own selves shall men arise, speaking perverse things, to draw away disciples after them. Therefore, watch, and remember, that by the space of three years I ceased not to warn every one night and day with tears." And again: "The Spirit speaketh expressly, that in the latter times some shall depart from the faith." Do not be shocked, therefore, and surprised that men are teaching error regarding the Kingdom. Paul told Timothy to "preach the word," but he also told him to "reprove and rebuke." It is as much the duty of every preacher to reprove and rebuke as it is to preach the word. Many brethren seem to think that no criticism should ever be offered against that which one considers error, but they are wrong in such a conception. Paul said to Timothy: "Them that sin, rebuke before all that others may also fear." It is pathetic to go into some churches and listen to the long string of announcements which require fifteen or twenty minutes, and then to hear this followed by a little sermonette made up of pretty phrases and smooth sentences which are absolutely void of real gospel truth. "The world seemingly wants a bowl of ice cream with a cherry on it, when in reality it needs a plate of beans with an onion on it." Such services are responsible for the indifference among the churches today. If you want a general revival of old-time religion and one that will stir up the brethren to greater determination, preach to them on the Great Commission, the first gospel sermon, the conversion of the Eunuch, etc., and follow such with real sermons on Christian living. Encourage brethren to stand four-square for that faith once for all delivered unto the saints. But this is enough for tonight.

The hour has passed, and in conclusion I beg of you to take what has been said and study it, carefully and prayerfully. Be like the Bereans in that you search the scriptures daily to see whether or not the thing spoken be true. Should there be one or more in this audience who understands the will of the Lord and who is disposed in heart and in mind to do it, the invitation is now extended.

PREMILLENNIALISM

My friends and brethren, in looking over this audience tonight, I have an idea that we have not fewer than 6,000 people assembled. I am tremendously impressed, not only with your presence, but with the significance of it in view of announcements made last night.

I want you to know that I feel, very keenly indeed, the responsibility that is mine, and I am praying God that, with the right spirit prompting every statement, nothing but good may come from our mutual study of those things that now challenge our concern.

I am talking to you tonight, as stated, about premillennialism, and some things connected with it. I might just say to you that that word means the reign or a period of a thousand years with Jesus Christ coming back to this earth before that thousand years begins, and after that, matters as I shall state, take place.

The leading spirit sponsoring this doctrine among the churches of Christ has been Brother R. H. Boll of Louisville, Kentucky. His teaching it among the people of God, has disturbed their peace and led to a number of things rather bitter in their nature and threatening to the unity of the body of Christ. But my friends and brethren, this matter, though considered by some of small moment and no importance whatsoever, except on the part of those who want to raise a fuss about things, cannot be confined to the church of the Lord, and only those make such statements, who have not studied the matter and really do not know just what is taught by the theory and the consequences that follow the same.

In all denominations the same trouble exists, over this land. The Baptist church of Fort Worth, Texas, of Dallas, of Detroit, Michigan, and wheresoever J. Frank Norris, and his influences have gone, is disturbed over the teaching of premillennialism. It's in the Methodist church to their hurt and to their sorrow. And right here in Nashville, I read in the *Nashville Tennessean* Sunday morning, of the Second Presbyterian church and of the trouble between the church and the preacher, Mr. Stroud, whom I do not know. But it seems that the church is trying to get rid of Mr. Stroud as their preacher, that they have preferred charges of various kinds against him, and in his statement of their trouble, he says one of the causes for the opposition is that he talks too much about premillennialism.

I mention all of that, friends, to show you that this theory, sponsored by a number of people, is affecting all religious bodies, everywhere. Now, I appeal to you, brethren, is a thing of that kind to be passed lightly by? Are we not of that type who have subscribed to the principle of investigating all matters, comparing them with the word of God, and making a careful study of all things? I assure you that, to me, it is an unpleasant task to talk about those things that cause differences, hard feelings, and ugly sayings among brethren. All of that is unfortunate. The only way on earth that I know how it may be possible to heal our breaches, and for us all to come together, is an open, frank, honest, and candid discussion of these things, and I appreciate the concern that you have about it, as evidenced by your presence tonight.

Now, as best I can, I want to state to you the theory of premillennialism, as I have been able to get it.

First, God Almighty promised Abraham that through his seed a great nation should exist upon the earth. Second, Palestine was to be their home and they should inherit it and inhabit it; and third, the Gentiles were to be blessed through Israel as a nation. Now, that's the original plan, in which there was no provision made for Gentiles except through the Jews as a nation. For the accomplishment of that purpose, God sent forth the prophets and the harbinger of Christ, announcing that He would establish a kingdom among men. Jesus Christ in company with John the Baptist, announced the same thing, and they broke the silence of the wilderness of Judea, by saying, "the kingdom of God is at hand." "The time spoken of by the prophet is fulfilled, and the kingdom is at hand," but the theory says God missed it, and Jesus Christ did not figure correctly. Why? Well, when the time came, as spoken by God through the prophet and announced by John and Christ as at hand, the Jews said, "No sir, we will not accept the Christ," and hence, God was unwise in the proclamation of it; John the Baptist miscalculated affairs; and Jesus Christ did not understand that his preaching would be rejected and his purpose thwarted. Why? Because when the time came, the Jews practically said: "We know the voice of the prophets has heralded the coming of the kingdom; John the Baptist has announced it; and Jesus Christ has proclaimed it; but we are not going to have it." Therefore, they upset the plan of God and of Christ, and rejected him as king. Hence, the purpose of God was not carried out.

Now, I just want to stop and insert some parenthetical things. Friends, if God miscalculated the disposition of the Jews then, and if Christ missed it in saying the kingdom of God was at hand, due to the fact that the Jews did not prove ready, how can God know that the Jews might be ready the next time Christ comes? What assurance could there be that any time on earth would meet with the approval of the Jews? God might be disappointed again! Well, with that program all upset, there was a readjustment. The theory suggests that when Jesus Christ found that he was rejected as king and could not set up the kingdom as he intended, he substituted for it, and established the church instead. Well, what for? Now mark it—that through the church, or what is called the gospel age, out of the Gentiles he might develop a ruling class. And when enough of the Gentiles are prepared for rulership, Christ will come back from heaven *for* his saints, and then both the living and the dead saints will rise and meet the Lord and go back to glory. That's the first resurrection, as the theory proclaims.

When they get back there, the respective places over which the Gentiles will exercise rule on this earth, will be assigned. Now you get that. The marriage feast will be on, and every Gentile Christian during the church age that proves worthy, will be appointed a place. One fellow will be appointed mayor of Nashville, another chief-of-police of Knoxville, and so on down the line.

In the meantime, the Jews will be gathered back to Jerusalem, the old service of the Jewish age will be re-established, and the temple will be re-built. Jesus Christ will be in preparation soon to occupy the throne, prior to which the Roman Empire, will have once again ruled the whole earth. Now, when all of that setting is complete, then, Christ will come back to this earth *with* his saints, destroy the Roman Empire and sit upon David's physical, literal throne. The Mosaic rites and ceremonies will all be continued, together with the burning of sacrifice, the observance of the Sabbath, and all things characteristic of the old law. All of this will continue for a thousand years, at the end of which time, the devil will be turned loose and deceive the nations, and the whole thing will end in a failure. Then the rest of the dead will be raised and judged.

Now, as best I have been able to gather, from quite an extensive bit of reading, that's the program of premillennialism. I just want to stop and ask, my friends and brethren, do you believe that or not?

With that program stated, I want to suggest some things further. That theory also says that God's promise to the Jews regarding their occupancy of Palestine has never yet been fulfilled. Well, I am disposed to read to you a number of passages from God's word right on that point, and I do that just to be careful about the matter, because I know this talk is being critically heard and observed. I thank God for the facilities for making it permanent, so that after I have gone from Nashville, there can be no misrepresentation of what Hardeman said on this night.

In the first chapter of Joshua, God is encouraging Joshua to be strong and of good courage. He said: "There shall not any man be able to stand before thee all the days of thy life: as I was with Moses, so I will be with thee: I will not fail thee, nor forsake thee." Now I am turning next to the 21st chapter of Joshua and am reading from the 43rd verse: Hear it—"And the Lord gave unto Israel all the land," wait a minute. Does that say the Lord *will* give? No. This is toward the close of Joshua's reign. Now then, Joshua said: "And the Lord gave unto Israel all the land which he sware to give unto their fathers; and they possessed it, and dwelt therein." Now what had God promised? That the land of Palestine should be theirs to possess. Joshua, before you died, what about it? Well, you've heard me read what he said. "And the Lord gave them the rest round about, according to all that he sware unto their fathers: and there stood not a man of all their enemies before them; the Lord delivered all their enemies into their hand." Now mark it—"There failed not ought"—now what does ought mean? Anything. "There failed not anything of all the good that God said he would do unto Joshua or unto the house of Israel, all of it came to pass." Well, what was the promise? That the seed of Abraham, with reference to the land promise, should occupy the land of Palestine. Well, Joshua, what do you say about it? Joshua said that's exactly what they did.

Well, I read the last part of Joshua, 23rd chapter, commencing with verse 14: "And, behold, this day I am going the way of all the earth; and ye know in all your hearts, and in all your souls, that not one thing hath failed of all the good things which the Lord your God spake concerning you; all are come to pass unto you, and not one thing hath failed thereof. Therefore it shall come to pass, that as all good things are come upon you, which the Lord your God promised you; so shall the Lord bring upon you all evil things, until he have destroyed you from off this good land which the Lord your God hath given you. When ye have transgressed the covenant of the Lord your God, which he commanded you, and have gone and served other gods, and bowed yourselves to them; then shall the anger of the Lord be kindled against you, and ye shall perish quickly from off the good land which he hath given unto you." Now, I just want to raise the point to an honest man: Does the Bible say that God promised the land of Palestine to the

Israelites? It does. Well, who was left to see to its fulfillment? First, Moses; second, Joshua. Well, Joshua said at the close of his career, there had not failed one single thing which the Lord God had said regarding their possession of the land, but when they turned from God and began serving idols, they should quickly perish from off the land. Well, I read again, this time, from Jeremiah, the 25th chapter, commencing with verse 9: "Behold, I will send and take all the families of the north, saith the Lord, and Nebuchadnezzar the king of Babylon, my servant, and will bring them against this land, and against the inhabitants thereof, and against all these nations round about, and will utterly destroy them,"—this is a prediction of the Babylonian captivity—"and will make them an astonishment, and an hissing, and perpetual desolations. Moreover I will take from them the voice of mirth, and the voice of gladness, the voice of the bridegroom, and the voice of the bride, the sound of the millstones, and the light of the candle. And this whole land shall be desolation, and an astonishment; and these nations shall serve the king of Babylon seventy years." Now watch—"And it shall come to pass, when seventy years are accomplished, that I will punish the king of Babylon, and that nation, saith the Lord, for their iniquity, and the land of the Chaldeans, and will make it perpetual desolations." Now note—"And I will bring upon that land all my words which I have pronounced against it, even all that is written in this book, which Jeremiah hath prophesied against all the nations." There's the prophecy regarding their captivity.

Now, I'm reading from the last chapter of Second Chronicles, "And them that had escaped from the sword carried he away to Babylon; where they were servants to him and his sons until the reign of the kingdom of Persia: To fulfill the word of the Lord by the mouth of Jeremiah, until the land had enjoyed her sabbaths; for as long as she lay desolate she kept sabbath, to fulfill threescore and ten years." Now note—"Now in the first year of Cyrus king of Persia, that the word of the Lord spoken by the mouth of Jeremiah might be accomplished." God appeared unto Cyrus and bade him write a decree that the Jews should go back unto the land of Palestine. Now, take the very next chapter, Ezra 1: and you'll find that thing they did. Now then, you ask, why are they not there now? I turn to the eighth chapter of Hebrews and there is this: "They continued not in my covenant, and I regarded them not, saith the Lord." Why is it, friends, that the Jews did not keep the land into which Joshua said he would place them at the command of God Almighty? Paul said the reason was that they continued not in God's covenant. Well, friends, observe; when a covenant, which is an agreement or contract, is made, both sides are bound to it so long as the terms are executed; but suppose one side fails and violates it, then what about it? That covenant is broken and the other party is under no obligation whatsoever. Now get it: because, they, the Jews, "continued not in my covenant I regarded them not, saith the Lord." Therefore, the Jews were lost to Palestine, because they failed to keep their part of the contract, and were scattered abroad upon the face of the entire land.

Now, it is declared that in the next phase the Jews are to be converted as a nation and, therefore, are to return to Palestine. Friends, may I say to you in all candor, this Bible does not teach that, and that thing is so clear that it seems to me there could be no possible misunderstanding. I beg your indulgence for I don't often read, but I am doing so tonight. This time from Romans the 11th chapter:

"Thou wilt say then, The branches," the Jews, "were broken off, that I," the Gentile, "might be graffed in." Well —; "because of unbelief they were broken off, and thou standest by faith. Be not highminded, but fear: For if God spared not the natural branches—" who is that? The Jews, "take heed lest he also spare not thee. Behold therefore the goodness and severity of God: on them which fell, severity; but toward thee, goodness, if thou continue in his goodness; otherwise thou also shalt be cut off." Then what's the next point? He tells just how the Gentiles got into the original vine, and that was by the process of being graffed in, and he said, therefore, if the Jews continue not in unbelief, they also may be graffed in. Well, how? Just like the Gentiles. One individual after another. Not as a nation. Are the Gentiles all converted as a nation? No. Well, how is it? I am reading from Romans, in the gospel age. We are converted one by one. Well, is it possible for all of us to be saved? It is, if we submit to God's process of graffing. Now Paul said, if the Jew does not continue in unbelief, he can be graffed into the promises of God just like a Gentile, "and so, all Israel shall be saved." What do you mean by that *so?* That's not the conclusion, but *so* is an adverb, and means in this way all Israel shall be saved. How? By being graffed in. That's the only hope for either Jew or Gentile. So that much of it.

Now then, friends, I want to talk to you tonight about the serious consequences of this premillennial theory, or Bollism, as sometimes it's called. And yet it's not peculiar to Brother R. H. Boll. It started in modern times by old William Miller, back in 1843, at the beginning of Adventism. It was brought on down the line by Charles T. Russell, by Judge Rutherford, and others, and R. H. Boll is but in company with speculators.

But, let's think about the consequences of it. First of all, I am charging that the belief of a doctrine of that kind nullifies, makes void, the commission as given by Christ unto the apostles. Now, I think there is not a member of the church who does not know that Christ said: "All power is given unto me in heaven and in earth. Go ye therefore, and teach all nations." I believe that you think that is binding upon all men. But, let me tell you friends, if the doctrine of premillennialism be true, that Commission does not and cannot apply to our Jewish friends. Someone asks why? Well, I'll just tell you why, and let me say that I don't generally shoot until I can "see the whites of their eyes," and know what I'm talking about. I have here a book written by R. H. Boll under the title, "The Kingdom of God." All right, now on page 84, here's the statement: "Moreover Israel is not in this judgment. It is the nations that are here judged before the King, which term means the Gentiles, and always means nations *as distinguished from Israel* who is not among *the nations*." Now let's get it, Brother Boll, when you talk about nations, whom do you mean? "I don't mean Israel, they are excluded from the term, the nations, and are not incorporated in it." Now what does the Commission say? Go teach *all* nations. But Brother Boll says the Jews are not in that, therefore, where is authority from God's word tonight to preach the gospel to a Jew? Friends, I speak candidly because of the intense earnestness. You know that Peter stood on Pentecost, after that Commission was given by Christ, and preached unto the Jews, but here is a declaration that says the Jews are not included in the nations—only the Gentiles. Then what? The Commission is nullified as it pertains to the Jew. And furthermore, this deponent saith not. Someone may say: You're misrepresenting. No, I'm not. That's what he says about it, that in the term *Nations*, the Jews are excluded. Well, to whom was the Commission? Go teach all *nations!* But the Jews are not in that. Well, all right, where is the Commission for the Jew? There is none according to this theory. Friends, what do you think about it? Someone says: I don't think there's anything in it. Well, there isn't for the Jew. If the theory be true, Christ treated them worse than Hitler will ever do.

Well, let me state another thing, friends, regarding this doctrine. It not only nullifies the Commission, but it makes the church of Christ absolutely an accident. Friends; Brother Boll, and other premillennialists, teach that the church is an accident, and not intended. Well, lots of folks are from Missouri, and I love to talk to them. I have here, R. H. Boll's magazine, the *Word and Work* March, 1938. All right, now you listen to what Brother Boll says right on that point. "If after all, God has solemnly promised and sworn to his people Israel that he does not fulfill his word in giving them the land of Palestine, but turns into a spiritual and figurative fulfillment to a new spiritual contingent, called the church." Now what does he say the church is? A contingent. Now then, look at the definition of the word "contingent," and here's what it is. It means "that which might happen, that which is incidental, that which is accidental, that which comes by chance." Therefore, friends, you who have relied upon the promises found in the church of the Lord, are in a thing that God never had in mind, and if the Jews had accepted Christ and let him establish his kingdom when he did come, there would have never been a church. So, but for the rejection of the Jews, that contingent never would have existed upon this earth. I want to ask you if you believe that? Is that church, bought with the blood of the Son of God, and filled with his spirit, and crowned at last by his matchless glory, just an accident, or a contingent, and did it come by chance? Friends, is that your hope tonight of the eternal promise beyond? Well, I want you to listen—that's Brother R. H. Boll, and there's his magazine; I'm not giving it to you second-hand. Anybody here is at perfect liberty to come after service and say; "Hardeman, I want to see it myself." I'll be glad to let you see it.

Now again, in contrast with that, I want to read to you from the third chapter of Ephesians, commencing with verse eight; Paul said: "Unto me, who am less than the least of all saints, is this grace given, that I should preach among the Gentiles, the unsearchable riches of Christ; and to make all men see what is the fellowship of the mystery, which from the beginning of the world hath been hid in God, who created all things by Jesus Christ: To the intent that now unto the principalities and powers in heavenly places might be known by the church the manifold wisdom of God, *According to the eternal purpose* which he purposed in Christ Jesus our Lord:" Now Paul, what do you say about the church? Paul said the church is according to God's eternal purpose. Brother Boll, what do you say about it? That it's a contingent, accident, that God never intended it. Friends, I am positively ashamed to have to make a statement of that kind. And if my brethren, before whom I have gone preaching the gospel of Christ as best I could, have decided that the blood-bought and heaven-born and world-wide institution called the church, is a mere accident, I don't know what to say further. If the preaching of God's truth regarding such does not bring my brethren to unity, and cause them to quit all that speculation, and theorizing, then I do not know what to do that our differences may be healed. Look at it—Brother Boll, what do you say about the church? It's a contingent, accident. Paul, what do you say about it? It was according to God's eternal purpose from the foundation of the world. And you say, "Oh, that doesn't amount to anything." Yes it does. It destroys faith in the church of the Lord Jesus Christ and robs us of our fondest hopes of a blissful crown because of our membership in the body of Christ. Now, I am appealing to brethren, without any feeling of a partisan; I am asking brethren; did you know that such is the doctrine of premillennialism? It destroys the commission to the Jews; it makes the church of the Lord Jesus Christ a mere accident, and an incident, and a matter of chance.

Well, that's not all. The doctrine of premillennialism denies, positively, Peter's statement on Pentecost, when he said: "This is the last days." Now let's see about that. According to the premillennialist theory, here we are in the church period. Well, when will the *last days begin?* After Jesus Christ comes back from heaven, sets up business in Palestine on old Mt. Moriah, and then begins to exercise authority. That will be the beginning of the *last days.* Now friends, 1900 years ago, Peter stood upon Pentecost after the Holy Spirit was poured out upon them and said to that excited crowd: "These men are not drunk as you suppose, but this is that which was spoken by the prophet Joel," namely, "it shall come to pass in the *last days.*" Peter, what do you say about it? That was the beginning of the last days. Brethren, that was the establishment of the church. God says it's the last days. But, if the doctrine of premillennialism be true, then it's not the last days. Why? There's to be a period of a literal thousand years after the days called the last ones. Now, I just want to ask you if you believe it or not? I am appealing directly to my brethren, for whose benefit this meeting is held. Do you believe that we are in the last days?

Well, again, Hebrews 1: 1, hear Paul, "God, who at sundry times and in divers manners spake in times past unto the fathers by the prophets, hath in these *last days* spoken unto us by his Son." Now do you believe that, or will you accept some man's speculative, theorizing, guessing conclusion?

Brethren, I've preached enough to know this; I know when I drive home an argument. I know just what it takes to sell my brethren and to convince them. Whenever I can show them God's word, that's the end of the controversy. Now then, I've read to you what Peter said; this is the *last days,* Paul said; God has in *these,* not those that are yet to come, but in *these last days,* spoken by his Son. That's God's word and, unless we are wonderfully partisan, and are determined to have some new-fangled affair, that's the end of the controversy with us.

Now I just wonder, if there is an under-current and a question being raised to this effect: viz., Brother Hardeman, if Brother R. H. Boll, or some representative were present to answer, would you say all of that? Now, if you are really inquisitive about that, suppose you try and see. I am perfectly willing for you to find out to your own satisfaction.

Again, I want to suggest, my friends, another thing right along this line. The idea of premillennialism dethrones Jesus Christ, demotes him, takes him from God's right hand, where he's crowned King of kings, and Lord of all, and destroys the idea of his ruling as our King in fact. In the second chapter of Acts, which my brethren ought to know by memory: When the argument had been made by Peter regarding the resurrection, there is this: "Men and brethren, let me freely speak to you of the patriarch David. He is both dead and buried, and his sepulchre is with us unto this day. Therefore, being a prophet, and knowing that God had sworn with an oath to him, that of the fruit of his loins he would raise up one to sit on his throne; he seeing this before spake of the resurrection of Christ." Well, what about him? That Christ was raised up, *to sit, now mark it*—to sit, for the purpose of sitting, that he might sit, in order to sit. Why did God raise Christ, who is of the fleshly seed of David? To *sit.* To sit where? On *his* (David's) throne. Friends, I don't know how to argue with some folks. If there is the disposition to deny that, I cannot say that I am like the proverbial boy that ran over the calf, I don't know whether I've got anything fitten to say or not. Peter said: Brethren, David is not risen, his sepulchre is right here, but being a prophet and knowing that God had sworn to him with an oath, that of the fruit of his loins he would raise up Christ to sit on his throne, therefore, seeing this, he spake of the resurrection of Christ, that Christ's soul was not left in hell, nor did Christ's body see corruption. But note again as I read further right along that line: "Therefore being by the right hand of God exalted, and having received of the Father the promise of the Holy Ghost, he hath shed forth this, which ye now see and hear. For David is not ascended into the heavens: but he saith himself, The Lord said unto my Lord, Sit thou on my right hand, Until I make thy foes thy footstool. Therefore let all the house of Israel know assuredly, that God hath made that same Jesus, whom ye have crucified, both Lord and Christ." Now Peter, where is Christ? He's raised from the dead. What for? To sit on David's throne. But premillennialists say, he's not sitting on David's throne. Well, what's he doing then? Don't you see that the resurrection could have been postponed until now. Where is Christ sitting? He was raised up to sit on David's throne. Peter said, there he is, Lord of lords and King of kings. And yet, I've got to come before you with a degree of embarrassment and say: "I have brethren who fly in the face of Peter and say, that's not so." Well, David said he shall sit upon his throne until his foes be made his footstool. Now listen at Paul's wonderful resurrection sermon, 1st Cor. 15, Christ must reign. Well, he's reigning, then. How long? "till he hath put all enemies under his feet." That's what the prophet said. "The last enemy that shall be destroyed is death." Jesus Christ is reigning at God's right hand, and will reign until the last enemy shall be destroyed. Now then, premillennialists say that's not so. That he is not doing anything of the kind. Brother Boll says: "Jesus Christ is King, *de jure et potentia,* but not King, *de facto et actu.*" That's wonderful, isn't it? Brother Boll, what do you mean by it? Of course, anybody that knows the Latin language knows what it means, but let's let him tell it. "Christ is king by *right,* but not in *fact* and in *act.*" Who said that? The fellow that wrote this book. Brethren, what about it, then? Is Christ your king tonight? Brother Boll says he is not; he's only a king by right, but not in fact. Well, all right, does he have a kingdom? Yes. How? By right, but not in fact. But Paul said: "God has delivered us from the power of darkness and has translated us into the kingdom of his dear Son." How are we in the kingdom? Only by right, not in fact. So, if you think you are in the kingdom of God, Brother Boll said you are mistaken about it. You are in no such thing. You ought to be in there, but you are not; you have a right to be in there, but you are not.

But I read again to you, and it but confirms the same thing. Now listen at this, Page 71, hear it—"so long as Satan's throne is on earth, Christ is not exercising the government." Well, is the devil's throne on earth? The same writer says it is. What about Christ? He's not ruling. Then who is your Lord, brethren, tonight, and whom are you serving? You say, I'm serving the Lord. No, no, he's not ruler; he's not exercising authority. He's not even king and doesn't even have a kingdom. Where are you—better put an *At* after it, to get the matter clear. Friends, that's the tragedy, and when I see what I know to be good brethren hold up their righteous hand, and say: "Oh, there's nothing to that; you brethren just want to cause trouble." I'm sorry to say it, brethren, but you simply don't know what you're talking about. Now, that's the plain facts about it. You haven't studied the matter; you haven't read all the speculation regarding it, and therefore, you have no right to criticize those that are exposing error of this kind. But it is characteristic of this cult to profess an extremely pious air, and to be negative on all questions, and not to try to expose any kind of an error, even out in the sectarian and denominational world. They can put their arms around folks in error and honey them up, and say: "Brother, kindly lead our prayer." Now that's the spirit of it. There's the harm. It's the sacrifice, brethren, of the old landmarks. It's the giving way to the least resistance, and it's loving the praise of men more than the praise of God.

Well again, this theory, friends, also denies most positively, salvation to the Gentile world. Now, if I don't read that, I'll take down my sign and never again appear before a Nashville congregation. I am reading now from the 15th chapter of Acts. In that great Jerusalem council, after various ones had spoken, James said this: "Men and brethren, hearken unto me: Simeon hath declared how God at the first did visit the Gentiles, to take out of them a people for his name. And to this agree the words of the prophets. As it is written, after this, I will return, and will build again the tabernacle of David, which is fallen down; and I will build again the ruins thereof, and I will set it up." Now what's going to happen? I am going to return and build again the tabernacle of David. What does the word tabernacle mean? Well, sometimes it means a tent, or a booth, or a house; again it means a descendant, posterity, those that are to come after. So what do we have in this connection? "I will build again the tabernacle of David, which is fallen down." Now with that, 2 Samuel 7: 12 is perfectly harmonious: "And when thy days be fulfilled,"—this is talking about David—"and thou shalt sleep with thy fathers, I will set up thy seed after thee, which shall proceed out of thy bowels, and I will establish his kingdom." Now whose kingdom? That of the seed of David. Therefore, I will build again the tabernacle of David that is fallen down.

Wait just a minute, while I present a matter. Friends, the kingdom was established over Israel in 1095 B.C. Saul reigned for 40 years, and upon his death David took the throne, 1055. He reigned for 40 years, and then Solomon 40. This brings the time down to 975 B.C. At that time, the kingdom divided. Ten tribes went down to Bethel, after

Jeroboam and two stayed at Jerusalem, with Rehoboam. These two were in the Davidic line; they were of the house or tabernacle of David, and his seed continued on down until 587 B.C., when Zedekiah, the last one that could trace his ancestry back to David, rebelled. Zedekiah was dethroned and the family of David went down and so remained for 600 years. Amos said; after this the sifting of the house of Israel, I will return and build again that family of David. No one of David's bloodline has been on the throne since the days of Zedekiah. But Christ is of the seed of David, and Peter said that God raised up Christ, of the loins of David to sit on his (David's) throne. After this, "I will return and build again the tabernacle of David, which is fallen down." Now what for? Let's get the purport. Here it is, "That the residue," what does that word mean? Well, the other, the remainder. "That the residue of men might seek after the Lord." Consider seriously. Couldn't they seek after the Lord until the tabernacle of David was rebuilt? No sir. Why are you rebuilding the tabernacle of David? "That the residue of men might seek the Lord." What else? "And that the Gentiles might seek the Lord." Friends, we belong to the Gentile nation. We are sons of Noah through Japheth, and the Jews are sons of Noah through Shem, hence, we are Japhethites or Gentiles. Now then, James, what do you say? David's family as ruler is gone. There must be another of David's seed on the throne or else the Gentiles cannot seek the Lord. I insist, therefore, based upon God's word, if Jesus Christ is not on David's throne, there is not a Gentile on earth that has a shadow of a show of salvation.

But let's pass to another passage. I am reading to you now Second Corinthians five, and verse 16, "Henceforth"—what does henceforth mean? From now on, and on, and on, and on. "Henceforth know we no man after the flesh: yea, though we have known Christ after the flesh, yet now henceforth know we him no more." Paul, what did you say? There was a time when we knew Jesus Christ after the flesh, but that time will never be again. Now look how premillennialists fly right in the face of that. They say: "Paul, you're mistaken; when he comes back and sets up business in Palestine, there he'll be in the flesh, exercising the functions of government and ruling with a sword in a bloody warfare." Don't you see that such flatly contradicts God's word? Paul said we will never know Christ after the flesh again, but the very heart of premillennialism is that Christ will come and reign in the flesh, and we'll know him in the flesh. Friends, it's a direct violation and contradiction of God's word. Notwithstanding such opposition to God's word, some deluded brethren think that kind of teaching amounts to nothing. Brethren, does error of that kind disturb the church? What do you think about it?

And then again and finally, watch this picture: Premillennialists think they know just how all will be when Christ comes again. But John says: "Beloved, it doth not yet appear what we shall be." Now John said that and he was the last to write. He said he did not know but premillennialists have heard from heaven since John did. They seem to know. John said: "it doth not yet appear what we shall be: but we know that, when he shall appear, we shall be like him; for we shall see him as he is." Friends, I thank God, that when the time shall come, I'll not look upon Christ as he was while traveling o'er Judean hills and across Samaritan plains; I'll not see him tired, footsore and weary; I'll not see him humiliated by a blood-thirsty crowd; I'll not see him as he was while on the tree of the cross suspended; nor yet in Gethsemane's garden praying with agony to the Father that all might pass: I'll not see him between the heavens and the earth as though rejected by both and fit for neither; but I'll see him as he *is* in a glorified state, having triumphed over the powers of the Hadean world and now at God's right hand crowned. That's the picture, and with that I am perfectly content. If, after life's dream is over and the time comes for the ransomed to be gathered home, I can be like Christ as he is, at God's right hand exalted, that will be glory enough for me. I thank God for the exceeding great and precious promise therein contained.

But I must close this talk tonight. Is there one, two, any number, who believe that the kingdom of God is in existence; that the church was really purchased with the blood of God's Son; that in the body of Christ, there is salvation and forgiveness of sins? If such there be, the invitation is once again gladly tendered while we stand and sing the song selected.

HOW GOD SPEAKS TO MAN

A fine audience like this, assembled from time to time, gives so much encouragement and enthusiasm as to make us resolve to carry on.

Far more than I am able to express it, do I personally appreciate that disposition on the part of so many men and women to long for and to study Bible truths that challenge our concern. Always on occasions like this, where good is being accomplished and where sentiment is aroused, there are some characters of very small caliber that would like to be galvanized into respectability. They make every effort to gain attention. Young people, if they don't mind, are disposed to get too smart too soon. Some of them have never learned that "while larger ships may venture more; little boats should stay near shore."

In the *Gospel Advocate* of this week there is a very fine article. I want to commend it to you. It's written by Brother F. B. Srygley. The article quotes from R. H. Boll on "What's It's All About," and then proceeds to expose the discrepancies, the deception, and the contradictions. I want to urge you to subscribe for the *Gospel Advocate,* and tell them to give you this week's issue that you may see a live topic discussed.

Let me say, ladies and gentlemen, that I preach the truth. Of that I have not, of course, a shadow of a doubt. I am exceeding careful in making statements, especially, when some other doctrine is discussed, but after I have made them, I want you to know this; I stand four-square for the defense of the truth, as I conceive it, against the lawful claims of all persons whomsoever. And that's enough to say.

I am reading to you tonight the first verse of Hebrews one. I bid you note the sentiment as expressed by the writer, supposedly Paul. "God, who at sundry times and in divers manners spake in time past unto the fathers by the prophets, Hath in these last days spoken unto us by his Son." Then he continues with an exaltation of that Son far above all and any who might have gone before.

Now the beauty of preaching, as I see it, is its absolute simplicity, and I want you to get just what's said, analyze it, and you'll appreciate it all the more.

That verse declares that God, at sundry, or at different times, spake in time past unto their fathers, and he did it in divers, or various manners. It wasn't always the same, but varied as circumstances and occasions demanded. But be it remembered that when God has ever wanted to transmit His will to man, He has not done it in some vague, mysterious way, but He has spoken unto man, and in the long, long ago, it was by or through the prophets. But in these last days, He is speaking "to us by His Son, whom He hath appointed heir of all things." First of all, friends, we ought to rejoice because we are privileged to live in the last days, where God is not speaking in divers and various manners, but rather speaking unto us by His Son, whom He hath appointed heir of all things, by whom He made the worlds; who being the brightness of His glory, and the express image of His person, and when he had by himself purged our sins, sat down on the right hand of the Majesty on high." Now through that kind of an exalted character we are privileged to hear God tonight in these the last days, the gospel age.

Be it remembered, friends, that after God had created man, He placed him in the garden, with but one prohibition round about him. To that, man proved unfaithful, and in order to uphold the dignity of high heaven and the sovereignty of God Almighty, something had to be done. God, therefore, drove man out and separated him from the tree that perpetuated his existence, and made him grope his way down the darkened aisles of the future, where there's yet not one star to cast its light upon the distant horizon. But, notwithstanding his being driven out, God loved him still and went about the inauguration of a system of religion suited to man and at the same time commensurate with Heaven's will and the Father's dignity. Well, the families were few, the human race was in its infancy, and God adopted a unit around which all things else centered, and that was the head of the family. Hence, he spake unto the father, and through the father, expected his will to be transmitted to the children. Now, very correctly, that has been designated a government of the father, hence, Patriarchy.

Now, be it remembered, friends, that in that kindergarten department man had no use for a book; as yet he had to be taught in divers manners. Therefore, you ought to appreciate and understand the fact that 2500 years in the history of the human family went by, during which time, there was not a line from high heaven penned to mortal man. There wasn't any Bible; there wasn't anything in a permanent form. How was God dealing with him? Just like a good teacher deals with a kindergarten department. It was by means of pictures, and of demonstrations, and concrete examples. Now it took 2500 years for God to get the human family prepared to receive a textbook.

Now think of some other matters. The revelation of God to man was a gradual affair, and it had to be that way for him to appreciate it. The obligations placed upon men were given one at a time, as they were able to receive them. Hence, you may commence with the first pair in Paradise and descend the stream for ten generations and you will find only one thing that God ever commanded man to do as an act of service or worship, and that was the offering of animal sacrifice, which so far as the definite record is concerned, dates back to the first pair born on this earth. I know good and well that God had commanded such an offering to be made, and I'm not stopping to go through with the whole affair, but Paul said, that "by faith Abel offered unto God a more excellent sacrifice than Cain." Therefore, since faith comes by hearing, God had spoken. Now whether he had spoken direct to Abel about that or whether he had spoken unto the father, Adam, respecting it, I am not absolutely certain. There is a suspicion, and I offer it only as a suggestion, that perhaps Adam and Eve offered animal sacrifice before Cain was born. Now if you ask where is there ground for any thought along that line, I'd suggest this. The Bible says in Genesis 3: 21 that after Adam sinned, God made for them aprons or coats out of the skins of animals. Well, I stop and raise the point: What use had they for animal skin? They were not allowed to eat flesh and yet, there they had the skins of animals, and the suspicion is not lacking, that they had offered sacrifices and had transmitted that very thought unto their sons, according to the system of God speaking to the father and in turn, the father committing the same unto the son. But be that as it may, that's the first thing that God demanded as an act of worship. Hence, he outlined exactly how that thing should be, and early in the morning of time taught us in a very definite concrete manner through Cain, as an example, that man can't substitute for God's word. You can't do something else and think that will meet with divine approval. If thou doest well, Cain, all is well; if not, sin lieth at the door, knocking ready to come in. That's the principle there involved.

Now then, let's pass down the line. You may commence with Adam and go on with Seth, Enos, Cainan, Mahalaleel, Jared, Enoch, Methuselah, Lamech, and Noah, ten long generations—and what revelation is made for man? None, other than that of animal sacrifice. But with the passing of those generations, wickedness began to multiply upon the earth and a state of almost total depravity prevailed. Finally, God saw that the wickedness of man was great in the earth, and that every imagination of the thoughts of his heart was evil and that continually. And then God decreed and announced, in the days of Noah, that everything that lives upon the face of the earth in whose nostrils is the breath of life should be destroyed and wiped from the face of this earth. There was the decree regarding the destruction brought about by that wonderful flood, which submerged the highest hill and over-topped the loftiest mountain.

Well, after Noah had prepared the ark as God had directed and had been piloted across that boundless ocean untouched by a single shore, there started out afresh, Noah and his wife, Shem, Ham, and Japheth and their wives—eight souls saved from the destruction and saved by means of water. Well, how? Oh, back before the flood they were tormented and vexed with wickedness and vice on every hand. Now then, by means of the flood, they were transferred from an old sin-cursed world into a new world purified by the great baptismal flood. After this, God commanded them exactly as he had Adam, "multiply and replenish the earth."

Now note, ten generations more are born before anything else comes to pass, and here they are: After Noah, then Shem, Arphaxad, Salah, Eber, Peleg, Reu, Serug, Nahor, Terah, and Abraham. Now we're ten generations from Noah and we may ask, what next? God speaks unto Abraham, He calls him out and establishes the covenant of circumcision, which was the placing of a physical mark on every male born in Abraham's house, and purchased with his money. Time rolls on; they are true to the circumcision covenant and likewise to the promise made concerning the land, and after a while, that posterity down through Isaac, Jacob, and his sons, drifts into the land of Egypt. There they multiply until the number becomes six hundred thousand men, beside the women and children. In Egypt they were made to serve with rigour until finally, God looked upon them and heard their murmuring, and saw their wonderful burdens. He set about to lead them out of the land of Egypt, in which they had been captives. This brought them across the Red Sea, and in about fifty days after leaving Rameses, they were at Mount Sinai. They have outgrown the family idea, and now they're big enough and prominent enough to become a great nation, hence, watch the development. They are now ready to receive permanent instructions and therefore, for them God wrote the Constitution upon both sides of two tables of stone, and then He told Moses to write out a book of the Covenant.

Think again. Under that first system, every father was a priest unto God; wherever he chanced to go, God gave him the right to stop and build an altar and there offer a sacrifice unto Jehovah. Hence, Abraham came into the land of Canaan, stopped first at old Shechem and built an altar. He then went on south to Bethel and did likewise. That was the order. Through the father the family approached the throne of God. That system was suited to their nature. They were wandering, nomadic in their disposition. Now God fitted that system of religion to their manner of life, and wherever they went, they could worship God with absolute assurance. The father was the priest and he could build an altar anywhere, and worship God acceptably. But after they had come out of Egyptian bondage and gone on to Mt. Sinai, they stayed there for an entire year, and I want you to note what all was happening. God was a God of system, "all things were to be done decently and in order." During their stay at Mt. Sinai four things were done: first, God gave the law, the decalogue; second, there was the worship of the golden calf and the punishment for the same; third, there was the building of God's tabernacle, a house of gold upon a foundation of silver; and fourth, they numbered and organized, ready to march on toward the land that flowed with milk and honey.

An entire new system has been set up and we inquire, what is it now? Instead of its being a family affair, it's now a National Religion. Instead of God speaking in divers ways and on various occasions, He now is speaking through His written word. They were to assemble time after time and hear the word of the Lord, which they gladly did. Not only that, but instead of having their altars builded just anywhere, it must now be in front of the tabernacle and no where else could they offer a sacrifice acceptable. Watch another change. Instead of each father's having the right to worship God by offering sacrifice, there must be a man of the tribe of Levi and of the house of Aaron. None other could approach the throne of God to offer a sacrifice. Can't you see a wonderful change and transition in matters and the unfolding and development of God's plan? Friends, that was a law given unto the sons of Abraham and to nobody else. I regret that I feel it necessary to speak of another thing.

It is strange to me that intelligent people imagine that

that law, in some of its phases, is applicable unto us tonight. There isn't any excuse for making a blunder of that kind. Let me say to you that the law of Moses has been abrogated for nearly 2000 years, but if it were in full force and effect tonight, it would not apply, in any of its provision, to us. Now why? Because it was never given unto anybody except the sons of Abraham, of whom we are not.

Now, may I just call your attention to this, in order to provoke you to think earnestly? Lots of people are interested in tracing back their family history. I never have been very much sold on a matter of that kind. I'm not especially interested in my ancestors. I just know that if I were to commence and go up that family tree, I wouldn't get far until I'd strike a limb that ought to have been sprayed a long time ago, and so I let it alone. But, to make the point that I intended, I want to say this: after the flood, there were three sons of Noah, from whom the entire human family sprang. Here they are: Shem, Ham, and Japheth. Would you be surprised and shocked if I were to ask you of which son you came? Are you a Japhethite, or a Shemite, or a Hamite? Now, let me tell you. I think this is about as intelligent an audience as usually gathers. I doubt if many of you know from which son of Noah you sprang, and yet, that's very important. Let me trace down just a minute: Noah, Shem, Arphaxad, Salah, Eber, Peleg, Reu, Serug, Nahor, Terah, Abraham, Isaac, Jacob, and then Reuben, Simeon, Levi, and on down the line of those who went down to Egypt. From whom do they descend? From Noah, through Shem. Well, what's our line of descent? Without going into the matter further, I want to say to you that the best evidence on earth is this: you and I get back to Noah through Japheth. Hence, we are not related to the others, except wonderfully far-distant cousins. Now then, who are the Shemites? They are not our kind. Who went down into Egypt? Sons of Shem. Who came up out of Egypt? Sons of Shem. To whom did God give the law? Unto the sons of Shem. Therefore, our ancestors were never a part of it, nor were they incorporated in it. It is inexcusable for a man to claim that any part of that law was given unto other than the sons of Shem. It did not apply to a son of either Ham or of Japheth. A knowledge of God's Book and a genuine appreciation of it depends upon a correct analysis of matters at the beginning. One must recognize its divisions and dispensations. Now, that law emanating from Mt. Sinai, which applied to the Jews, lasted for 1500 years. I raise with you this point: under what was the rest of the world worshipping during the existence of the law which applied to the sons of Abraham? Were all the sons of Japheth and of Ham left out? Was there no way by which they could worship God while the Jews were gathered about the tabernacle? The giving of the law at Sinai to the sons of Abraham does not necessarily, declare that there was no system by which the rest of the world could worship. How do you know that Patriarchy ceased until we reach the house of Cornelius? God, by the death of Christ, was to make of the twain one new man. The law of Moses lasted 1500 years and during that time the prophets stood upon the hilltops of Israel and pictured the coming of the Christ. John the Baptist came during that time, and it was during the law of Moses that Jesus Christ came and preached the coming of the kingdom. It was under the law that not only Christ Jesus our Lord lived, but during the law of Moses, he suffered and sorrowed and ultimately bled and died, and on the tree of the cross he said: "Father, it is finished." Well, what's finished? That thing that I came to fulfill. What was it? Turn back to the Sermon on the Mount, Matthew 5: 17, Jesus said: "Think not that I am come to destroy the law, or the prophets: I am not come to destroy, but to fulfill. Till heaven and earth pass, one jot or one tittle shall in no wise pass from the law, till all be fulfilled." Remember on the cross, he said, "Father, it is finished." What is finished? The law and the prophets pertaining unto me. If that be true, friends, and true it is, what about the idea then of claiming those same prophecies as yet unfulfilled? Christ said, on the morning when he walked with the disciples: "These are the words which I spake unto you, while I was yet with you"—now mark it—"how that all things

must be fulfilled, which were written in the law of Moses, and in the prophets, and in the psalms, concerning me." Think about it a minute. Lord, what are you saying? All things written in the law and all things written in the prophets have been fulfilled. What about our premillennial friends? They say, "Lord you never made a greater mistake in all of your life; things concerning you have not begun to be fulfilled yet." Friends, that doctrine of premillennialism is contrary to God's word at almost every angle and from every point. Christ said the law is fulfilled. Paul said that he blotted it out; that he took it out of the way; that he nailed it to the cross and that he gave unto us a better covenant founded upon better promises. Can't we thank God for that? "For," said Paul, "if that first covenant had been faultless, no place should have been sought for the second." But finding fault with that one, he said, "Behold, the days come, saith the Lord, when I will make a new covenant with the house of Israel and with the house of Judah." Well, how is it, Paul? "Not according to the covenant that I made with their fathers." When? "In the day when I took them by the hand to lead them out of the land of Egypt." Why? "Because they continued not in my covenant, and I regarded them not, saith the Lord. But this is the covenant that I will make with them, saith the Lord: I will put my law in their minds." Well, where is the old one? On tables of stone, but now I will put "it in their minds and write it in their hearts. I will be to them a God, and they shall be to me a people; and they shall not teach every man his neighbour, and every man his brother, saying, Know the Lord: for all shall know me, from the least to the greatest. For I will be merciful to their unrighteousness, and their sins, and their iniquities will I remember no more." What about the other? In those sacrifices there is remembrance made again of sin every year. Why? Because it was not possible for the blood of bulls and of goats, which they offered, to take away sin, but unto this, their sins and their iniquities will I remember no more. "In that he saith a new covenant, he hath made the first old. Now that which decayeth and waxeth old is ready to vanish away." Friends, that's the end of the national system.

And then what? Beginning first with a family where the father is the priest, he offered sacrifices 2500 years. Then came the inauguration of a national system at shaking Sinai, destined to last for the next 1500 years, and after that, when the fullness of time was come, Jesus Christ was born upon this earth. He lived thirty and three years. He came to break down the middle wall or partition that had stood between Jews and Gentiles for, lo, these 1500 years, and "that he might make in himself out of the twain, the two nations, one new man, so making peace; and that he might reconcile both unto God in one body, by the cross, having slain the enmity thereby; and came and preached peace unto you who are afar off, and also unto you that are nigh." Therefore, you Gentiles "are no more strangers and foreigners, but you are fellow citizens with the saints, and of the household of God; And are built upon the foundation of the apostles and prophets, Jesus Christ himself being the chief cornerstone." Again Paul said: "Unto him be glory in the church by Jesus Christ throughout all ages, world without end." And what do premillennialists teach? That the church will end when the next age begins. But God said, "Unto him be glory in the church throughout all ages; world without end." My friends, don't insult my intelligence by saying that the church is incidental, accidental, a contingent, and will cease to be when the kingdom shall have come, not only *de jure*, but *de facto*, and *actu*. Brethren, you ought to know that the church was from the beginning, according to God's eternal purpose. Paul so declares in Ephesians 3.

Conscious of the fact that the Patriarchal and Jewish dispensations have passed, we now have a world-wide, heaven-born, blood-bought institution through which the wisdom of God is to be made known unto all the world. Hence, in anticipation of its being fully established, Jesus said to those disciples who were to become its charter members, all power in heaven and in earth is mine, not *de jure*, not simply by right, but as a matter of fact. I am on

David's throne, not only by right, but also by actuality. "Go, therefore, and teach all nations." Friends, no such a declaration had ever been made, from the morning of time until now. Even John the Baptist preached only to the Jews. In the personal ministry of our Lord, he said, "I am not sent but to the lost sheep of the house of Israel." But after the tragic death of the cross, the burial in a borrowed tomb, and the triumphant resurrection over the powers of the Hadean world, Christ came forth and said for the first time: "Preach the gospel unto every creature." Friends, that's where we are tonight, and I rejoice together with you, and thank high heaven, that we are not under the system of our fathers, nor are we under the system of Levitical priesthood, but we are under Christ Jesus our Lord, who is at God's right hand exalted, crowned King of kings, and Lord of lords, and that he is really and actually exercising the power and sovereignty of a ruler. Christ not only said: "Go preach the gospel to every creature," but he added the terms of salvation. "He shall be saved." Now, suppose Christ had put it just that way, unmodified? Go into all the world and preach the gospel to every creature, "he shall be saved." Well, Christ did say that, but he limited that to a certain kind of *he*. "He shall be saved!" Lord, what *he?* Just any *he?* No, not that. Well, what *he* now are you declaring salvation unto? Of what *he* do you predicate salvation? "He shall be saved!" What *he?* Now mark it, Lord, did you say he that believes, shall be saved? No. Did you say he that is baptized shall be saved? No. Well, what did you say then? I said, it's the "*he* that believeth *and* is baptized." What about him, Lord? That "he shall be saved." Friends, you tell me that I can't understand that? I want to tell you and it may be a shock to you. I could not misunderstand it to save my life, even with expert help. I just couldn't misunderstand that. What did the Lord say? "He that believeth and is baptized"—he that does two things. Lord, were you talking about an innocent babe? No. An untaught heathen? No. An unfortunate imbecile? No. Then, Lord, whom are you talking about? "I'm talking about a certain *he* who believes

and is baptized." What do you say about him, Lord? "That man shall be saved." "He that believeth," number one, "and is baptized," number two, "shall be saved," number three. Friends, look at it honestly, candidly, seriously, soberly: where did God put baptism, *before* or *after* salvation? Did the Lord put salvation before or after baptism? If there's anybody here who can't understand that, I'd be afraid to let him run loose in Nashville. The Lord said belief *plus* baptism equal salvation. Man says, belief *minus* baptism equals salvation. Now, which way do you believe it, as the Lord put it or as man puts it? There are some who may think such issues are dead and ought not to be preached. They think we should go on. God knows we ought to get back there where the truth is. You can't insult God's word by reflecting upon it, with impunity. Jesus Christ, in his farewell message, in his final doxology, and valedictory to mankind, said to those disciples, "Go ye into all the world, and preach the gospel to every creature." The soul that believes it and is baptized stands upon the promises of Christ Jesus our Lord.

Friends, I must meet these issues on the plains of eternal judgment. I'm not afraid to appear and answer for this preaching. I have preached what the Bible says and that's all we know about it. I am appealing, therefore, to those who honor me with their presence and lend patient, polite, and courteous attention, to do just what Jesus said. We'd better accept the terms by Him laid down, and stand upon His everlasting promise. It is a wonderful privilege to preach the gospel; it is grand to believe it; it is glorious to obey it. The invitation is yours while we sing.

THE FIRST SERMON UNDER THE COMMISSION

I know of nothing, my friends, more gratifying than the continued presence of this company which is made up, practically, of the same people night after night. And, your presence, I repeat, is the greatest encouragement that could be given.

This meeting, as has been said before, had a definite object in view. I tried to state that at the first service. Carrying out that objective, every service has had its bearing upon it.

I want, before it closes, to present some of the old-time, simple gospel stories, so familiar to all of you people who chance to be with us from time to time.

Tonight, I am talking about the first Gospel Sermon ever preached in the name of the risen Lord. I recognize the fact that, to many of you older brethren, this is exceeding familiar ground. I'll have nothing new to reveal to you, but just bear in mind, there was a time when you and I did not know it, due to the lack of opportunity. There are possibly hundreds of people in our hearing tonight, and on various nights, who likewise have not been blessed with the privilege of hearing these elementary matters discussed, and that's the reason for the repetition of these old-line talks.

In harmony with that outline of last night, be it remembered, that I reviewed God's dealings with man from the very beginning. He saw His plan unfolded and developed through the different ages, until the fullness of time was come, when Jesus Christ was born upon the earth. He lived a third of a century; walked among men; and left us an example that we should follow in His steps. After the tragic scene of the cross, He came forth triumphant o'er the powers of the dead and brought life and immortality to light, and then, for the first time in all the history of the world, there was the glad announcement that the gospel was to be preached unto every creature on this earth.

I want you to think just a moment how simple that matter is as planned by God, executed by Christ, and revealed by the Holy Spirit. God drafted the plan of human redemption. When all was complete, He transmitted that blue print to his Son, with direct specifications to come to this earth and carry out that which the Father had planned. And then the Holy Spirit stepped in with his particular work and made known what God had planned, and what Jesus Christ had executed. Hence, the work of the three, and yet, all of them are one.

Of course, you believe that God's plan was adequate for the purpose intended. You would not think of asking Jehovah to draft another scheme of redemption, but with what He has done, those who believe the Bible are satisfied. You wouldn't think of asking Jesus Christ to leave heaven again, and come to Palestine to carry out the Father's will and to suffer, sorrow, bleed, and die once again for a lost, a ruined, and a recreant race of mankind. Why? You believe that he did that and tasted death for every man. Then, my friends, when the Holy Spirit comes to consummate the work of redemption, and has finished his revelation to man, and closed the record, it's an expression of a lack of faith for any man to pray God's Spirit to make known to us any other than that which already has been revealed. What we need, therefore, is to study God's plan, Christ's execution, and the Holy Spirit's revelation. So, when Christ gave the great world-wide commission to the apostles, to teach all nations and to preach the gospel to every creature, he said to them: Go to Jerusalem and there wait until ye be endued with power from on high. Why that? Simply because of this: the message that you are to deliver to mortal man is fraught with such momentous importance, that I do not want to leave it to you unaided, but wait till power comes upon you, and then it'll not be you that speaks, but God's Spirit that speaks through you. Therefore, wait in the city of Jerusalem. Thither they went and with them we are, tonight, ready to begin the execution of that Great Commission but recently received.

I propose the following method of studying this first sermon: namely, I want to find out, first, the time of it; I'd like to know next the character of the audience assembled; then I want to study who the preacher was; and next, I want to analyze that sermon thoroughly, and then, after it's proclaimed, I ask what the effect was, and what the further results that followed? Now, can you think of any other vital topic that ought to be included in an investigation of this kind? I think those cover it, and to them I address myself tonight.

I am raising a point: when was this first sermon delivered to mortal man? The record says: "When the day of Pentecost was fully come." That's the time. It's the first Pentecost, of course, after the resurrection of our Lord. Now Bible students remember that Pentecost was one of the three annual feasts of the Jews; that it always came on the first day of the week. There never was a Pentecost on Monday, nor on Thursday, but always on what we call Sunday, the first day of the week. This Pentecost, especially, was the time of many prophecies, and the inauguration of various things there came to pass. It's the day when God's Spirit was to come; it's the time when Jesus Christ was to be crowned at God's right hand; it's the time when the administration of our Lord was to begin upon this earth; it's the time when the church of the Lord, or the Kingdom of God, was established upon this earth. Hence, it was a wonderfully memorable occasion. Thus, we are at Jerusalem, according to God's announcement, on the first day of the week, around 9 o'clock in the morning. Well, with that answered, note the next.

What kind of an audience was here assembled? Here is what the Bible says: "There were dwelling at Jerusalem, Jews, devout men, out of every nation under heaven." Now, we read that carelessly, and it makes not much of an impression, but, notice it, where did you ever see or hear of an audience like that? You've been in big crowds where multiplied throngs of people came together, but you've never seen an audience wherein there were devout men, representing every nation under heaven. I've preached to big crowds right here in Nashville, many times this auditorium has been packed to its capacity, but we've never had a crowd like that. We've had perhaps various nationalities, but not all of them assembled, and furthermore, our crowd has not always been made up of men as devout as they might have been. But here is a select crowd of honest, upright men devoted to religious matters, and they had gathered from every nation under heaven to attend this Jewish feast of Pentecost. I know that there are brethren who sometimes visit in Nashville and, while here on some other business, they might drop in to church. Friends, that wasn't the character of the audience there assembled. They went there for one definite purpose, and that was to worship God Almighty. Hence, they were men devoted and they were there out of every nation under heaven. Then the writer of the book of Acts enumerates fifteen different nationalities, and if you'll draw upon your memory with reference to geography, I want you to see the countries. From away up yonder northeast of the lands of the Bible, around about the Caspian Sea, there were representatives; then sweeping on down toward the Persian Gulf, and up the rivers of Tigris and Euphrates, you'll find men from there. Passing across the great Wilderness of Wandering into the country of Africa, you'll observe representatives from parts of Libya about Cyrene, and on west as far as Rome, there were strangers, Jews and proselytes. That's the most wonderful audience of which I have ever read, and it is so fitting, for Christ had said: "Go teach all nations." That's the fine audience thus assembled.

Now, watch the next point. I am asking, who was the preacher? Just naturally, you would center upon Peter. Why? Because Christ had said to him, I'm going to give unto you the keys of the kingdom of heaven, and, therefore, it'll be your task to inject the key, turn the lock, open wide the door, and bid characters to enter in. Peter is the preacher. But it is not the Peter who wavered; it's not the Peter who followed afar off; it's not the Peter who denied the Christ and boasted of what others might do, but he never would. That's not he, but it is Peter as a new man, filled with the Spirit of God, who stood like a stone wall, with powers from on high granted unto him. It was not Peter speaking but the Holy Spirit using him as a medium through which the truth of God was to be proclaimed. That's the preacher of the occasion.

Well, you note the next point, the sermon that was delivered. But be it remembered, that before Peter could get their ears, gain their attention, and begin that address, there were certain difficulties that had to be cleared away. When the noise from heaven was sounded abroad, as the result of the Holy Spirit's coming, and filling all the house wherein they were sitting, the people were all in confusion. The Bible says "the multitude came together, and were confounded," they marvelled, they were amazed, they were in doubt, saying one to another, what does all this mean, how is it, there here we are listening to every man in our own tongue, wherein we were born? Now, to them, that was a real problem. They understood it not, and therefore, they were bothered, confounded, confused, amazed, and wondered, how can these things be? But did you ever note, that in any kind of a crowd, there are always some smart enough to explain almost anything? So, some mockingly said: all these men are drunken. "These men are drunken," "they are filled with new wine"; and for that reason, all of this amazement, and confusion. Well, when Peter got their ears, he lifted up his voice, and said: "Ye men of Israel, these men are not drunken as ye suppose." Well, why? "It is but the third hour of the day." Now, that's Peter's explanation in refutation of their charge that these men are drunken. "It's but the third hour of the day." I am not sure that I understand all about that. I don't know whether it was just simply contrary to their custom to get drunk before nine o'clock in the morning, or whether some other explanation is due. I just know that that wouldn't hold good here in Nashville, or in West Tennessee; we've got stuff that will make a fellow drunk before nine o'clock. But, be that as it may, Peter's statement that they are not drunken because it was the third hour of the day, was perfectly satisfactory to that crowd. They argued it no more. Now, Peter, if that's not the explanation, what is it? Peter appealed to them through their Old Testament, the scriptures which they were forced to believe. He said to them: these are not drunken, but here is the explanation: This is the fulfillment of that which was spoken by our Jewish prophet Joel, namely, "I will pour out my spirit upon all flesh." While Peter, therefore, unfolded Joel's prophecy the audience regained their reason and were soon ready to hear what further Peter had to say. Now then, with explanations having been made and with their ears tuned, Peter began: "Ye men of Israel, hear these words; Jesus of Nazareth, a man approved of God among you by miracles and wonders and signs, which God did by him in the midst of you, as ye yourselves also know." Now that is rather lengthy, but it is the statement of one proposition. Now what is it? You know that Jesus Christ of Nazareth is a God-approved man, and the proof is, the performance of miracles, wonders, and signs that he's done right in your midst. You know it. Now Peter never did refer to that again. He simply stated that proposition and clinched it by saying, you know it. Well, all right, what's the second one? "Him, being delivered by the determinate counsel and foreknowledge of God." Now, that's the second proposition laid down by Peter. All of this is according to the foreknowledge of God, and our Jewish scriptures abound in statements to that one effect, that God has foreordained and according to his foreknowledge, Jesus Christ was thus to be. Well, now what's the third one?

Here it is: "Ye have taken, and by wicked hands have crucified and slain." That's the third statement. Now, I just want to ask you, do you think that needed argument? There they were, who a little more than fifty days before, had seen Jesus Christ on the cross, and had said to old Governor Pilate: "Crucify Him, Crucify Him; away with Him." Well, that didn't need any argument. Nobody on earth knew that any better than did they. Hence, the mere recitation of it was sufficient.

Well, what's the next statement? "God hath raised him from the dead. It was not possible that death should hold him." Here we have a model sermon outline. First, the introduction, including the clearing away of all misunderstanding, and preparing the audience for the reception of the more sober and more solemn declaration. Then, step by step, there was the statement of his four propositions.

Now, let's get them again. First: Jesus of Nazareth who went among you, is approved of God by the performance of miracles, wonders, and signs, which he did in our midst, and you know it. Next, what is number two? That he was delivered according to the foreknowledge of God. And again, what is number three? You have crucified him by wicked hands, and they are right now dripping in the innocent blood of the spotless Son of God. Finally, what is the fourth one? God has raised him from the dead.

Now friends, I want to submit to you this simple thought, and I think all of us ought to get some lesson from it. Sometimes we are in the habit, as preachers, of stating a thing that everybody knows, and which nobody denies, and yet we'll argue that point for fifteen minutes. Now, all such ought to be eliminated, and here is a fine example. Peter never argued the fact that Jesus is God-approved. He said, you men know that. Neither did he stop to argue that Christ was delivered according to the foreknowledge of God. He simply stated the fact.

Well, what's the next point? You have crucified him by the hands of lawless men. Now, why talk five minutes on that? Anybody doubt it? Nobody knew it better than did that crowd. Therefore, Peter passed it by and he said, God has raised him from the dead. Now, that's the only point among the four that Peter's crowd denied. They were bound to accept three of the propositions, and hence, he spent no time in arguing matters of that sort, but he devoted his time to the proposition that needed support, and that was the resurrection from the dead. Now, may I submit to you that Peter adduced three arguments in behalf of the resurrection of Christ from the dead, and here they are: I read from Acts the second chapter: "Whom God hath raised up, having loosed the pains of death; because it was not possible that he should be holden of it." I want you to note how skillful and how accurate Peter's argument is. It wouldn't do for him to turn to some Gentile and introduce him as authority. So he goes right back to that crowd's own prophet David, whom they recognized, in whom they had confidence, and whose testimony they must accept. Peter said, you killed the Christ and God has raised him from the dead. You deny it but that's the thing I'm going to prove to you, and I'll commence with our own prophet David. Hear him: "David speaketh concerning him, I foresaw the Lord always before my face, for he is on my right hand, that I should not be moved: Therefore did my heart rejoice, and my tongue was glad; moreover also my flesh shall rest in hope: Because thou wilt not leave my soul in hell, neither wilt thou suffer thine Holy One to see corruption. Thou hast made known to me the ways of life; thou shalt make me full of joy with thy countenance." Now that's what David said. He declared that somebody was going to die, but that his soul was not to be left in hell, and that his flesh would not see corruption. Now they were bound to admit that David said that.

Now, watch Peter's comment: "Men and brethren, let me freely speak unto you of the patriarch David, that he is both dead and buried, and his sepulchre is with us unto this day." Possibly Peter pointed out exactly the spot where David's body was lying. David "therefore, being a prophet, and knowing that God had sworn with an oath to him, that of the fruit of his loins, according to the flesh, he would raise up Christ *to sit* on his throne." "He seeing this before spake of the resurrection of Christ, that his soul was not left in hell, neither his flesh did see corruption." Christ's soul was not left in Hades and the body of Christ did not see corruption. That's Peter's argument. He said to them: if you'll accept our own David, you must admit the resurrection, for he prophesied this very thing. He said somebody would not be left in hell, nor would his flesh see corruption. But David wasn't talking about himself, for David knew that God had sworn to him, with an oath, that of the fruit of his loins, he would raise up someone to sit upon his throne, and, therefore, seeing this before, he spake of the resurrection of Christ, that *His* soul was not left in Hades, nor did Christ's body see corruption, but God raised up Christ. For what intent? *To sit* on his, David's throne. That's Peter's argument thus far, but he presented another and here it is: "This Jesus hath God raised up." What's the proof of it, Peter? "Whereof we all are witnesses." Now I want you to see just what an array of testimony this statement included. That audience to whom he is preaching, must say either that all of you twelve apostles and you 120 disciples are liars or else it must accept the statement thus given. So that's argument number two. Watch argument three. "Therefore, being by the right hand of God exalted, and having received of the Father the promise of the Holy Spirit, he hath shed forth this, which ye now see and hear." Hence, the outpouring of the Holy Spirit with its like demonstration is the third argument in behalf of the resurrection of Christ. I submit to you, again, the four statements of Peter's sermon: First, Jesus is God-approved among you and you know it. Second, he was delivered by the determinate counsel and foreknowledge of God. Third, you have crucified him. Fourth, God hath raised him from the dead.

What's the evidence of the resurrection? First, the evidence is David's own testimony, when he prophesied not regarding himself, for there his body lies as yet, but he is talking about Christ. Second, all of us testify. Third, look at this wonderful demonstration.

Friends, that's the sermon. Now then, I want you to think, what effect did it have? "When they heard this." This what? The climax of Peter's sermon. Well, what was it? "That God hath made that same Jesus, whom ye have crucified, both Lord and Christ." Now Peter, what has been your procedure? "I have stated matters fundamental, three of which you do not doubt, and the fourth one I have produced evidence to support. Hence, I want you to know that God has made that very Jesus, whom you crucified, both Lord and Christ." Now note the effect of that address.

"When they heard this they were cut to their heart," conviction to them was brought. They were affected by the proclamation of the gospel of God's Son. There was God's Sword of the Spirit bringing conviction of their guilt. Therefore, they cried out to Peter and to the rest of the apostles: "Men and brethren, what shall we do?" Now let's just see matters as they are. What has been the program? First, Peter has preached. Second, that multitude has heard. Third, conviction to their hearts has been brought, and it expressed itself by their inquiry, "What shall we do?" I want to ask, were they believers or infidels? To ask that is to answer. Where, friends, did you ever hear of a set of infidels cut to the heart by the preaching of God's word? Where did you ever see a set of unbelievers crying out, saying: "Men and brethren, what shall we do?" Now then, if Peter had subscribed to certain doctrines he might have said: "Gentlemen, you can't do anything; all was fixed before the foundation of the world, and the number to be saved is definitely settled," or he might have said: "If you men believe what I have preached you are already saved and nothing else is required. You know we are justified by faith only, and that's a most wholesome doctrine." Now this audience knows that Peter did not subscribe to anything that even sounded like such doctrines. I want you to see it, friends. Sacred and serious matters are confronting us tonight. Those Jews heard the gospel as preached by Peter, and the effect of it was, they were cut to their hearts. It brought conviction unto them. It stirred them up. It made them conscious of their guilt, because they were made to believe that their hands were stained in the innocent blood of the Son of God. Therefore, they cried: "What shall we believers do?" Now watch it—"Then Peter," speaking by God's Spirit, "said unto them, Repent, and be baptized every one of you in the name of Jesus Christ for the remission of sins, and ye shall receive the gift of the Holy Spirit." Friends, I just want to ask you, is that perfectly clear and easily understood? Is there anything difficult about that? Can a man responsible to God Almighty misunderstand it? What is the program?

First, preached the gospel unto them; they heard it; as a result of hearing, faith was theirs, and due to that faith they made the move and cried: "What can we do?" For what? "To rid ourselves of the heinous crime, that you have charged upon us in that we have killed the Son of God. What can we do about it?" Now God's Spirit, speaking through Peter, said unto that crowd of believers: "Repent and be baptized." Now it's strange to me that folks resent a matter of that kind, that a great many preachers, with high-sounding titles and terms attached to their names, would not tell a Nashville audience just what Peter told that multitude on that memorable Pentecost.

My friends, are you here tonight believing that you have heard the gospel of God's Son? Do you believe in the Lord with all your heart? If so, are you anxious about your eternal welfare? If you are, and want to go to heaven when you die, Peter said, my dear sir, "repent and be baptized." Do what? Two things, repent, *and,* what does "and" mean? Addition, plus, something else. Repent *plus* be baptized. "Repent *and* be baptized." Well, why? "For the remission of sins." Why repent? "For the remission of sins." Why be baptized? "For the remission of sins." That's God's word about it. Someone may saw, now, Brother Hardeman, that's just your opinion and your view of it. No, my friends, that's not my opinion; that's what God said; that's not nearly it, that is *it,* and everybody knows that's exactly what God said.

Friends, it isn't a question of understanding. It is just a question of whether or not you and I believe what God said, and are willing to take Him at His word, do what He requires, and then trust Him for every promise. Now that's the story. He said to them: "Repent and be baptized every one of you in the name of Jesus Christ for the remission of sins, and ye shall receive the gift of the Holy Spirit." It's not popular to proclaim Peter's answer to that guilty crowd on Pentecost. It's not popular to stop and tell our friends today just what to do "for the remission of sins." Some would much rather hear a psychological discussion. If I were to announce to you that I'm going to preach on "The Physiological Analysis of the Psychological Anthropos," many would say, I want to hear that; I imagine that will be deep. Yes, so deep you'd never know one thing on God's earth about it. But when I come and announce the simple story of redeeming love, and tell it just as the Bible tells it, men say: "Well, I'm disappointed in that, I just can't see it that way." Friends, yes, you can see it that way. Don't insult your intelligence; don't deceive yourselves by saying: "I can't understand that." Yes, you can. What does it say? God says to every believer: "Repent, and be baptized for the remission of sins." The man who can't understand that reflects upon his own intelligence.

Peter said further: "For the promise is unto you, and to your children, and to all that are afar off, even as many as the Lord our God shall call." Note again: "And with many other words did he testify and exhort, saying, Save yourselves from this untoward generation." How save yourselves? Surely, not in procuring the salvation, nor the means of it, but by laying hold of that which he had presented for their consideration.

I once stood on the American side of Niagara Falls, and a gentleman told of some boys once coming down the river beyond the danger point. Fortunately, their boat ran against a boulder and there they were suspended. From the Canadian shore, there was thrown out the life line, with the command: "Boys, save yourselves." They laid hold of it and were brought to the shore and saved. God provides, but man must appropriate. It's Jehovah-jireh all the way along the line. God provides water, by which our physical thirst is slaked. He provides us with a drinking apparatus, and all round about us there is water. But, suppose, I just refuse to drink. Don't you know that I'll die of thirst? Friends, I have sense enough to know this, if I get the benefit of that water, so abundantly provided by Jehovah, I must appropriate it, drink of it, apply it, and work with God to bring about the physical blessings. The atmosphere is all round about us. It is about fifty miles in every direction from the surface of the earth. Well, here I am with a breathing apparatus, nostrils, a pair of lungs, the ability to inhale and exhale. Well, does God want me to have air? Certainly. Do I have to have it to live? Yes, sir. Well, when do I get it? There it is, without money and without price, and whenever I accept it, the physical blessing is mine. Paul said: "We are labourers together with God." Watch the point: God provides the means of human redemption. By God's grace men are saved, but while it's a matter of grace on the part of God, it's a matter of faith and trust on the part of man. Do I have sufficient faith in God to lay hold of that means provided? If so, I can come to shore, stand justified, purified, washed and cleansed in that fountain filled with the precious blood of His spotless Son.

Now, you ask what was the further effect of Peter's sermon? They, on that Pentecost day, that received God's word "were baptized, and the same day there were added," put together, "about three thousand souls." But who did that? "The Lord added to the church day by day."

Friends, that's the system. I am hoping tonight, as we come to sing the invitation hymn, that there is not only one, but two, three, and many, in this audience who will gladly duplicate the experience of these Pentecostians and rush to the outstretched arms of Him who said: "Come unto me all ye that labor and are heavy laden, and I'll give you rest." Friends, do you believe the story tonight? If so, why linger any longer? Render that obedience demanded by God. But you say, "I just don't see any reason for being baptized." Friends, the very fact that God said it, that God commanded it, is the highest reason possible for man. Out of deference to His authority, out of regard for His word, do it and trust Him for every promise.

THE CHURCH

It is exceeding fine, friends, to be greeted by an audience of this kind again tonight. You have been quite faithful in coming to our engagements, and I am persuaded to think that you are enjoying all that comes to pass here.

How any soul cannot be stirred by the singing of such songs as these just sung is almost beyond my conception.

I am talking to you, tonight, about the Church of the New Testament.

I am reading from Eph. 3. Paul said: "Unto me, who am less than the least of all saints, is this grace given, that I should preach among the Gentiles, the unsearchable riches of Christ; And to make all men see what is the fellowship of the mystery, which from the beginning of the world hath been hid in God, who created all things by Jesus Christ: To the intent that now unto the principalities and powers in heavenly places might be known by the church the manifold wisdom of God, according to the eternal purpose which he purposed in Christ Jesus our Lord: In whom we have boldness and access with confidence by the faith of him. Where I desire that ye faint not at my tribulations for you, which is your glory. For this cause I bow my knees unto the Father of our Lord Jesus Christ, of whom the whole family in heaven and earth is named, that he would grant you, according to the riches of his glory, to be strengthened with might by his Spirit in the inner man; that Christ may dwell in your hearts by faith; that ye, being rooted and grounded in love, may be able to comprehend with all saints what is the breadth, and length, and depth, and height; and to know the love of Christ, which passeth knowledge, that ye might be filled with all the fulness of God. Now unto him that is able to do exceeding abundantly above all that we ask or think, according to the power that worketh in us, unto him be glory in the church by Christ Jesus throughout all ages, world without end. Amen."

Now, in the sixteenth chapter of Matthew, I want you to hear again: "When Jesus came into the coasts of Caesarea Philippi, he asked his disciples, saying, Whom do men say that I the Son of man am? And they said, Some say that thou art John the Baptist, some, Elias; and others, Jeremias, or one of the prophets. He saith unto them, But whom say ye that I am?" Never mind about the other fellow, what do you think about it? "And Simon Peter answered and said, Thou art the Christ, the Son of the living God. And Jesus answered and said unto him, Blessed art thou, Simon Bar-jona; for flesh and blood hath not revealed it unto thee, but my Father which is in heaven. And I say also unto thee, That thou art Peter, and upon this rock I will build my church; and the gates of hell shall not prevail against it. And I will give unto thee the keys of the kingdom of heaven; and whatsoever thou shalt bind on earth shall be bound in heaven; and whatsoever thou shalt loose on earth shall be loosed in heaven. Then charged he his disciples that they should tell no man that he was Jesus the Christ." The time had not yet come. In those passages, together with a host of others, specific reference is made to the church about which I am proposing to talk.

My friends, I have just called your attention again to the statement of the Christ, when Peter said, "Thou art the Christ, the Son of the living God," the response made by Jesus was a benediction pronounced upon Peter for making that confession. I regret to say that the effort of the unbelieving world is to rob Christian people of their faith in that one fundamental statement, that Jesus Christ is the Son of God.

All of these books and lectures exalting Jesus, the man; Jesus, the Great Teacher; Jesus, the Matchless Man of Galilee; Jesus, the Great Philosopher, are laden with downright infidelity. You may not see that at first mention, but the effort is to exalt Christ as a man towering above his fellows in his ability to teach, to instruct, and in his philosophy of life. But they never mention the fact that he is

God's Son. Let me say to you, brethren and friends tonight, I'm not especially interested in Jesus as a man, nor as a teacher, nor as a philosopher, but I am tremendously interested in Jesus Christ as the Son of God, and the Saviour of mankind. There's where the emphasis needs to go. "Thou art the Christ the Son of the living God." "Blessed art thou, Simon." Where did you get it? Flesh and blood didn't reveal it, but my Father did. Now Peter, I'm telling you, "Upon this rock," that is, upon this great fundamental truth which shows my relation to the Heavenly Father: "I will build my church; and the gates of hell shall not prevail against it." I think there is the strongest determination expressed. "I will build my church." I've had it in mind; it's according to God's pre-arranged plan, and from the foundation of the world, it was the intent of Jehovah, that unto principalities and powers in heavenly places, might be known by the church, the manifold wisdom of God, and for that reason, I expect to build it. All the powers of the Hadean world shall not prevail against my so doing. Now let's analyze just what he said in that. Christ said: "I will build my church." Who is the builder? Jesus said: "*I* will build." Now, don't you see this, that any church built by anybody other than Jesus Christ is not the one of the Bible? I, Jesus Christ, "will build my church." Well, suppose N. B. Hardeman were to start out and organize or build a church, could it possibly be the one mentioned by Christ? Don't you know that's not the thing that Christ was talking about? Well, note again.

This church mentioned by Him was builded in the year 33, according to our calendar. Well, again, in Zechariah 1: 16, we love the prophet's declaration: "I am returned to Jerusalem with mercies: my house shall be built in it." In what? In Jerusalem shall my house be builded. Now mark three things: Who built the church? What's the answer? Jesus Christ. When did he build it? In the year 33. Where did he build it? In the city of Jerusalem. Now that's just as simple as it can be.

Without going into details I'm referring you to the origin of all the denominations on this earth. You'll find an account of them, not in the Bible of course, but in the "Federal Statistics of Religious Census," a book your Congressman will send you on request. Now then, after you've investigated, you'll find this: each one of them was built by some other *man* than Jesus Christ, at some other *time* than the year 33, and at some other *place* than Jerusalem. Well, what is the conclusion? They were, therefore, begun by the wrong *person,* at the wrong *time,* in the wrong *place.* Therefore, they cannot be the thing which Jesus Christ had in mind when he said: "Upon this rock, I will build my church." I think that's very important, and that much depends upon it. Such things ought to challenge our most serious concern, research, and investigation.

Now, note another thing. Jesus Christ said in Matthew 16: 18 in the year 32: "Upon this rock," a great fundamental fact, "I will build my church." Well, that means that he had not done it previously. "Will build," certainly cannot point backward. It refers to something not yet done. Now, I just want to say, that unless people in general will get the basic idea, and the fundamental conception of affairs, we can't make much progress in our efforts to come together. All of you, who perchance, are attached to some organization which teaches that the church was organized and set up previous to the time mentioned in this connection by Christ, are bound to be wrong about that. Christ said, I *will* build it. Now may I say to you this, that practically all the leading denominations represented in the city of Nashville, are based upon the erroneous idea that the church started back in the days of Abraham, or in the days of John the Baptist, or during the personal ministry of Jesus Christ our Lord. There lives not a man on earth, who can prove the correctness of such contentions. Now we've got to plant our Jacob's staff at the right corner and get our tripod correctly set, or else, we never can run the line aright and come out with no dissension and no controversy. Let's everybody, therefore, march back to Jerusalem, to the year 33, and recognize Jesus Christ as the builder of that great institution. The church was organized on that day of Pentecost. It was filled with the Holy

Spirit and started out upon its great mission as God's institution through which His wisdom was to be revealed unto mortal man.

Now, let me say to you next, that the establishing of the church of God was the main purpose of Jesus Christ our Lord. It was contemplated by the Father. Already have I read that from Ephesians 3. Hear it again, "Unto me, who am less than the least of all saints, is this grace given, that I should preach among the Gentiles the unsearchable riches of Christ." Now watch it—"And to make all men see what is the fellowship of the mystery, which from the beginning of the world hath been hid in God, who created all things by Jesus Christ; to the intent that now unto the principalities and powers in heavenly places might be known by the church, the manifold wisdom of God, *according to the eternal purpose* which he purposed in Christ Jesus our Lord." Now what do you have? The very medium through which, from the foundation of the world, and according to God's eternal purpose, His revelation was to be made known to mortal man. Brethren, friends, based upon that, let me say; for any man to come along and say, that the church was a "spiritual contingent, an incident, accident, or a mere chance," is but little short of blasphemy in the sight of God Almighty. And yet, such statements are made and they are disturbing the peace of God's Israel tonight.

Well, look again. Paul said, 1 Timothy 3: 15: Timothy, I hope to come unto you shortly, but if I do not get to come, then I'm writing. Well, what for? "That thou mayest know how thou oughtest to behave thyself in the house of God," now mark, "which is the church of the living God, the pillar and ground of the truth." You ask tonight, friends, upon what did God intend the truth to rest, upon what is it founded, and what is its support? God says the church is not only the pillar, but it is the very foundation, the ground of the truth. Now then, for me to minimize the church and talk about it as a contingent, or as a mere chance, a mere accident, I repeat, is quite contrary to the very sentiment that prevails everywhere in the Book of God. The church is the ground and the support of the truth, but when I tell you brethren, now, that the church is made up of men and women who have been born again, born of water and of the Spirit, it imposes on you that responsibility, and I tell you but that which you ought to recognize and feel very keenly. I am making the appeal, are you upholding the truth, do you stand four-square like a stone wall in defense of God's word? To you elders and deacons and members, are you standing in support of God's truth? All over this land, are brethren upholding the hands of preachers who are "fighting the good fight of faith"? What about it brethren? Are you behind them 100 per cent? Are you supporting the truth? If you constitute the church, there's your responsibility. You ought to be like Aaron and Hur who held up Moses' hands all through the battle and until the victory was won. I sometimes fear that brethren, through lack of courage, or lack of information regarding matters that disturb us are not as firm in support of those contending for that faith once for all delivered, as they should be.

Since this meeting has been on, several members of the church have been to see me. They are saying: "I did not understand all this quite so clearly, but now, since I have a conception of it, I'm into it 100 per cent; I'm standing as I could not have otherwise done." Therefore, the obligation rests upon preachers to teach the church. Let's tell them what it's all about. They should know about all kinds of opposition, every phase of error, and how to expose the same and defend the truth. Hence, the church of the Lord is God's great organization through which His wisdom is revealed unto mankind.

I am calling your attention now to just what the church of the New Testament is. That's not intended to reflect upon anybody's intelligence. But here we are, in the midst of the twentieth century, and I am persuaded to think that it is perfectly in order to talk about what the church is. Friends, what is that thing which you read about in the New Testament, called the church? Well, of course, it's not a material building, and yet that idea has always been prevalent. We see a meeting house towering heavenward, and we talk about the church upon the corner of the street. That's not uncommon. Back in the days of Paul and of Stephen such an impression was corrected. Stephen said in Acts 7: 48: "The most High dwelleth not in temples made with hands." Paul said on Mars Hill: "The God that made the heaven and the earth and all things therein, seeing he is Lord of all, that God does not dwell in tabernacles made by the hands of men." So the church is not a material building wrought out of stone, marble, lime, and mortar. That's not it.

Well, again. The church is not that old Jewish institution perpetuated on down the line. How do you know it isn't? I know from the third chapter of John that Jesus said to Nicodemus, who was a ruler of the Jews and a member of the Jewish organization, "except a man be born again, he cannot see the kingdom of God." And then to impress the matter, he said, I tell you, Nicodemus: "Except a man be born of water and of the Spirit, he cannot enter into the kingdom of God." Now then, the fact that you are a member of the old Jewish church does not give you a passport into the kingdom of God. But although a member of that, if you ever see the light of this, you must "be born again, of water and of the Spirit." What does that argue? The church is not a continuation of that organization gone before, but it's a new institution. Absolutely and positively it is different.

Well, again, my friends, the church of the New Testament is not a denomination. That's the hardest matter to put across that I've ever yet tried. Why? In this country of ours, we've been bred and born and reared in the denominational idea until it has become such a mass of confusion that it's next to impossible for any man to make clear the distinction between the church of the Bible and a human organization, founded by some uninspired man, at some other time than the year 33, at some other place than the city of Jerusalem. Just ask yourself where, in the Bible, did I ever read about a denomination existing by the authority of Jesus Christ our Lord? Now don't you know that regardless of how many times you've read the Bible, you cannot think of a single passage where anything that even intimates a thought of that kind can be found. Such an idea, friends, is a total stranger to God's Book. If you think the church that Jesus said: "I will build," is a denomination, then I have this question to ask, which one was it? There are more than 200 in our fair land. Now which one was Christ talking about when he said: "Upon this rock, I will build my church." Friends, the idea of a denomination does not attach to a statement of that kind. When Christ said, "Husbands, love your wives, as Christ also loved the church and gave himself for it," I raise the point, for what denomination did Christ give his life's blood? The answer is, absolutely none, positively none. Brethren, friends, can I become a member of the church of the New Testament? I think you are bound to say, yes. Well, all right, Do I have to become a member of a denomination in order to become a member of the church of the Bible? Everybody answers, No. Then you have exactly where I want to stand, namely, a member of the church of the Bible and at the same time, not a member of any denomination on earth. And if you were to meet me or privately ask me, Hardeman, of what denomination are you a member? I'd be certain to say, None. Well, are you a member of the church? Yes. Well, what branch? I'm not a member of any branch, I am a branch myself, and a member of the true vine. That's what the Bible teaches right along that line. Now, it would be a glorious day if all of us could forget such a thing as denominationalism, and march back to Jerusalem, to the year 33 and claim membership in the institution there and then organized by Jesus Christ. There is the only possible ground of all coming together without the sacrifice of a single principle.

I now want to state further that the church of the Bible is the only place wherein all of God's children are. It is difficult for many to appreciate this statement. They just can't conceive of the idea that all of the saved people of this earth are members of the church. The common idea is, that a man first becomes saved, and then later on and by a different process, he becomes a member of the church.

Now, that's all wrong. That idea is not in the Bible. Let me read to you just one verse, Ephesians 5: 23: "For the husband is the head of the wife, even as Christ is the head of the church, and he is the saviour of the body." Well, what is the body? It's the church of the Lord. Now then, of whom is Christ the Saviour, and of what? Of the body, but the body is the church, therefore, Christ saves those in the church. Now do you know what folks say when I preach that way? "Oh, the church doesn't save anybody." Well, who said it did? I never. Now, let's get two or three things. First, who is the saviour of mankind? The answer: Jesus Christ our Lord. When does Christ save? He said: "He that believeth and is baptized shall be saved." Where does he save them? In the church, which is his body. Who, when, where? Christ, at the end of obedience, in the church, the pillar and the very support of the truth. But someone is ready to say: "I think a man can be saved outside of the church just as well as within it." I have heard that so many times. I know that the man who thus says, doesn't understand what the church is. Friends, think about it. If a man can be saved outside of the church, he can be saved without the blood of Jesus Christ. Acts, chapter 20 and verse 28 explains why. Paul said: "Take heed therefore unto yourselves, and to all the flock, over the which the Holy Spirit hath made you overseer to feed the church of the Lord which he hath purchased with his own blood." And again, Ephesians 5: 25: "Husbands, love your wives, even as Christ also loved the church, and gave himself for it." Now, we are saved by the blood of Christ. "What can take away my sins?" Answer: "Nothing but the blood of Jesus." But friends, what became of the blood of Christ? It went into the purchase of the church. How much of it? The last drop. What became, therefore, of the blood of the Lord? It went for the purchase of the church. Therefore, if I ever get the benefit of the blood of Christ, I must get it in that institution into which it went, and with which it was bought.

Now, illustrative of that, let me say, that if I had five dollars, and with that five dollars, I purchased this coat, giving every penny of the five dollars for the coat, I want to ask you, how can I get any benefit out of that five dollars? You may say you got it out of your shoes. No, sir, it didn't go for the purchase of shoes. All the five dollars went into the coat. Therefore, if I ever get the benefit of that five dollars, I surely must get it, in some way, out of the coat into which I put it. So it is, beyond a shadow of a doubt, Christ's blood went for the purchase of the church. If, therefore, I become a beneficiary of the blood of Christ, I must contact that institution bought by it, and into which the blood of our Lord went.

Furthermore, the church is called the family of God; hence, it is God's family upon this earth. It is God's household. Now, if a man can be saved outside of the church as well as within it, then, he can be saved outside of the family of God Almighty, but that's going to get one into wonderful trouble, because of this fact. There are just two families on this earth, one of them is the family of God, the other is the family of the devil. Now, I maintain, friends, all of God's people are in His family. I insist that God does not have children over in the devil's family. What do you think about that? Is it complimentary to a man to say that he has children not members of his family? God's children are in God's family. Now if you want to ask just how they get in, I'm going to suggest this. In the Bible there are three statements right along that line, each of which is illustrative of our membership in the family of God. Sometimes, it is pictured as if we were married unto the Lord Jesus Christ, and, therefore, enter the family by marriage. Married unto our Lord; Christ the bridegroom; the church the bride. In that likeness, there is an acquaintance, then, a cultivation of such as results in faith and finally deepens into love, and trust, and confidence. Then there is a resolution to turn away from all else and let that ceremony be said which climaxes a change of relationship. The bride now has the right to the husband's name and to share his estate. The marriage has been completed. Just so, under that likeness and that figure, when a man hears of Jesus Christ, and cultivates an acquaintance, it will result in faith, confidence, trust, and love. He then decides to turn from the power of Satan and flee to Jesus Christ. He next comes to one properly authorized, to say the ceremony which, in the name of the Father, Son and Holy Spirit, marries him into God's family.

After the marriage, can you imagine a wife's wanting to wear some other man's name? What would you men as husbands think about that? Would it be satisfactory? "A hint to the wise is sufficient." You ought to make the application. Lord, I love you with all my heart, I'll put my hand in your wounded palm, I'll pledge fidelity as long as I live upon the earth, I'm married to you; I'm leaning upon you and trusting you; but, Lord, won't you let me wear your cousin's name, or that of some other man? Friends, what do you think about that anyhow? Women, you doubtless say, "Oh, Hardeman, that doesn't make any difference." I'll tell you how to put it to a test. You try it on hubby tonight. Tell him you are going to wear your neighbor's name. You are Mrs. Higginbottom, for instance. You tell him that you are going to be Mrs. Joe Jones, and see what he has to say about it. "There'll be a hot time in the ole town tonight!" No man, with self-respect would agree for his wife, to whom he is married, to wear the other fellow's name. I don't blame him. Now, let me tell you women; if you love your husbands as you should, you don't want to wear anybody else's name.

Now then, the man who loves Jesus Christ as he ought to love him does not want to and will not wear any other name under heaven than that by which we must be saved.

There is another figure suggesting our entrance into God's family. The Bible says that we are born again into the kingdom or family of God. Well, how born? As in all cases, there are two elements, and in this case it is, "of water and of the Spirit." What does born imply? It is a coming up and out of, into a new relationship. A child in its mother's womb is shut out from the material world and the light of God's day, but when it is born, it emerges into a different sphere and into a different relationship. So then, when a sinner is born of water and of the Spirit, he enters into a new realm which is the kingdom of God, the church of the Lord, God's family, God's house.

Now, we not only become members of God's family under the likeness of marriage, and under the similitude of a birth, but the Bible says: "By one Spirit are we all baptized into one body." This is God's family, the church of the Lord. Friends, that's it, and there's no doubt about it whatsoever; that's what God's Book teaches.

Well, note some other things right along this same line, and in connection with matters of this sort. Had you ever stopped to think, friends, of the different names by which this heaven-born, and blood-bought institution is called? Let me just call to mind as I may, a few of them. First, it's called the church of God. It's called the church of the Lord. It's called "My Church." It's called the household of faith, the body of Christ, the pillar and the ground of truth, God's building, God's temple, and so on. More than a dozen different names are mentioned in the Bible, either of which would meet the demands of Holy writ. Now then, here's what I can't understand. Why people will know all of those dozen or more names in the Bible, reject everyone of them, and get over in another list and pick out a name that God Almighty never one time mentioned, and write that over the door of their meeting house. They will then glory in a name nowhere mentioned in the Bible. Why do men do that?

When Jesus comes to reward his servants, will he find us watching and faithful to his teaching, or will we be off wearing certain church names that are total strangers to anything that Jesus Christ ever knew?

Now, you ask what are the individual members to be called? That depends upon certain things, and if I may extend the time just a moment, I'd like to get that before you. In the Bible, members of the church of the Lord are sometimes called disciples, sometimes saints, again brethren, and again Christians. Now analyze just a minute. What does the word disciple mean? A learner, a student, a pupil, a follower. If brethren are students and learners and followers of God's Book, it is in order to call them disciples.

Now, if you want to emphasize their saintly character, and their purity, the word "saint" is more fitting to express a relation of that kind.

If you want to talk about our relationship one with another, then what? "We be brethren." What does that word mean? Members of the same family.

But, if you want to emphasize our relation to Christ, the word disciple doesn't express it, the word saint does not fit, the word brethren carries not the thought. When emphasizing the fact that I am related to Christ, then the word "Christian" is the most suggestive of any term known to mortal man.

Friends, these are the things that I want to mention to you tonight regarding the church of the Bible. Are you a member of it? Do you stand upon the merits of the blood of Christ that purchased the church? Are you in relationship with God's family? If so, I bid you faithful endurance until the end. But if not, you stand absolutely without God and without hope in the world. You have, tonight, the opportunity of rendering obedience unto Jesus Christ our Lord and to stand upon his promises. Won't you do it while, once again, the invitation is tendered?

THE VINE AND THE BRANCHES

On this Saturday night, I think one could hardly expect an audience superior either in number or character to that which has assembled. You have been so faithful to come that I am under everlasting obligation to you.

I am reading to you a very familiar passage from John 15. "I am the true vine, and my Father is the husbandman. Every branch in me that beareth not fruit he taketh away: and every branch that beareth fruit, he purgeth it, that it may bring forth more fruit. Now you are clean through the word which I have spoken unto you. Abide in me, and I in you. As the branch cannot bear fruit of itself, except it abide in the vine; no more can you, except you abide in me. I am the vine, you are the branches: He that abideth in me, and I in him, the same bringeth forth much fruit: for without me you can do nothing. If a man abide not in me, he is cast forth as a branch, and is withered; and men gather them, and cast them into the fire, and they are burned. If you abide in me, and my words abide in you, you shall ask what you will, and it shall be done unto you. Herein is my Father glorified, that you bear much fruit; so shall you be my disciples."

That is what is called, and possibly correctly, the parable of the vine and the branches, stated in a little bit stronger terms than some of the parables. Christ does not say that he is *like* the vine, using what we call a simile; but he uses the metaphor, and says "I am the true vine, and my Father is the husbandman." A parable when read seems to be as simple a thing as could be constructed, but if you undertake to create one, you will find it exceeding difficult. Teaching by parables was a favorite method of our Saviour, and for that reason, we should try to learn what a parable is and also its purpose. May I say then that a parable is the presentation of some simple matter with which the people were acquainted, and alongside of that is the spiritual application of the same. In a parable, all matters stated are realities. All the personages presented are real persons, and the things stated either did or could come to pass. I am stating that in a parable there are no fictitious things, but all are realities. To illustrate: The kingdom of heaven is like unto a man who called unto him his servants, delivered unto them his goods, and finally took his journey into a far country. Now that could have happened. It's a reality, and not simply a mere fanciful presentation. The parable therefore differs from a fable in that one regard. A fable is ascribing, either to animals or inanimate things, the doings of men and the characteristics of humanity. No fable ever happened, but it is used purely to illustrate a matter. Therein is the chief difference between a parable and a fable.

Now you ask, as I do when studying, why speak in parables? The disciples asked the Lord that question once. I want to suggest to you a few reasons for speaking in parables. First, for those who love the truth, it tends to clarify the same, and to make plainer the teaching. To those who do not love the truth, it tends to blind their minds, to obscure the matter under consideration. Third, a parable tends to embalm the truth. You know a thing told in the form of a story will be remembered much longer and more easily than any abstract fact presented. And then in the fourth place, a parable is given to gain the assent of the party before the real truth and application of it are made known. Will you keep these points in mind?—You will read them in the book later, and have time to meditate further upon them.

So, Jesus Christ is presenting something known to his audience—with which they were perfectly familiar—and from that he passes to a wonderfully sublime application of the truth. I think it safe to say that the beautiful white grape represents 60 per cent of all things cultivated in Palestine. Jesus had been talking, in part of his address preceding this, about the fruit of the vine, and maybe that suggested to him this simple lesson that we are studying tonight.

Now, that your eye may assist your ear, I just picked up this (speaker holds up small vine with branches before the audience) as a concrete illustration, I trust, of what the Saviour had in mind. Hear it again: "I am the true vine, my Father is the husbandman." I think it doesn't require any strain on intelligence to see that this (speaker points to the one vine) represents the Christ. "I am the true vine." All right, that locates him. Now he says "my Father is the husbandman." Well, what is a husbandman? He is the character who nourishes and prunes and looks after the growing of the vine and the bearing of the fruit. So, Christ is in this lesson; and also God is in it. I wonder if you would think I was stretching the matter if I should say that the Holy Spirit is also in it—by necessary inference? It isn't mentioned directly, but beyond the shadow of doubt, the implication is there. Well, why? In every trunk where there are branches and where there is fruit, there is that thing which flows and circulates underneath the bark, which ordinarily we call the sap. With a circulatory system complete, it rises from the trunk and flows into every branch and causes the bud to appear, then the blossom and, finally, the fruit. Farmers understand that. We talk, in the Fall of the year, of the sap's going down—whether that is scientifically correct or not, I am not stopping to argue. But we speak of it that way. When all nature is brown and sere and the leaves are falling and all is passing into the winterland, the sap goes down. Well, in the Spring, we say the sap rises. And watch what happens. There is that life current beneath the bark and it brings life, growth and fruit.

Now the figure would not be complete unless you would understand that not only is Jesus Christ the true vine, and God Almighty the husbandman, but the Holy Spirit is the life-giving current that brings vitality and force to all the branches, and produces the fruit. Well, the fruit never grows on the vine itself, but it is found only on the branches. Did you ever imagine that the sap ignores the true vine and goes out to the branch and produces fruit independent of the vine? Now, nobody who is allowed to run loose, would dare think of a thing of that kind. But watch how the sap does its work: it comes up through the main vine, out through the different branches, and through the medium, of the trunk and of the branches, it produces the fruit. Hence, you can see the indirect working of the sap, or the operation of it, through these definite means, to accomplish the purpose. Just so, the Holy Spirit does not operate separate and apart from Christ and the medium ordained, but always coming through our Lord, it operates upon the branches, and thereby produces the fruit as a result.

So, then, Christ says "I am the true vine, my Father is the husbandman." And may I add that the Holy Spirit is the life—the fruit-producing element. There never was any fruit but that it was affected by the operation of the sap—that is literally true. There never is any fruit, spiritually speaking, without the operation of God's Spirit. And I might just as well say here, as later, there never has been any question as to whether or not the Holy Spirit operates in the conviction and conversion of a sinner. No one doubts that. Yet, you have heard all kinds of misrepresentation and confusing ideas regarding the same. Everybody, so far as I know, believes that in the conversion of mankind, God's Spirit operates upon the heart of that one to be converted.

But the point of controversy has been: By what method does the Spirit operate? I submit to you that there are but two possible ways by which it can be done. I want to illustrate these two ways. Let this (places white tablet on pulpit stand) represent the sinner's heart. Let my hand repsent the Holy Spirit. Now, I'll operate upon the heart of the sinner (brings hand in contact with tablet). That did it—but how? Directly, straightforward, immediately, separate and apart from everything else, with nothing intervening. Now that is one theory presented in the religious world. Here is the other teaching: I lay that Bible on this white booklet—between my hand and the thing to be operated on. Again, I operate on the tablet. But how? This time through the book. Now these are the two views regarding this matter.

If you believe that the sap in the natural realm ignores all means and goes direct to the fruit out on the branch and begins to do its work, then you are prepared to accept the unreasonable, the unscriptural, and the wholly foreign idea of a direct and immediate operation of the Holy Spirit. If, on the other hand, you get the idea that the sap, in the natural world, comes through the trunk and branches, then you are prepared to accept the truth that the Holy Spirit operates upon the heart of the sinner through a medium, and that medium is the book of God!

Now with that setting, let us read further. "Every branch in me." I want you to get that—I am stopping on purpose, not to take a drink or to cough but for you to think. "Every branch *in me*." I am underscoring i-n, in, and m-e, me. In me! Not just stuck on superficially; not a water spout; but really, actually, genuinely, in me! That bothers lots of preachers. They would give thirty cents, with the proverbial hole in it, if the two little words "in me" were not in the Bible. It spoils a human theory. Every branch *in me* that does not bear fruit, the husbandman will take it away. But, someone says, you can't take one away if he is ever in him. That's preacher talk, not Bible teaching. I want you to get that, and I am impressing it for that reason. If one does not bear fruit, God, the husbandman, takes it away! But every branch that beareth fruit, he will purge it that it may bring forth more fruit. Friends, that is exactly as it is and as it ought to be.

If you start out to help someone, and he responds to the opportunity, and enters heartily into the affair, and does his part—what about it? Why, you are ready to help him more, to lend him further assistance. But suppose you try to help someone and he falls absolutely down on it, and proves himself not worthwhile, then what? If you have good judgment, you'll take that help from him and give it to somebody who is worthy. That is exactly the principle involved. Unto him that hath, I'll give more! He shall have more abundantly. But to him that hath not, I'll take away even that which he hath. Every branch that beareth not fruit he taketh it away, and every branch that beareth fruit, he'll help it, purge it, that it may bear more fruit.

Well, note again: "Now you are clean." How? "Through the word which I have spoken unto you. Abide in me, and I in you." Now watch: "As the branch cannot bear fruit of itself except it abide in the vine," I just wonder if we appreciate that statement? On this (pointing again to the vine and branches used for illustrative purposes) are many branches. I'll pick the best-looking branch on it. This one doesn't have any appearance other than a healthy, living, fruit-bearing branch. Now let's sever it. Here we have it. "Every branch that does not bear fruit, he takes it away." "And as that branch cannot bear fruit of itself except it abide in the vine—no more can ye, except ye abide in me." Can it or not? Why, take the best branch on any vine or from any tree and separate it from the main trunk, and tell me how much fruit it will ever bear. That's the end of it. There is nothing hopeful or possible for it. That branch, isolated or separated from the true vine, never can produce any more fruit. Friends, you know that is true. The biggest, finest, most attractive branch on God's earth, separated from the true vine, is not as good as the most insignificant one imaginable that is still attached to the trunk. There is much more hope for the puny, sickly-looking branch attached to the true vine than there is for any, isolated and cut loose.

Some old fellow once said that he had always noticed that when cholera broke out among his hogs and one of them lingered on and on it was more likely to get well than one that took it and died right away. I think he was correct about it. So, you can take the humblest branch in the vine. It may look unattractive in comparison with this one that stands aloof. But there's more hope of that one's producing fruit than there is of the one isolated. Now get the application: as the branch cannot bear fruit of itself, except it abide in the vine, no more can you except you abide in me. Now you can take the best man that ever walked the streets of Nashville, an upright gentleman splendid in personality, clean in habit, noble in moral affairs, but if that man does not have vital connection with the Son of God, he *cannot* bear fruit that will redound to his credit on the other shore.

I have lots of fine, moral friends, who should get that lesson. They are splendid citizens, upright in all respects. They are fine fathers, good husbands, public-spirited, charitable, philanthropic in nature, and yet they are not members of the true vine. When that kind of man dies, the preacher gets up over him and makes a big ado. He eulogizes the spirit of this great man, who has done so much for Nashville; who gave so much to charity and from whom no one was ever turned away, either hungry or naked. That man, says some preacher, is basking in the sunlight of God's eternal smiles. Friends, that's not so! No man on earth has ever been saved on his intrinsic worth or on his own merit. The gospel is God's power to salvation—not my good deeds. I am going to be saved or lost according as I retain a positive connection with Jesus Christ, the true vine. I wish I could impress that on so many people whom I know, and in whom I am interested. Yet they are deceived and deluded. "Here I am—I don't do this, and I don't do that, and I do not do the other; therefore, I must be all right." Friends, that's the wrong check-up. Well, "I speak the truth and pay my debts and I am public-spirited —what's the matter with me?" Simply this: Salvation is in Christ; redemption is in Jesus Christ; and the Holy Spirit comes to the man who is *in* him. Be you ever so good, ever so attractive and powerful; so long as you stay aloof from Christ, he says, just as that branch cannot bear fruit of itself except it abide in the vine, no more can you except you abide in me.

It just seems to me that this is so clear, I could not help but see the point. But note again: I am down to verse 6. "If a man abide not in me he is cast forth as a branch and is withered and men gather them and cast them into the fire and they are burned." Now that raises the point as to what the branches are. There is no doubt on earth as to what the true vine is—Christ said "I am the true vine." God is the husbandman; the Holy Spirit is the life; now what are the branches? And do you know that the best argument ever made for the existence of denominations is the point which preachers try to make to the people, that they, the denominations, are the branches contemplated by the Christ? Now he is the big church and all denominations are branches. Think of that a minute. That cannot be so for several reasons: First, at the time when Christ said "I am the vine and ye are the branches," there was not a denomination on the face of God's earth. Hence, he could not address a thing that was not. Second, denominationalism, as we have it in our land tonight, did not come into existence until fifteen hundred years after Jesus spoke the parable of the vine and branches. Third, Christ said "abide in me"—well, who is "me"?—"I am the true vine." Now let me ask you: Where are you abiding? Someone says: "Hardeman, I'm a member of a certain branch." Well, God said, my dear sir, get out of the branch! Don't hang onto a limb, but stick to the true vine. I just want to ask you: Are you connected simply with the branch, as some church over here, which you say is a branch church? Where are you? "I'm out here in a branch." Christ said, "abide in me." We ought to be able to see that Jesus Christ speaking to men said this: "If a *man* abide not in me *he* is cast forth as a branch." What are the branches? Men! That's the idea. To whom is he talking? The apostles. And it is *ye* abide in me, individually.

Friends, the world can't appreciate the truth. Error has been prevalent so long and gained such a footing, that even up to 1938 this old world is unprepared to accept with open mind the truth of God Almighty.

If I meet with men, as frequently I do, and they ask me, "Hardeman, are you a member of the church?" I answer "Yes." "Well, of what branch of the church are you a member?" My answer is, "I am not a member of any branch on earth," and they look as if they thought I was not all at home. Why? I talk as the Bible talks and they are not used to that.

I read a story once, that I have told time and again. A gentleman stepped off the steamer in our Southern city, New Orleans, and some boys were at the wharf ready to carry his baggage that they might make a dime or a quarter. All the embarrassment from them had gone, and as they walked along with him carrying his luggage, they raised a conversation with him. For some reason or other one of them suspected that he was a preacher, and asked him, "Aren't you a preacher?" "Yes, sir." "Well of what church are you a member?" "Oh, Son, I'm a member of the church of the Bible." "Yes, I know, but of what branch of the church are you a member?" He said: "I'm not a member of any branch; I'm a branch myself." That boy turned to his little companion and said, "I'll bet you five dollars he's a Campbellite." Now, why say that? Just because the man talks as the Bible talks. He didn't use the language of Ashdod, but he spake as the oracles of God speak. So Christ said, "I am the vine and ye are the branches; if a man abide not in me, he is cast forth as a branch, and is withered; and men gather them, and cast them into the fire." Now sometime we pass over words without noting their bearing. I have had men, when I quote that to ask, "Well, Hardeman, why is it then that you fellows will call for backsliders, if they are to be cast in the fire and burned? Why that invitation to come back to be restored?" They think we are inconsistent. Now, let me give you a thought on that. The Saviour said: "If a man abide not in me, he is cast forth as a branch, and is *withered.*" What does that word "withered" mean? Now you know this, you can take some branches off from the main trunk and go and set them out again or cover them over, and they will keep on growing, although severed. I have a suspicion that Bermuda grass is of that type. But let me tell you one thing: if even Bermuda is ever withered, if its life is gone and it is completely dried up, you can do for it what you will; it is forever gone. Now that's what Christ said. So long as a man, though he sin, does not reach that point beyond which restoration is impossible, there is a hope of that man's coming again, but let him cut loose from Jesus Christ our Lord, pass out and *wither;* I want to say to you friends, there is no power in heaven nor on earth by which that man can be saved. It's impossible to renew him. Why? He's reached that point beyond which, his conscience being seared as with a hot iron, the penetrating rays of God's gospel truth cannot reach nor affect him. That's what Christ said. "If a man abide not in me." Well, there's one that didn't. What about him, Lord? "He is cast forth as a branch." Look at him, what about him? "And is withered," all hope of life is gone, all signs of life are gone, every vestige absent—Lord, what about him? What will finally happen? "They are gathered." Who are gathered? "The branches." What branches? "Those once in me." Wasn't that branch one time "in me"? "Yes." Who took it away? "God did." Why? "It didn't bear fruit." What happened to it? "It withered." Then what? "Men gather it and throw it in the fire and it is burned." Friends, if that is not the thought, language has no meaning at all. It is mighty hard to get some preachers to notice an illustration of this kind.

Well, note some other things. I just wonder what kind of branches these are which are left in the true vine? Is one a pumpkin, another a watermelon, and still another a cucumber, etc? Now friends, do you know that there isn't a man living who believes that? Not one. You do not know of a single individual with little enough judgment to think that from the true vine, different kinds of fruit grow. That would be so ridiculously preposterous and so absolutely nonsensical as to make an intelligent man shudder at the possibility of anyone's imagining that a thing like that ever could happen. On the same vine, every branch bears exactly the same kind of fruit. Shall I look, for instance, upon a tree that bears apples and expect to find that, while it bears apples, they are of different kinds? Look upon it and note the great number and then ask: "What kind are they? Is that a Ben Davis, and that a Winesap, and that a Virginia Green, and is this an old Horse apple?" No, that won't work, and you know that just as well as I. Now we all see that alike, don't we? That whatever this is, that will be accordingly, and so on. Note again, every fruit bears the name of the main trunk. That's an apple tree, all right; what about the fruit? They are apples. That's a peach tree. Well, they are all peaches of the very same kind. Now, there isn't any difference on that. Well, how is it that all of us see that alike? Just because we are unbiased and we haven't had any theology to becloud or hinder our seeing it. Now apply it religiously.

"I am the true vine." Yes, and this branch is a Mormon; this other is an Episcopalian, and there another is a Lutheran, etc. Men can accept that. How can you, friends? Now, just think, how can you? Do you not know that something has been working on you, to cause you to accept a thing in religion, that would be repulsive to you in natural affairs? What was Christ teaching? Was this given to illustrate that he is the true vine and that different denominations were the branches, and that men should abide in a branch? Christ is the main trunk and every branch in him takes the name of the trunk. Hence, they were called Christians. What does the "Christ" mean? The true vine. What does the "ian" mean? The one attached. Men will say, I'm a member of a certain branch. Why do you want to be a member of the branch, when you can be a member of the trunk? If all the denominations, about 200 in U. S., are branches, I just want to ask you: where is the main trunk? You can't have branches unless there is a trunk somewhere. My effort is to try to find and to restore the main trunk in our land. Friends, the assuming of different names and titles is more responsible for our divided condition than any other one thing. People will argue that there's nothing in a name, but everybody knows that's not so. You may argue that there's nothing in it, and then when I appeal to you,

in behalf of unity, to give up yours, you become offended and positively refuse.

Friends, I want to read to you, some statements about matters of this kind, I bid you hear this, before I tell you its author and where you can find it:

"I look forward, with pleasure, to the day when there will not be a Baptist living. I hope they will soon be gone. I hope the Baptist name will soon perish; but let Christ's name endure forever." Who do you suppose said that? I want to repeat it: "I look forward with pleasure, to the day when there will not be a Baptist living. I hope they will soon be gone. I hope the Baptist name will soon perish; but let Christ's name endure forever." Friends, that was said by Charles Spurgeon, the greatest Baptist preacher that ever lived upon this earth. This quotation can be found in "Spurgeon Memorial Library," Volume 1, Page 168. Someone may say: "I don't believe it." I don't care whether you do or not. He said it just the same, or else the Baptists misrepresented him in publishing that book. Now what is Mr. Spurgeon's idea? "I hope the name Baptist will pass out of existence, that there won't be a Baptist living." He doesn't mean some individual, but he means the name, and the wearing of it. "Let it perish forever from the face of the earth, but let Christ's name endure forevermore." Someone thinks the word "Baptist" is in the Bible. Yes, "Baptist," is in the Bible, but the plural, *"Baptists"* is not in God's Book from beginning to end. There never was but one Baptist on earth, and he said he was going out of business. John 3: 30. "I must decrease."

Well, look again. "I pray you to leave my name alone, and call not yourselves Lutherans, but Christians. Who is Luther? My doctrine is not mine. I have not been crucified for anyone. St. Paul would not let any call themselves after Paul, nor of Peter, but of Christ. How then, does it befit me, a miserable bag of dust and ashes, to give my name to the children of God? Cease, my dear friends, to cling to these party names and distinctions: away with them all; and let us call ourselves only Christians after Him from whom our doctrine comes." That was said by Martin Luther, in the book called, *The Life of Luther,* by Stork, Page 289. The reason I am giving this is because it will be put down, and made permanent in the book of sermons. And yet, some Lutheran glories in the name Luther. Friends, old Martin Luther said: "Cease, my friends; don't call yourselves Lutherans, nor Paulites, nor Cephasites, nor Apollosites, nor any other name, except the name Christ." Isn't that wonderful preaching?

Now I am reading from John Wesley, and all you Methodists should prick up your ears and take notice: "Would to God," hear it—"that all party names and unscriptural phrases and forms which have divided the Christian world were forgot; that we might all agree to sit down together as humble, loving disciples at the feet of a common Master, to hear His words, to imbibe His spirit, and to transcribe His life into ours." Friends, look at them: Charles Spurgeon, a noted Baptist; Martin Luther, the founder of Lutheranism; John Wesley, the founder of Methodism, all forbid, as much as they possibly can, the wearing of their names, and yet, here we are, glorying in them. You may think you are honoring John Wesley and Martin Luther. My friends, these men resent that. What are we going to do about such matters? Are we content to live and move and pass off the stage of action and leave the world in a state of confusion, with no effort on our part to try to bring about a unity and a oneness? I never saw the day that I wanted to be distinguished from any other Christian on earth. I recognize God as our common Father, Jesus Christ as our elder brother, and all who have been "born again, of water and of the Spirit" as God's children. Therefore, we ought to be as one, wearing the name of Him who died that we might live. If Christ is the bridegroom, what name ought the bride to wear? If he is the head of the body, what ought the parts of the body to be? Every sort of an illustration imaginable, but emphasizes and stresses the need of all coming together, and of our being as the vine and the branches.

Friends, on this Saturday night, I have talked to you long enough. Are you a member of the true vine? If not, this is a wonderfully fine time for you to march quietly down any of the aisles, extend your hand to someone, and make known your wishes. Won't you do it while we sing?

IS CHRIST WITH US?

My friends and brethren, I am very deeply moved this afternoon by the presence of such a magnificent audience. When I call to mind that this is the sixth series of gatherings in this auditorium, wherein I have had a part, I find myself wholly unable to express the genuine and profound gratitude that is mine. Those six occasions have been as follows: four meetings, five nights in a discussion with Dr. Ira M. Boswell, of Georgetown, Kentucky, and then three nights for the delivery of some lectures on Palestine, Egypt, and lands evermore made sacred.

You have been exceeding and wonderfully kind in your response to our assemblies, and if this auditorium will seat eight thousand people, that number is here this afternoon. The lower floor, the galleries and platform, are filled to capacity.

We have come, friends, to the last day service of this meeting, and as a basis of what I have to say, I am reading to you from Luke the second chapter, commencing with verse 40: "And the child grew, and waxed strong in spirit, filled with wisdom: and the grace of God was upon him. Now his parents went to Jerusalem every year at the feast of the passover. And when he was twelve years old, they went up to Jerusalem after the custom of the feast. And when they had fulfilled the days, as they returned, the child Jesus tarried behind in Jerusalem; and Joseph and his mother knew not of it. But they, supposing him to have been in the company, went a day's journey, and they sought him among their kinsfolk and acquaintance. And when they found him not, they turned back again to Jerusalem, seeking him."

That's a part of the story in connection with Jesus Christ at the age of 12 years. When his parents left their home in Galilee and went up to Jerusalem to attend the Feast of the Passover, they took the child Jesus with them. After they had worshipped and started home, the child tarried behind, but his parents knew not of it. I stop to raise the point: Could they have known whether or not he was with them? They could. What was the trouble? "But they, supposing him to have been in the company, went a day's journey" and then missed him. I just wonder, friends, if that does not illustrate matters today fairly well. All people who claim to love God and respect his word, think that Jesus Christ is walking with them down the pathway of time and, ultimately, will introduce them into the glories of "over there." Are you right certain that he is traveling in your company? Have you ever stopped to make due investigation? That would not say that you are dishonest, or necessarily unconcerned. His mother did exactly that. She thought that he was along with them. She knew not of his staying behind, but went along all the day, supposing that her precious boy was in the crowd, but she was mistaken about it. He wasn't in her company and had not been since she started. Do you think there are people today journeying on toward their eternal destiny, only supposing that Christ is in their midst? After review of such a story as this, with all of its sadness and worry, don't you think it timely that we should carefully examine to see whether or not Jesus Christ be with us? A day's journey passed, during which time Mary, the mother, and Joseph, the father, were walking by supposition. It never dawned on them that they were wrong, that Christ was not in their midst, and had you asked them, "Is Jesus with you?" "Certainly," would have been their reply, but he wasn't. They went till the close of the day and when they began to pitch tent for the evening, they looked round about to gather their company, and found, to their surprise, that Jesus Christ was not in their midst. That didn't arouse them very much. Mary, the mother, thought: "Just over there is the camp of our kindred. He is with Uncle John, or with Aunt Elizabeth." But when she went over to the camp of her kindred, and made inquiry, and they took a search, he was not there. And then she said, "Well, we have some mighty good friends and they are camping just across on the other side.

I suppose he is with them." But when she went to look, lo and behold, he wasn't with them, and never had been. Then business picked up, and, of course, there was no sleep that night. Everybody was aroused, Jesus Christ is lost to his parents and his friends. After searching all around to find him not among them: "They turned back again to Jerusalem," and there they found him. Friends, why is that in the Bible? Is that simply to fill in space, with an idle story, to no profit, regarding a little incident of the Saviour at the age of twelve? I certainly think not. From it there is a most wonderful lesson, that I believe all of this audience ought to consider.

Think, today, of the different encampments marching along down life's way, supposing, each of them, that Christ is in their midst. It would be well to turn introspective and make research. Raise the query: "Did Christ ever hear of the company with which I am journeying?" Now, you know about it. "Did the Lord ever say anything about the crowd with whom I am marching?" Did he or not? Where did you ever read anywhere in the Bible about the crowd with which you are traveling? There is a challenge to your intelligence, and it's intended to provoke thought on your part, and to cause you to determine to investigate the crowd with which you are journeying. Is Christ in it? Was he ever in it? Did he know anything about it? Has he ever said a word regarding it? Friends, there's the tragedy of religious affairs today, and many an honest man and honest woman are going along, like the parents of Christ, not knowing but that Christ is in their midst. They just suppose he is. It is possible for us to pass on to the judgment and there to wake up, only to realize for the first time, as did his mother at the close of the day, that Jesus Christ has not been with us all the day. I am asking all of you brethren, what are all of our efforts about? What are the congregations in the city of Nashville trying to do? Is it to organize or form some special organization unknown to the Bible? What is our purpose? If I can discern and properly understand it, our great objective, brethren, is to cut loose from things of human relations and hark back to Jerusalem, and there again, start out determined and firmly resolved to make all things according to the pattern revealed in the New Testament. You know, as well as I, that under the guidance of inspiration there was an institution established on the first Pentecost after the resurrection of Christ. That institution is called the Church of the Lord, or the Kingdom of God. You are fully aware of the fact that men and women were members of it; that God added them thereunto; and that they continued in the doctrine taught by the apostles as they were guided by the Holy Spirit. Now what did it take to make and bring about a company of that kind? I am submitting to you with all the simplicity that I possibly can an analysis of matters pertaining to just such.

Friends, in order to have a crop, there must be two things: first, a soil adapted to the nature of that committed to its kindly bosom; and second, there must be seed planted in that soil. Then by virtue of the warmth, and sunshine, and gentle showers, there comes forth the product from that seed. It starts its growth, adding fruit as on it goes. That's the simple story. Apropos of that, may I suggest this: that on Pentecost, when Jews, devout men out of every nation under heaven were assembled, there was the soil, the human hearts. The word of God is the seed of the kingdom. The Holy Spirit saw to it that Peter and others, on that day, put that seed into the soil of those people there assembled. What the result? They that received the seed were baptized and Christians were born that day, "of water and of the spirit," to the number of about 3,000 souls. God called that the "church of the Lord," the "house of God," the pillar and the ground of the truth. The gospel was the thing that produced the crop. With the passing of time and the corrupting influences of uninspired men, before the last apostle died there were evidences of apostasy. All through the Bible there are warnings to the church against such. Paul said to Timothy: "The time will come when men will not endure sound doctrine," and "In the latter times some shall depart from the faith." There will be those who will overthrow the faith, and make shipwreck of it. Paul said, "the mystery of iniquity," and the man of sin had already raised his head and appeared, a threatening menace to the church of the Lord. The years were not many after the days of inspiration before there began to be an hierarchy, an organization drafted by men. to supplant the church that God ordained. In addititon to that, there was a corruption of the practice of the original body by the introduction of both Jewish and pagan ideas into the church of the Lord. They sought by worldly means to embellish and adorn the church and thus enlist public interest. Six hundred years passed away and there was scarcely a shadow of an organization on earth like that planted by inspiration. Popery had raised aloft its head, and the human ecclesiasticism was riding high-handed. It was swaying the scepter over the lives and destinies of men both in civil and in religious affairs. That period is known as the Dark Ages, into which the world passed. It was characterized by corruption and crime and the blackest deeds that have ever disgraced the pages of human history.

Things went on for about a thousand years, until conditions became intolerable and decency could no longer endure. The world became tired and restless, and at last men began to throw off their shackles and to think for themselves. A new era was about to dawn and a new light was soon to shine. Men of vision looked out and fancied a new world bright with hope and prospect. Such a transition is known in history as the period of the Renaissance. The world was emerging out of darkness into a more marvelous light.

Responsible for that, most of all, was the invention of printing by means of movable blocks. As a result, religious and other literature began to be spread abroad; men began to read and think for themselves. One of the greatest leaders of that old religious body became sick, tired and disgusted. He determined that no longer would he hold his peace, but he would speak forth that which was in his heart. Hence, at the risk not only of being ex-communicated, but also of being executed, Martin Luther braved the organized forces of the time, marched out and swore allegiance unto God, rather than unto any human organization upon earth. That's the beginning of what we call "The Period of the Reformation." Martin Luther was an educated young man. He was born, reared, tutored, trained, and disciplined in the "Faith of the Fathers," but when he saw the corruption and the exceeding sinfulness and rottenness characteristic of the church of which he was a member, let it be said, that he displayed a courage equal to that of Jesus Christ before Pilate, of Peter before the Sanhedrin, and of Paul before Agrippa. Therefore, he proposed a discussion of the merit of that hierarchy wherein he was born and reared. One debate was held with old John Eck, but that one proved to be sufficient. I just wonder if it would be amiss here to call your attention to a matter. In 1923, our friends of the Christian church, in convention up at Ovoca Springs, resoluted, whereased and therefored that they would arrange for a discussion of Instrumental Music in every county seat of Tennessee. A committee waited upon some brethren of the opposition here in Nashville and agreed upon the terms. These were that such a debate should be wherever both sides were represented. The first debate was held at the Ryman Auditorium. Some of you remember quite well that the debate was on for five nights, with immense crowds packing both the lower and the upper floors of this historic old building. At the close of that discussion, brethren said to those who had resoluted so much, "Where will the next one be?" They have not answered until this good hour, and that was fifteen years ago. Now that's but a parallel to the experience of Martin Luther, when he came out to attack and to question the doctrine of the church of which he had been reared a member. Martin Luther's idea was that, since the church was so corrupt, he wanted to reform it. He had no idea of establishing a denomination. But, friends, let it be said to his disappointment that the thing refused to be corrected; it refused to be reformed. A thing so corrupt that it cannot and will not be reformed must be destroyed. Martin Luther had that very sentiment; therefore, when brought before the powers that be, and the great accusation presented written out with the charges, instead of bowing as a puppet, he stood up and said, "There's your scrap of paper and do what you please, God being my helper, I can do none other than stand for what I believe to be right." Friends, that resulted, in 1521, in the establishment of the Lutheran denomination upon this earth. So Luther's work, although quite valuable, was a failure so far as getting anywhere in reforming the church of the Fathers. Well, you know the restless spirit that would grow out of that. John Calvin, at the same time, also had become tired and skeptical of many of the things found, as did Luther, but not agreeing with his contemporary, started out upon a different line, writing his Institutes, setting forth reasons for his belief and announcing the five points of Calvinism that have come down through the ages. The result of the work wrought by John Calvin was the organization and the introduction of the great Presbyterian denomination, which never existed either in the Bible or out of God's word. Well, time rolled on. Old Henry VIII answered Martin Luther in such a wonderful way, that the Pope commended his book and announced that the author be styled "Defender of the Faith." He stood there—a towering character in defense of the excommunication of Martin Luther; but with the passing of time, Henry VIII looked upon his wife, Catherine, six years older than he, saw that she hadn't been to the beauty parlor, that her hair was all stringy, and that she was getting wrinkled, and stooped, and didn't care much; and there was young Anne Boleyn of just nineteen summers, a beautiful, blushing maid, with perhaps both cheeks and lips painted, and her dress abridged at both ends, who attracted his attention. Indeed so much so, that he and Anne had a kind of a quiet understanding, and that was, "if I can get rid of my wife, Catherine, business will pick up in our affair." When he applied, therefore, for the divorce, it was very correctly refused on the part of the papacy; but "love will find a way," and in the course of time, he had Thomas Cranmer appointed archbishop of Canterbury; then as King of England, he demanded that his appointee write out a bill of divorcement. That was done, and as a result there was born upon this earth, as I have said from this platform before, the great Episcopal body. Now, what do you find? Denominationalism springing up. What is it all about? An effort to reform the Catholic church, which absolutely refused to yield.

Well again. With the passing of time, Episcopalianism grew cold, wonderfully formal, ritualistic, frigid in its nature, and some young men in college, members of that body, who wanted warmth, zeal, fervor, and feeling in their religious affairs, undertook to inject some of the warmth that they had into the cold Episcopal organization. What was their effort? To try to reform Episcopalianism. Leading that body was none other than John Wesley. When that effort failed, Methodism was born on this earth, 1729. What was the purpose of Wesley? "I am trying to reform the Episcopal church." Thus he lived and died a member of the Episcopal church, working at it, trying to reform it; but when it refused, those who believed as did Wesley organized and looked back to Wesley as the founder and the beginning of that denomination.

Well, you can hardly quit, when you talk along those lines. In the course of time, two questions arose. Now be it remembered, that with all denominations thus far had been the idea of the baptizing or the sprinkling of babies and, therefore, the subject of baptism, namely a baby, and the actual baptism, namely sprinkling, became a practice among them, as borrowed from the Catholics who adopted it on a parity with immersion, at the Council of Ravenna, 1311. All right. There grew up within these different bodies, Lutherans, Presbyterians, Methodists, and Episcopalians, this sentiment: namely, nobody but an adult is a subject of baptism, and nothing but immersion meets the demands of God's word; therefore, those elements from various parties believing that only adults should be baptized and that immersion was the act, accumulated, and gathered force until, about 1608, the Baptist church came into existence, with its name based upon the baptismal act. That was an effort to reform some of the churches gone before.

Friends, things went from bad to worse; human names and party spirit reigned high-handed, human creeds were everywhere prominent and each of them, bitter in denunciation of the others. Again, the doctrine of total hereditary depravity, sponsored by various ones, was obnoxious to those who used their heads for thinking and for study. Based upon total depravity, there comes, of necessity, the doctrine of a miraculous conversion. Hence, the world lost its head; conversion was a mystery; and every man's birth born into God's family was the result of a great miracle—so that confusion became more and more confounded upon the earth.

The years went by; the nineteenth century opened up; and then from various quarters of our globe, came a general demand that something must be done. "The world cannot go on with its partisan spirit, with its divided condition, with each having his own particular creed, and each bearing some human name. Can't we do something about it?" May I say to you, that, as a result of the failure of the reformers and the disappointment of those who had gone before, good men from various denominations reasoned together, and began to wonder why there could not be upon this earth again, an organization like that back in the days of the apostles. That thought fastened itself upon them; they couldn't get rid of the idea. "Is it possible that there can be such an organization?" Well, they looked about their respective company, and the various denominations, and found that Christ was not in this one. They turned to the next and said, "This one is a total stranger to Jesus Christ; he said not a word about it." They looked at a third, "Neither is he here. Brethren, what can we do?" Then there was that duplication of the thought of Mary, the mother of our Lord, when they said: "Brethren, something is radically wrong. Let's go back to Jerusalem." Hence, there was begun another great movement, different from anything hitherto found upon the earth. What was it? A determination to *restore*, not to *reform*, but to *restore* that which one time existed, which had been lost and buried under the rubbish of human affairs. It needed to be brought to light again. Therefore, the great Restoration Movement was launched upon this earth.

Well, I want to lay down to you some principles upon which they began their work. First: "We will not try to organize some human affair." Everybody said that there were far too many organizations, that man had no right to go into the business of establishing churches. So, they said: "Let's go back to Jerusalem and there take the Bible as our guide, and by it, let's see if we can't duplicate the old paths and restore the ancient order of affairs." Again, "These creeds so prevalent among men, and so contrary one to the other, are but human products. Brethren, let's cut loose from every creed on earth and adopt the Bible as our only creed, our only discipline, our only confession of faith, our only church manual." Now that's a platform broad enough and big enough for every God-loving man to occupy and yet not sacrifice any principle whatsoever. That same thing can be done today by every man, woman, boy and girl in all this land of ours. "God's word as our complete guide without human addition, without human supplement—just the Bible and the Bible alone." Then "Let's subscribe to the idea of speaking where God speaks, and where He is silent, let us likewise be." Friends, those are mottoes early adopted in the effort to bring about a restoration of the ancient order of things. They saw each one over in his little denominational pen, not only with a human creed, but wearing, boasting, and glorying in a human name, unknown, unheard of, unwritten, in all the Book of God. They decided: "Let's lay aside the name Lutheran, as Luther himself bade them, which exhortation I read to you last night. Let's lay aside the name Presbyterian; let's no longer march under the banner of the name Baptist; let's go back. What were they back on Pentecost? What were they in the city of Antioch? What were they in the household of Cornelius?" And therefore, the thought seized upon them, "They were Christians," and that covered every child of God on earth. "That name is nonsectarian; it's undenominational; it's not narrow; it's not limited; it does not build a pen of human construction around anybody and say 'unless you subscribe to our creed, and adopt our human name, you can't be one of our number.' Friends, that's narrow; that's little, that's dwarfed, and dwindled; let's march out on the broad, universal platform; God's word as our guide; the name Christian as that by which we will be called, and under the banner of Jesus Christ our Lord, let us pass gloriously on."

Well, that's not all. They said: "In our practice let there be absolutely nothing required of any man other than that which is taught in the Bible either by direct statement, or by approved example, or by necessary inference." Those are planks laid down, and then to guarantee the matter, they said: "In all things of faith, let there be unity; in all matters of opinion, let there be liberality; in all things, let there be charity." Friends, that's the only hope of this sin-cursed world; that's the only hope of healing the breaches in the religious realm today. We ought to stand as a solid phalanx on matters of faith. If God has declared a thing and we can read it from His word, I would not move one-thousandth of an inch; I could not compromise one idea of faith taught by God's word; but if it be merely a matter of opinion, let me have it, but let me hold it to myself. I have no right to force my opinion upon anyone else. I am out of order, a disturber of the church, if I go about from house to house, or publicly try to push my opinion upon any other member of the church. Let's hold that opinion as private property. And then, in all things let there be charity, and let brotherly love prevail so long as there is not a sacrifice of faith demanded. Friends, I believe confidently, that we have come to the time in our religious affairs, that these old principles, seemingly forgotten, need to be restated over and over again. While I have preached to you practically this same outline before, and have gone over this same matter, I have been in the schoolroom long enough to know that people forget things, that they have to be told over, and over, and over. With these young men here from Freed-Hardeman College, and about double their number that have not come, over and over, and then again, from varied and sundry angles, these matters are discussed, and then: "To the library, boys, for confirmation of all these notes, so that when you get out, you can say it boldly as you ought to speak, and be confident that you know what you are talking about, and with courage preach the ancient order of affairs, and let no uncertain sound go forth." Repetition is a basic principle in teaching.

We are today in a condition possibly without a parallel. I am talking now about matters in general. Friends, in the whole world there is a spirit of anarchy prevailing. I want you to think just a moment. In our homes, rebellion is in evidence far more than it was, a generation gone by. In our cities, counties, states, nation, men do not want to be subjected to authority. Every man wants to be free to do as he pleases. I regret to say that same spirit has found its way into the church of the living God, when no longer are men content to bow in subjection to the authority of Jesus Christ. Modernistic trends are in evidence on every hand, and that means the rejection of established authority.

Another trait of the times is the consuming ambition to start something new. There are just plenty of people who aspire to prominence on the ground, "I've discovered some new thing." This is a wonderful age of invention, as everybody knows. Unfortunately, that same idea has not been kept out of the body of Christ. Paul said: "The time will come when they will not endure sound doctrine, but after their own lusts," for prominence, for prestige, for publicity, "they'll heap to themselves teachers with itching ears" that just must be scratched. They can't stand it any longer; they'll turn away their ears from the truth, and take out after fabulous stories, and attractive suggestions. Too, there have developed, within these last years, two different types of preaching, two different philosophies of proclaiming the gospel, two methods of telling the story. One of

them is, to put on the soft pedal, to preach what you believe to be right, but to do it with modification and sometimes with apology. "Be certain that you respect and give due deference unto your friends, and say nothing, even though you think it correct, that might be offensive; seek popularity and the applause and the commendations of your fellows." Victims of the current mania to preach over radio are often guilty of such an attitude. They modify what otherwise they might preach. They give some little, nice, liberal talk on modern affairs or educational matters, or social customs, and develop the habit of preaching after that fashion, till the gospel, God's power to save, is absolutely gone from their line of proclamation. Hence, they seem to love the praise of men more than the praise of God. They recognize all people who even claim to wear the name Christian. Now then, I want to say something, and if I were off by myself I would say it.

Friends, there is not a man on God's earth that has more respect for his fellows and their convictions than do I, but I believe some things; I preach certain things; I'm criticized for certain matters. Now mark it—you people who have very kindly been attending our services know this: I preach just what the Saviour said, namely: "He that believes the gospel and is baptized, shall be saved." Now you know I teach that. My brethren subscribe to it whether they all preach it firmly or not. They teach that faith is the condition of salvation, that baptism is "for the remission of sins," that salvation follows obedience to the gospel of Jesus Christ, and that no man enjoys forgiveness of sins until that man has believed the gospel with all of his heart, repented of his sins, acknowledged the Christ, and been buried in the name of the Father, Son, and Holy Spirit. Now, I teach that; I believe that; those are my convictions; and as the boy said, "Them's my sentiments."

Now then, here's a mighty good friend of mine, a man that I love and appreciate—but he has not done that. For me to recognize him as a Christian and call upon him to have a part in the service, to pray unto God Almighty for me, is, in my way of thinking, a reflection upon that man's good sense, and presents quite an embarrassing situation. First, if I recognize him as a Christian I slap in the face all the preaching that I have been doing for the past twenty-five years. By my recognition of that man as a Christian, I virtually say, "I am a hypocrite; I don't believe what I have been preaching all these years." I simply say to him whom I count as a friend: "Sir, I cannot be consistent and recognize you as a child of God." May I tell you this: I was reared with a boy who is now a preacher of a denomination. He is quite prominent and holds place among his people. He likes me and it's quite mutual. He comes to hear me preach sometimes, and one day on the train, he said to me: "Hardeman, I just want to ask you something. I think you like me," I said, "I do. I wouldn't mistreat you at all, I'd do anything I could for you." Then he said: "You never do recognize me, never call upon me, never give me any mention, or recognition as a Christian when I am in your service." I thought that was the time to come clean, so I said: "Just look here! I teach that a man has to believe the gospel, repent of his sins, confess his faith, and be baptized in the name of the Lord Jesus Christ to be a Christian. You haven't done that; therefore, if I recognize you as such, I go back on my teaching." He slapped me on the knee, and said: "That's the first time that I have ever been made to see and appreciate that fact. Here's my hand! I respect you ten times more; I think you would be hypocritical to do it otherwise."

Let me tell you, friends, we'll never get anywhere by a compromising spirit. Brother J. D. Tant is an old preacher of the gospel of Christ. A man whose wife was a Christian, though he was not, once said to Brother Tant, "I am some kin to you. I'm a brother-in-law to the church. My wife is a member and that makes me a brother-in-law." Brother Tant said, "Well, that will work both ways; that means then that your wife is a sister-in-law to the devil." Friends, I am just as certain as in your midst I stand, that we have drifted away and departed from that type of preaching which is responsible for our existence in the city of Nashville. I know that if you would hark back to the days, for instance, of Brother J. A. Harding, and others like him, there would be a different ring from that you hear too frequently today. I have brethren who say: "Hardeman, I believe exactly like you do, but—" But what? "I don't think you ought to say some things." Preach the truth; say nothing about anybody else! Now at the first service of this meeting, I reviewed that principle and showed how inconsistent it is. I'm against gambling; I'm against betting; I think marble machines, all such devices, are out of order; but I mustn't say anything about them. "Just go ahead and preach the truth and let the gambling and the saloon-keeper alone!" There are brethren who will maintain that kind of principle with reference to religious matters; and then criticize the outside matter unsparingly. Brethren, let's be consistent and, above all, let's stand four-square for the ancient order of things.

Let me say to you, as one of the parting messages of this meeting: It has been my heart's desire and prayer to God, that by the recitation of these fundamental matters there might be a cementing together, in closer bonds, the great brotherhood of Nashville, Tennessee, people that I love, and in whom I am deeply interested. We must stand together against the powers of denominationalism, of all kinds of error, and as Jude said, "earnestly contend for the faith once for all delivered unto the saints." You ask how can that be? We have the same soil that they had on Pentecost, the hearts of men; we have the same seed of the kingdom, God's word. If brethren will put that seed into the hearts or soil, it will bring forth exactly what it did back there; if we'll continue in the apostles' doctrine, and be not wise above that which is written, and not be lured after teaching with itching ears, there'll be unity, peace, joy and happiness, as once there was in the land wherein we now dwell.

Let me say again that all the ground we occupy is indeed sacred; the ground whereon we stand is holy ground. What is it, brethren, that has brought to us the prestige and the prominence that we have here in Nashville? Has it been the denominational world, opening up its arms and saying: "We want you in our midst"? Absolutely not, but it has been a fight from beginning to end. God recognized that, and so Paul charged to Timothy, "Son, buckle on God's armor, raise aloft the banner, unsheathe the sword of the spirit, fight the good fight of faith, lay hold upon eternal life," regardless of opposition. That's the type of men and women needed today, those who stand firm for their conviction and until convinced that they are wrong, sacrifice it not. Heed not the siren song of compromise anywhere, but bear down, impress God's truth, because the salvation of a soul depends upon it. I have heard of men who said: "Hardeman, I believe exactly as you do. I believe those things precisely, and I want you to preach them." I have had word sent to me by preachers: "Hardeman, lay on! I want you to do it; but I can't and stay where I am." Can a man be saved who thinks more of his job than he does of God's truth? I bid you think on matters of that kind.

Friends, I appreciate your encouragement and your exhortation, but put it down: N. B. Hardeman will be preaching it exactly that way twenty-five, forty, even forty-five years hence, if God but spares me. But I have talked to you long enough this afternoon. If there is one in this entire company who wants to hark back to Jerusalem, return to the old paths, embrace the old faith, and walk with Christ in the straight and narrow way, it is our happy privilege to remind you again of the Lord's invitation to come unto him. If you have understood the teaching and have developed a faith that urges you to obey the Lord; if you will to turn from your evil ways—repent—and here before this audience, confess your faith, thence to be buried with the Lord by baptism, to rise to walk in newness of life; will you not come as an expression of your interest? Do it immediately, as we again sing the invitation song.

THE FINAL EXHORTATION

Phil. 1: 27, 28

This brings us, friends, to the last service of the meeting as scheduled. I just want to say now, this meeting has transcended the fondest hopes I had when I first came to have a part in it with you two weeks ago. It has steadily grown in interest and in number attending. This afternoon there was scarcely a seat to be found after all were in; that same condition prevails tonight, with some standing.

When people about seven or eight thousand strong come together from time to time for no clap-trap entertainment, but the rendition of these fine old gospel songs, so well directed by Brother Ben Murphy, and then to hear a simple presentation of gospel truth, it's evidence of their interest in things sacred and sublime.

I have been the recipient, together with Mrs. Hardeman and members of the family, of so many kindnesses extended on your part. Friends from various places and different parts of the city have extended invitations, best wishes, etc. We have been guests at the Sam Davis Hotel. I have stayed in many a hotel, but with no disregard for any other, I think I have never had, on the part of the manager and all the employees, more courteous treatment, more interest and anxiety to look after every need and to see that every comfort was extended, than has been mine to receive from that splendid hotel of your city. I want all to know that I am profoundly grateful for courtesies of that kind.

I was requested by Brother Redmond to announce the meeting at Russell Street, to begin on the second Sunday in November, with Brother E. W. McMillan as the preacher. At the same time Brother I. A. Douthitt will be at Charlotte Avenue. I am glad to make these announcements and to commend to you all gospel truth and hearing wherever it may be.

I have been interested in Nashville since first I came into your midst. I was delighted last spring when I learned that you were to have meetings at all the congregations in the city, about the same time, and thus put on a campaign for the extension of the gospel of Christ. I understand Brother Paul Miller suggested that idea.

My friends, it is many times fine to look back. Our spirits are saddened and we are made to feel our loss when we think of those who were with us in other meetings but since have slipped away. Time is so rapidly passing. It doesn't seem to me possible that it has been sixteen and one-half years since I first came to you. Of course, I cannot remember all, but I want to let you know of those that I do recall, most of whom occupied the platform: Brother E. G. Sewell, Brother Scobey, old Brother Blaine, Brother George Porch, Brother Elam, Brother McQuiddy, Brother F. W. Smith, Brother Moore, Brother Alex Perry, Brother Dr. Boyd, Brother J. W. Grant, Brother J. Petty Ezzell, Brother Lawson, Brother Allen, Brother Dennison, my good friend, Brother James T. Anderson, of Waverly, also Brother David Lipscomb, of Fanning School, together with Governor McMillin, Governor Taylor, Judge Meeks, Judge Pitts, and Mayor Hilary Howse. All of these have passed on. Brother Smith, who was then Chief of Police and who was greatly interested, has been unable to attend this meeting. They once occupied this platform and with all of those back tonight, they would fill these seats that are now occupied by others. I just mention that because in thinking about it, I made note of some whom I recall with a degree of pleasure, and whom I counted among my friends and those interested in what I am trying to do.

This meeting, friends, from various angles, has been exceeding pleasant, and I am quite certain that profit has resulted from our studying together those things that challenge our attention. So far as I know, these lessons will go on down through the ages. Hundreds if not thousands of young men and older ones will read the sermons, meditate upon them, revise them, and present those thoughts on down to boys and girls yet unborn upon this earth. Unto

God Almighty be all the praise and the glory and unto us the encouragement.

I am reading tonight the 27th and 28th verses of the first chapter of Philippians. Hear it: "Only let your conversation be as it becometh the gospel of Christ; that whether I come and see you, or else be absent, I may hear of your affairs, that ye stand fast in one spirit, with one mind striving together for the faith of the gospel; And in nothing terrified by your adversaries; which is to them," that is, which faith on your part, is to them "an evident token of perdition, but to you of salvation, and that of God." That text is a little lengthy, but I want to read it again and impress upon you: Only this, brethren, "let your conversation be,"—some versions put it, "let your manner of life," others, "your citizenship"—"let your conversation be as it becometh the gospel of Christ; that whether I come and see you, or else be absent, I may hear of your affairs, that ye stand fast in one spirit, with one mind striving together for the faith of the gospel: And in nothing terrified by your adversaries; which is to them an evident token of perdition, but to you of salvation, and that of God."

The Philippian church was the first one established on European soil. Preachers went there in response to a Macedonian call. They lingered round about the city for some little time and learned that some women were accustomed to meet out by the riverside. Thither they went. The result of that contact was the preaching of the gospel to Lydia and to her house. They were converted, and these became the nucleus of the Philippian church. To that, the jailer and his house were later added, and others as the power of God had its effect. Paul stayed with this church and planted it correctly, established it firmly, and then went on his journey southward, through Amphipolis and Apollonia and on to Thessalonica, Berea, Athens, and as far south as Corinth. After awhile, during imprisonment, Paul wrote to the Philippians this short letter of four brief chapters. In that he spoke the words of our text tonight: "Only let your conversation be as it becometh the gospel of Christ."

I am calling attention, friends, first to the fact that this letter was not addressed unto preachers, and yet to them it is so wonderfully applicable. You will not disagree with me when I declare that any man who stands before his fellows and talks about things that transcend the realms of time, when souls are at stake, and heaven or hell may be the destiny—surely when he is thus honored by the presence of his fellows and enabled to speak to them, his words ought to be of such a character as becometh the gospel of Christ. Any preacher who is called into the sick room to offer words of encouragement, and of sympathy, ought to let his conversation and manner of life be such as are becoming to the gospel of Christ. And that man who stands at the sacred casket and speaks the last word regarding some departed soul, that man, surely, ought to have his conversation such as becomes the gospel of Christ. But, friends, I said this was not written to preachers, and it wasn't, only as they are members of the church. Nor was it written to elders as though they were in a separate class, and needed instruction other than all the membership. Brethren, this letter was written unto the church at Philippi and it includes both men and women, boys and girls. Paul said: Brethren, I know not whether I will ever see you again or not, but be that as it may, I want you to get this: "Let your conversation," let your manner of life, let your citizenship, "be as becometh the gospel of Christ." Friends, I think all of us like things becoming. We want matters fit, suited. The world about us is wonderful in its harmony, in its fitness, in the relation of all things one with the other. I have often thought of the absolute fitness of things with which divinity has had to do. Now Paul said, Brethren, "let your conversation be" fitting, let it be suited, let it be adapted, let it be becoming. Becoming to what? To the gospel of our Lord. We are particular about our garb and the paraphernalia in which we are clad. We want our wardrobe, if you please, all harmoniously blended; we want things suited and in harmony. I have seen women in the millinery shops, and I have sat, as patient as possible, and watched them try on one hat after another. I have seen them fix the hair and touch it up nicely, and the saleslady would ask: Isn't that a darling little hat? and I thought, "Indeed, it is!" They would try this and object on the ground that it isn't suited to my complexion; this doesn't fit my type; and it isn't adapted to my height, etc. Well, that runs throughout the whole realm of our affairs. If you are going out for a rough job, and to do manual labor, you don't want to be dressed like preachers, in their finery, and superior garb (?). If you want, therefore, to do hard, dirty work, dress accordingly, and be becoming to the nature of the thing that confronts you. And so it is, in all the affairs of life. Paul said, Brethren, "let your conversation be as it becometh the gospel of Christ." I'll tell you, friends, you can get a pretty good idea of how a man estimates the gospel of Christ by watching his conversation. He claims to be a Christian, but from his mouth there goes forth a continued sluice of slime. What do you know about him? He may, perhaps, sit on the front seat and sing, "I'm Bound for the Promised Land," but you know his ideal and his conception of the gospel are indeed quite low. Now if that's in harmony with what you think the gospel is, it's away down below par on the market of the world, and I think there has never been a time when our attention needs to be called to these matters more than now. The world is loose and lax in its manner of speech. Our vocabulary is not of that particular type as will always adorn the doctrine of God. The name of the Lord is used quite loosely. By-words and slang phrases too frequently abound in the conversation of most of us, and thus I really think we belittle the gospel of Christ and the church of the Lord. If, according to some of our actions, we think they're in harmony with the gospel of Christ, the impression goes out, that the church doesn't stand for much and doesn't mean much.

I want to ask you, friends, how can we, as a body of people exalt the church of the Lord in Nashville? By just letting matters of every type go along unprotested? Shall we let all kinds of conduct prevail and nothing be said about it? Shall we allow those on the outside to point their finger and say: "Some in the church are unfit, some are unworthy, about some we know enough to put them in the penitentiary"? Can we expect the church of the Lord to be elevated, adorned, and highly regarded? Friends, there's no outside power on earth, nor are there enough demons in hell to hinder the onward march and the progress of the church of the Lord. It must survive or perish, live or die, according to what those on the inside may do. The enemy from without can do but little harm, but if there rise up an enemy from within, he can stick the dagger that will break the body and cause its life current to flow as in the days gone by. May I say to you tonight, what I have said before: I would rather be the man that injected the spear and tore asunder the body of Christ on the cross than to be the man in Nashville, or anywhere else, responsible for the dividing of the spiritual body of our Lord. Friends, let's have our conversation, our manner of life, our united citizenship in the kingdom of God, such as to be becoming unto the gospel of our Lord; let's elevate the church in the conception of the world; let's make it realize that the church stands for something; that it is God's institution; that Christ is the head of it; and that the King of the kingdom is reigning over the destinies of men. So Paul said, Brethren, "Let your conversation be as it becometh the gospel of Christ: that whether I come and see you, or else be absent." Paul didn't know what the future held for him. He was at that time a prisoner, in the custody of the enemy, and, I presume, like all prisoners, he indulged the hope that, perhaps, he might be freed, and again go to the Philippian brethren. "But, brethren, whether I do or not, I want to hear of your affairs." Friends, may I make that sentiment mine. I have been with you now for two weeks. This is the eighteenth successive effort on this platform in your midst. Life is fraught with so many uncertainties, pitfalls, dangers, incidents, and accidents all along the line, that I don't know whether I will ever stand on the platform of Ryman Auditorium again or not. I may never behold the faces of you who have so kindly come and lent your presence, your prayers, and your influence to make pleasant these relationships, but candidly, and with a degree of feeling that I am wholly unable to express, may I say, whether I ever come to you again, brethren, or not, I want to hear of your affairs. I'm interested in the cause of Christ, not simply at Henderson, Tennessee, not simply in the county where I chance to dwell, not merely in the state of my citizenshp, but everywhere, from the rivers to the ends of the earth, I'm interested in the cause that Christ died to establish. I want to hear of the affairs of brethren. But, Paul, what do you want to hear? Paul said, I want to hear this: "That ye stand fast in one spirit, with one mind striving together for the faith of the gospel." Now, no man on earth could put a stronger statement down than that. Paul, what do you want to hear? That the Philippians *stand fast*. If I had been writing it, I might have said, I want to hear, brethren, that you stand *pat*, but I mean exactly the same thing. Now, do you get just what that implies? It doesn't mean to be a weakling, a negative sort of fellow, afraid of his shadow, looking out with his ear to the ground to see what public sentiment says, figuring out what is the best policy. You brethren *stand fast*, stay put! That's the idea. I have rooted you and have grounded you, I've stayed with you until the tap root has gone directly down and there has a footing, and then I have stayed with you until the sprangle roots, the guy ropes, are out in every direction.

For more than a hundred years we have preached upon unity, but our appeal has been to the denominational world. Now it has come to pass, and I say it with profound regret, that in these last days, we must preach on "Unity" and apply it to our own brethren. May God help us and cause the time soon to come when, again, all discrepancies, all cross-firing, and all reports of every slanderous nature may pass away, and God's truth may be so sacred that we stand uncompromisingly for it, "earnestly contending for the faith once for all delivered," and that there will be no division among us.

Paul said, I want to hear of your affairs, "that ye stand fast in one spirit, with one mind striving." Now, friends, if I may say it, I have always been, I presume, what the world would call a rather positive sort of fellow. That's just my nature. I have never been afraid, regarding any matter that I ever heard of, to tell the world where I stand. And why not? Sometimes you find brethren who are afraid to express themselves on issues that threaten the peace of congregations. They usually say: "I just haven't studied that." Brethren, that is not so. That's an alibi, an excuse to get by without committing themselves. May God forbid the time will ever come when that any matter appertaining to the church of the Lord Jesus Christ may be presented, and N. B. Hardeman doesn't know where he stands. My friends, I believe that in the kingdom of God there's no place for a negative character; there's no place for a weakling; there's no place for an apologist; there's no place for a compromiser. Fancy the peerless apostle Paul, Peter, James or John, of any other type than that of a positive, firm, aggressive character, willing to stand four-square for God's truth against the claims of all opposition whatsoever and whosoever they may be. Now Paul said, Brethren, I want you to strive. Someone may say: "I don't think there should be any strife." Well, I don't either. God never said strife, s-t-r-i-*f*-e; he said, brethren, I want you to s-t-r-i-v-e, *strive*. I just wonder what purpose some people have. They are wholly negative in nature, not doing this, that, or the other. Take, for instance, the one-talent man. What have you against him? What did he do? Nothing. What accusation? "I ain't done nothing." Well, what can you say against him? Wherein was he a transgressor? Nowhere. Yet the Lord cast him out into outer darkness. Why? Because he hadn't done anything. Now, let me tell you, friends, there will be more folks in hell for not having done what they ought, than for flagrantly and openly violating God's word. Matthew 25 gives the picture of the last judgment. To them on the right hand, "Come, ye blessed of my Father." Why? "I was an hungred." What did you do about it? You got busy and gave me something to eat. "I was thirsty." You acted. "I was naked." You moved. "I was sick and in prison," and here you came. All right, "Enter in." But to them on the left hand, "Depart from me, ye cursed, into everlasting fire." Why, Lord, what have they done? Let's see. "I was hungry." What did you folks do? Nothing. "I was thirsty." Then what? You kept on doing nothing. "I was sick and in prison," and you did more of the same. To hell you go. Why? Just because you haven't done something.

Friends, don't you know there are two ways of sinning? One is by *commission,* the other is by *omission.* Many people sit and take an inventory of their lives, and they nearly always take it negatively: "I haven't done this, or that, or the other. Hence, I am all right." Friends, the religion of the Lord Jesus Christ is not simply to *be* good, but the religion of the Bible is to *do* good. It's an active, aggressive, progressive sentiment starting in the hearts of men, finding expression out in their relationships to their fellows. Paul said: "Brethren, I want you to strive." How, Paul? "I want you to strive *together.*"

I was reared away back in the country. I don't usually have to tell that. I used to drive oxen, and some of you old-timers know the kind of vocabulary it takes to get anywhere with them. It was a pleasure to crack the whip over the backs of Tom and Jerry and see them step together. I often boasted that they could pull anything loose at both ends. But I remember to have had steers that strived hard, but they were pulling against one the other, until a great knot was on the outside of their necks. Of course, you city folks don't know a thing in the world about such things. They were striving, but they were striving one against the other, and they needed swapping off or selling to the other fellow.

After the days of the ox my father used horses, and we had a good team of beautiful bays that stepped together. I liked to drive them, I took pride in getting up fine harness with brass top hames, leather tugs, back-bands, belly-bands, choke-straps, flank-straps, etc. But I have seen teams much better than I ever had. I have seen big Percherons stepping down the street in perfect unison until the wagon wheel dropped in a hole up to the hub. There they stopped. Of course, I know what's on hand now. The driver talks kindly to them; he walks around and pats them on the neck and says nice things, and then by and by, he gets back and gives the word "go." Then the off horse lunges forward while the lead horse doesn't budge. Well, that got nowhere. The wheel is still resting on the hub and in the mud. Well, the driver goes around and tries to quiet them down again. He says nice things to them when he really feels like beating the life out of them. After a while, he picks up the lines and gently gives the word "go," and the lead horse lunges, while the other one stands stock still. Then both horses and driver get in a mood of excitement and anxiety. The horses begin to see-saw, back and forth. Perspiration breaks out in great drops of sweat, and they get to foaming and champing the bits. Finally, one of those horses lays his chin over on the other one's neck right in front of the hame. Do you know what that means? That means, "I'm balked, nothing further doing." Now, after that failure to strive together, I have seen some fellow drive up with a pair of little peg-leg mules that weigh about 800 pounds. They have rope bridles, shuck collars, cotton back-bands, iron traces, no breeching, no belly-bands, nor flank straps. Without any great big show, this man just drives his little mules across the tongue, hooks them up, while he sings, "Blest be the Tie That Binds." He then gets back and picks up the lines. They set their little legs; he gives the word; and they move together, all eight feet in the same direction; and that old wagon comes out of the mire and moves on down the street, while the big horses, finely harnessed, look like thirty cents with a hole in it. This shows what can be done by striving *together*. That's the philosophy; that's the keynote of success. I care not how inferior, or how small a matter may be, a business, an organization, or a congregation. If every member in it will strive together, that thing is going to succeed. Paul said: "I want you to strive together." For what? "For the faith." Not for some new-fangled idea, not for some modern philosophy, not for some fancied theory, not for something speculative in nature, concerning which you cannot be certain, and which at best is only a guess. I'm not asking you to strive together for that, but for that "faith once for all delivered unto the saints." Brethren, put your shoulders to the wheel, get your feet properly set, and when the word is given, let's strive *together,* and as a solid phalanx we can make heaven and earth move, for the accomplishment of God's purpose among men. In all of that, Paul in effect said, Don't be terrified now, don't be disturbed, nor agitated by your enemy. Of course, there will be opposition; there will be those to hinder your progress; there will be those to throw the proverbial monkey wrench in the wheel; but don't you be "terrified by your adversaries: which is to them—" Which what? Which contention for the faith "Is," to your enemy, a "token of perdition." They think you are going to hell. They see you working hard and striving together for the faith. They say: "That's dead sure to lead to perdition." Don't you be worried about that. While they interpret it that way, let me say to you, brethren, it is to you a token of salvation and that of God.

Friends, those are the sentiments tonight. Now the final verse that I transmit to you is also from Paul. "Brethren, be ye stedfast, unmoveable, always abounding in the work of the Lord," now mark it—"forasmuch as ye know that your labour is not in vain in the Lord." Paul wasn't a wishy-washy character; he wasn't a policy man; he cared nothing about what the world said. "I count all that but as the refuse of earth that I may win Christ." "None of these things move me, neither count I my life dear unto myself so that I might finish my course with joy and the ministry which I have received of the Lord Jesus that testify the gospel of the grace of God." Therefore, brethren, "be stedfast, be unmoveable." Think of it: those characters whose pictures have adorned the pages of profane history have been men, first, of convictions; second, of courage; third, of faith. They neither doubted nor were they afraid of any adversary. They are the type that has moved forward all the affairs of the world. That's what we need in every department of life. There need to be, may I suggest, in the home, fathers and mothers who stand for the best interest of their children. I think you know that. In the schoolroom, there needs to be a firm hand, and yet one characterized by sense. It won't do to turn matters over to our children in the home; they have not had their senses exercised as yet, to discern between good and evil. The old-time discipline has faded away, hence, we are leaving things for the schools, for the courts, and for the state to rectify, and our penitentiaries are overflowing with boys and girls who, if correctly governed and disciplined back at home, would not be on the state and behind prison bars. In our city and county administration we need men who will stand four-square for their convictions. In the State of Tennessee, as governor, as executive, we need men who have conviction, who are nobody's puppets, not mere echoes, not "me too" fellows. It's a tragedy, friends, in matters political, when we have a candidate put out by some great politician, and then, perchance, nominated or elected. What's the common sentiment over Tennessee? "Some man will run him. He's but a puppet in the hands of somebody else." The governor of Tennessee rarely ever lives in Nashville.

Sometimes as elders in the congregation, we have men who are weaklings, who yield to every kind of a suggestion, and who are afraid to do their duty. In the pulpit we need men who believe God's Book, who stand like a stone wall against all error, who are neither afraid nor ashamed to denounce that which is antagonistic to the body of Christ. Lord, give us men of that type. "Be ye stedfast, unmoveable, always abounding," not simply as Job said, "by the skin of the teeth," but "abounding in the work of the Lord." Why? "Forasmuch as ye know that your labour is not in vain in the Lord." We work at lots of things, friends, put in our time and money and our very best effort; yet all the while we are not absolutely certain. Things come along and destroy the crops, after the hard days' labours have been expended; fire breaks out and destroys the goods piled up in our storehouses; the Cumberland River overflows and submerges large parts of our stock—labor in vain. There's but one thing that I know about wherein there is an absolute certainty, and that is the work of the Lord. Stand fast in that, because we know that when we labor in His name, and according to His word, it will not be in vain; but on fairer fields and in brighter climes, in the glad sweet by and by, in a land across which the shadows have never come, a home of an unclouded day, we shall reap the handsome reward. I am saying, therefore, friends, to all of you that love the truth: buckle on God's armor afresh tonight, raise aloft the sword dipped in the blood of the spotless Son of God, unsheathe the sword of the Spirit, march faithfully on under the leadership of Him who has never yet lost a single conflict; and by and by, when life's dream is over, when its race is won, its battles fought, and its victories won, He'll bid us lay aside our old battle-scarred armour on the glad plains of eternity, hang our swords upon the jasper walls of that eternal city, while with palms of victory and with crowns of glory, we sweep through the gates into the beauties and grandeurs that passeth understanding. In the sweet by and by, what will it mean to be there?

If there's one or any number, tonight, not yet bound for the Promised Land, not yet headed toward the sweet by and by, I bid you come; make preparation for that just now, while together we stand for the song.

CPSIA information can be obtained at www.ICGtesting.com
Printed in the USA
LVOW040756091012

302071LV00001B/27/A